ARE YOU IN LOVE WITH MR. WRONG?

1. Does he flare up and lose his temper over small things and at times threatens or becomes violent? ❑ yes ❑ no

2. Does he become inordinately jealous or resent your relationships with others and frequently becomes picky, controlling, and rigid? ❑ yes ❑ no

3. Is he unable to break his allegiance with his mom and her feelings, desires, and demands, leaving you feeling like the "other woman" in the relationship? ❑ yes ❑ no

4. Are his stories and explanations hard to believe and you often feel in your gut that he is hiding something and deceiving you? ❑ yes ❑ no

5. Do you end up paying for most of the things you do together because he sponges off others, using you and them financially and otherwise to cover his irresponsibility? ❑ yes ❑ no

6. Is he so passive and preoccupied that communication with him is either impossible or like pulling teeth? ❑ yes ❑ no

7. Has your relationship with him taken a backseat to his obsessive and compulsive relationship with work, chemicals, alcohol, sex, gambling, pornography, sports, or even church? ❑ yes ❑ no

8. Is he indifferent to matters of faith, values, and morality; intimating that church and religion are for women and the weak? ❑ yes ❑ no

9. Does he seem "too good to be true" and able to charm anyone he meets? ❑ yes ❑ no

10. Is he afraid to take a stand or set boundaries with you or the kids and is such a people pleaser that he goes along with the crowd, even when he knows it is not right for you, him, or your relationship? ❑ yes ❑ no

Each question refers to a specific Mr. Wrong who will make your life miserable. So if you answered yes to any of the questions, you are most likely in love with a Mr. Wrong. If you checked more than one, he must be really wrong. Here is the key to discovering which Mr. Wrong is in your life:

(1) Mr. Angry, (2) Mr. Cor
(4) Mr. Deceiver, (5) Mr. F
(7) Mr. Addiction, (8) M
(10) Mr. Cowardly Lion

AVOIDING MR. WRONG

[AND WHAT TO DO IF YOU DIDN'T]

STEPHEN ARTERBURN
AND
Dr. MEG J. RINCK

TEN MEN WHO WILL RUIN YOUR LIFE

THOMAS NELSON
Since 1798

NASHVILLE   DALLAS   MEXICO CITY   RIO DE JANEIRO

Published in Nashville, Tennessee, by Thomas Nelson. Thomas Nelson is a registered trademark of Thomas Nelson, Inc.

Thomas Nelson, Inc. books may be purchased in bulk for educational, business, fund-raising, or sales promotional use. For information, please e-mail SpecialMarkets@ThomasNelson.com.

Published in association with the literary agency of Alive Communications, 7680 Goddard St, Suite #200, Colorado Springs, CO 80920.

Scripture quotations noted NKJV are from THE NEW KING JAMES VERSION. Copyright © 1979, 1980, 1982, Thomas Nelson, Inc., Publishers.

Scripture quotations noted NASB are from the NEW AMERICAN STANDARD BIBLE®. Copyright © The Lockman Foundation 1960, 1962, 1963, 1971, 1972, 1973, 1975, 1977. Used by permission.

Scripture quotations noted NIV are from the HOLY BIBLE: NEW INTERNATIONAL VERSION®. Copyright © 1973, 1978, 1984 by International Bible Society. Used by permission of Zondervan Publishing House. All rights reserved.

Scripture quotations noted NLT are from the *Holy Bible, New Living Translation,* copyright © 1996. Used by permission of Tyndale House Publishers, Inc., Wheaton, Illinois 60189. All rights reserved.

Library of Congress Cataloging-in-Publication Data

Arterburn, Stephen. 1953–
    Avoiding Mr. Wrong (and what to do if you didn't) : ten men who will ruin your   life /
Stephen Arterburn and Meg J. Rinck.
      p. cm.
    Includes bibliographical references.
    ISBN 978-0-7852-6646-4 (pb)
    ISBN 978-0-7852-6889-5 (hc)
    1. Man–woman relationships. 2. Women—Psychology. 3. Men—   Psychology.
HQ801.A792000   00268970
                                                    CIP

Printed in the United States of America.

10 11 12 WC 17 16

To my wonderful daughter, Madeline, who deserves a wonderful
Mr. Right. May all the Mr. Wrongs get held up in eternal
traffic on their way to our door. I pray her mother and
I will be able to teach her the difference between
Mr. Right and Mr. Wrong, and that she will feel
deserving enough to wait for Mr. Best.

—SFA

To my Dad, Paul E. Josephson, who has consistently been
Mr. Right for my mom, Bee, his wife of fifty-two years.
May his godly example continue to bear fruit in the
lives of all ten grandchildren, and indirectly, in
the lives of all who read this book.

—MJR

CONTENTS

Acknowledgments   ix

Introduction   xi

  1. The Detached Man   1

  2. The Control Freak   21

  3. Mr. Wonderful   47

  4. The Cowardly Lion   66

  5. The Angry Man   85

  6. The Mama's Boy   111

  7. The Deceiver   130

  8. The Addict   150

  9. The Eternal Kid   178

10. The Ungodly Man   195

11. Avoiding Mr. Wrong If You're Still Single   212

12. Helping Mr. Wrong Get Right   221

Afterword: The Last Word on Mr. Right   231

Notes   236

ACKNOWLEDGMENTS

A huge thanks to our initial editor, Brian Hampton, for taking a lot of time on this project and less on others so he could help us. Also, thanks to our final managing editor, Cindy Blades, who brought this in whole, complete, and on time.

Another huge thanks to friend and colleague Paul Meier, M.D., for his assistance on the clinical perspectives behind our ten men.

Even huger thanks to Victor Oliver, who helped conceive the book and successfully ran it up the Thomas Nelson flagpole.

And the hugest thanks to Sandy, Stephen's great, wonderful, wise, creative, fun, and unpredictable wife, who stuck with him as he transitioned out of being Mr. Wrong.

INTRODUCTION

Wait! Do not turn that page! Even if you have never read an introduction to a book before, *please,* read this one! Usually, intros are boring and it is *so* tempting to rush ahead to one of the chapters—especially if you think you know someone who fits the chapter's title. We urge you to resist that temptation—it will be good for your character to delay gratification, and we *do* have some important things to say first. Honest!

WHY DID WE WRITE THIS BOOK?

Does the world really need another "male-bashing" book? No, it doesn't—so we didn't write one. While these men may be a minority, it seems everyone knows someone they regard as "Mr. Wrong." All of us in the counseling profession would be just as happy if we never had to deal with difficult or destructive relationships again. Yet every day we encounter the problem, and, it seems, so do a lot of other people. (Just in case you think we are just *picking on* men, be sure to read our next book, *Finding Mr. Right.*)

We should be "wise as serpents and harmless as doves." Unfortunately, we are usually harmless to a fault and not very wise when it comes to getting into relationships. The church community is particularly naive in this regard. The men we describe in this book can be destructive—to themselves, to their wives, to their children, to society. They are not "safe people." Some are blatant about who and what they are; others are more like "wolves in sheep's clothing." In any case, we need to understand who they are and what to expect from them.

We have written this book for at least four reasons: (1) to give women the quickness and accuracy of discernment and keenness of insight they need to not become ensnared in hurtful relationships; (2) to give women who are already married or involved with such men a helping hand with how to cope in a healthy manner; (3) to challenge men to learn about their hurting male friends and help them; and (4) to invite men who are struggling with the characteristics of Mr. Wrong to see themselves as they really are and do whatever it takes to change.

While some of these examples may seem extreme to those who have been insulated from the realities of life, more of these men are around than you might guess. For example, we know that on average, 1 out of 10 people has a sexual addiction. So in a group of 200, there are about 20 sex addicts. If half of these are men, then this typical gathering of men would have 10 men who are struggling to not allow sex to completely destroy everything they hold sacred. Of course, there are even more who are struggling with pornography or some other sexual acting out behaviors, but not yet addicted to it.

We will try to answer the following questions: What are the ten types of men all women should avoid? What are the signs that someone may be developing these problems? What kind of women are they interested in? Why do women fall for them? What are the chances they will change? What can you do if you are already in a relationship with one of these men? What can you do if you are already married to one?

In trying to communicate the distinctives of the ten types of men with tough problems, we have used labels. Labels can be used destructively, reducing a person to a category, depersonalizing them and completely negating their existence. That is not our intent. We use these ten labels to help communicate the one overriding problem that will destroy the relationship, the man, and, perhaps, even you. In some cases, we present the extremely dark shades of a man's character to better help identify whether or not a man is in big trouble or merely broken, needing acceptance and understanding.

Most, if not all, of the men we will describe in this book have issues with masculinity. Indeed, probably all men everywhere have some problems understanding what it is to be male. The roles, at least in Western civilization, that seemed so sure and stable just fifty years ago have changed and are changing every day. Many men are confused, hurt, angry, and scared coming out of the past thirty years of social upheaval. Roles for women and men have changed and, in some cases, seemingly reversed. It's been pretty confusing for everyone.

One reaction to all this upheaval has been polarization: development of extremes. Some men, embarrassed by the generations of male abuse against women, internalized the shame of their progenitors. They tried to make up for having too much power in the past by giving up all their power in the present. Some also became disillusioned with their own fathers. They became angry and overwhelmed by having to face life alone and without any reliable rules. Their fathers were not there to teach them the ways of the world and the methods of men. They floundered and took on destructive roles in the absence of a father who cared or was at least there. These men also felt pressure from their moms, if only covertly. Mom needed a male who could feel, who could understand her, and too often she subtly communicated to the boy that he should be that male. Yet because she secretly despised men because they disappointed her, she also communicated that being male was not such a good thing. Dad, on the other hand, needed the son to run interference with Mom, since he was too frightened of and overwhelmed by her needs. Uncomfortable with vulnerability, Dad delegated this task to his son. Son became the surrogate spouse, who was sensitive, gentle, and listened to Mom's problems. However, there was a caveat with Dad's delegation of responsibility:

> One more thing. Because you will become a sensitive male, I will not like you. I will fear you as I fear your mother. I will see you as *wimpy* and I will secretly hold you in contempt. But son, it will all work out. Trust me.[1]

Other men have gone to the opposite extreme. Feeling a secret shame from not being "blessed" by their fathers, they mess up their lives, their families, and society in their never-ending quest to be man "enough." They are not exercising true masculinity, but rather a grotesque caricature of what they think masculinity is. Afraid of their own inadequacy, their show of exaggerated maleness is an attempt to ward off anyone who could come along and measure their shortcomings. Longing for the love and approval of a father, these men fear women and use anything, from philandering to competition with other males, to become the ultimate controllers in an attempt to win their fathers' approval. Often they are angry, selfish, not above mishandling the truth, and prone to addictions and acting out. We will examine them one by one.

Our intent is to offer hope in the midst of brokenness and struggle. We know that people can change. A man can change from being destructive to being productive. A woman attracted to a sick man can become a woman who cares less about being a couple than about being whole and healthy. If you are attached to a man who should have been avoided, you can run from him, or you can try to rescue him. After reading this book we hope you will be motivated to reconsider those options. Hopefully, you will find the insight here to make decisions that will lead to the healing of the relationship and the healing of your soul. After all, if you don't work out what motivated you to attach to one sick man, you will probably find yourself attached to another one, sooner or later.

CHAPTER 1

THE DETACHED MAN

Rob could be classified as a classic detached man. He has a responsible job for a large company as head of the sales department. He deals with people and problems all day long and wants to "hide" when he gets home at night. A nondrinker, Rob grabs a Pepsi and the newspaper or the mail and heads for his den. Later, he wolfs down his dinner and makes only token conversation with his wife and children, if they are even there. (Sometimes he does not get home until 7:30 P.M. and they are already finished with their meal.) After dinner, he goes to the den and does paperwork or watches television. His wife puts the kids to bed and cleans up the kitchen.

Usually, Rob falls asleep with a book or the television remote in his hand, right there in his easy chair. About 1:00 A.M. he stumbles into bed, his wife already asleep. Rob is not that different from his friends. They are typically into the same pattern, or they stay out until 11:00 P.M. either at work or at some meeting, coming home only when they are sure their family is all asleep. Rob and his friends are all articulate, active, and energetic at work, but sluggish, mute, withdrawn, and inert at home. It is a puzzle to their families because otherwise they are likable and reasonably prosperous.

Rob and his friends look at the situation this way: "Look, I have been out there working my tail off for this family day after day. I am sick of problems, and I am sick of people. I work hard to provide what my family needs. Why can't she be happy with that?"

Carol, Rob's wife, and *her* friends look at it this way: "Hey, I haven't been exactly sitting all day. I've been up since 5:30 A.M. with the kids; I cook breakfast, pack lunches, clean up. I am carpooling so much I feel closer to Tom Bodett of Motel 6 than to you. Besides that, I have Brownies and Cub Scouts and PTA. I go to the soccer games and the basketball practices. When was the last time you went to a game? I sell Mary Kay on the side, so it is not like I don't bring in *any* money. All I want is some time with *you*. Is that so terrible?"

He wants to hide and she wants his hide. Connecting with him is the most important part of her day, while being at work is his most important part of the day. When he comes home, her day begins, emotionally. His day is over as far as he is concerned. All he wants is to disconnect. All she wants is to connect: emotionally, sexually, intellectually. She uses words like *closeness, intimacy,* and *togetherness.* He just wants her to go away—not for good, just to the other room so he can have some "peace and quiet."

The detached man is ill-equipped to do the hard work of being in an intimate, connected relationship. He was not taught how to connect with women and children. He did not learn these skills at school or from his peers. He and other men will joke, tease, cajole, slap one another on the back or the fanny, or punch one another on the biceps. He does not realize that these masculine ways of showing affection do not work with women and kids. Women and children are often hurt or put off by these gestures, and then he feels confused. The detached man does not usually associate physical touch with much other than sexuality. (Other than when involved with sports or in the teasing mentioned above.) So when the wife wants attention and affection, he may misunderstand and think she wants sex. Or she may come out and directly ask for sex and he is "too tired" or "too busy," when in reality he is too scared to connect even in that manner. Only when slightly intoxicated or exhausted does he find himself able to express feelings, but too often the only emotion of which he is cognizant is anger.

Once the wedding is over, the detached man often goes on to focus his energy and emotion on other pursuits. "Well, I got that need met. Now on to the next challenge." Being task-oriented, he tends to see wooing and wedding as a goal, just like any other goal. You pursue it, and once it is accomplished, you move on to the next project. Relationships are difficult because of the cultural pressures to be tough, strong, independent; not needy, not emotional, not dependent. On one side, he needs closeness, intimacy, and warmth, just as women do. (Though he has been emotionally disconnected for so long, he often is not aware of what he needs or feels.) On the other side, he intuitively experiences these needs as somewhat weak and too feminine, rather than merely human. So he distances and ignores his feelings and his needs.

He comes home defensive, if he even comes home early enough to run into his wife. He gets involved with the computer, or the Nintendo, or the *Wall Street Journal*—anything to escape what he sees as her continual pressure to give more, be more, do more. He begins to feel trapped, resentful, furious, and even rage-filled. He wants acceptance and cheerleading for who he is. He wants appreciation. He wants someone to dote on him, give to him, do for him. He wants someone who will meet his every need but never demand anything in return. He wants Betty Crocker, Meg Ryan, Madonna, and Mother Teresa all in one. But, please, don't ask him to do anything more. It is already too much just for him to be here. Well, he is here all right, but he is also not here at all.

When you were younger did your teachers ever have you read a paragraph and then underline all the verbs and nouns and personal pronouns? Well, let yourself drift back a few years and try the following exercise. Read the Scriptures listed, and then jot down on a piece of paper the verbs you find.

If you love Me, you will keep My commandments. (John 14:15 NASB)

This is My commandment, that you love one another as I have loved you. Greater love has no one than this, than to lay down one's life

3

for his friends. You are My friends if you do whatever I command you. (John 15:12–14 NKJV)

Let love be without hypocrisy. Abhor what is evil; cling to what is good. Be devoted to one another in brotherly love; give preference to one another in honor; not lagging behind in diligence, fervent in spirit, serving the Lord; rejoicing in hope, persevering in tribulation, devoted to prayer, contributing to the needs of the saints, practicing hospitality. Bless those who persecute you; bless and curse not . . . *If your enemy is hungry, feed him, and if he is thirsty, give him a drink; for in so doing you will heap burning coals upon his head.* Do not be overcome by evil, but overcome evil with good. (Rom. 12:9–14, 20–21 NASB, emphasis added)

Now we who are strong ought to bear the weaknesses of those without strength and not just please ourselves. Let each of us please his neighbor for his good, to his edification. (Rom. 15:1–2 NASB)

In reference to your former manner of life, you lay aside the old self, which is being corrupted in accordance with the lusts of deceit, and that you be renewed in the spirit of your mind, and put on the new self, which in the likeness of God has been created in righteousness and holiness of the truth. Therefore, laying aside falsehood, speak truth, each one of you, with his neighbor, for we are members of one another. Be angry, and yet do not sin; do not let the sun go down on your anger, and do not give the devil an opportunity. Let him who steals steal no longer; but rather let him labor, performing with his own hands what is good . . . Let no unwholesome word proceed out from your mouth, but only such a word as is good for edification . . . Let all bitterness and wrath and anger and clamor and slander be put away from you, along with all malice. And be kind to one another, tenderhearted, forgiving each other, just as God in Christ also has forgiven you. (Eph. 4:22–32 NASB)

What did you notice? Look again and note the verbs that specifically call for action in relationships. Words such as *keep, do, love, lay down, be devoted, bear, contribute, bless, be fervent, be kind* all involve action in relation to someone else. Yet an active relationship is something foreign to the detached man.

I (Steve) dated a wonderful young woman from a very respected family. Her father was a physician whom women loved. He had a large practice, and the house would fill up on the holidays with gifts from current and former patients. From all outside appearances this was a relatively normal family. When I got to observe the family up close and personal, I discovered it was anything but normal. It was a family run by Dr. Detachment.

His routine was pretty amazing, allowing him to avoid almost all contact with the family. He arose at 4:30 A.M. and was out of the house and on his way to the hospital by 5:15 A.M. After that he held normal office hours, got a bite to eat for dinner and saw his hospital patients a final time before heading home. He would arrive around 7:30 P.M., greet everyone, shower, turn on the noise equalizing machine and go to bed, where he read until he fell asleep. On Saturdays he made patient rounds early, played golf, and was home in time for dinner, his time for family. After dinner, off to bed he went.

On Sundays he took the family to church, lunch at the country club, and then home to watch golf, read the Sunday paper, have a light dinner, and back to bed. I figured he was able to limit his interaction with his family to less than five hours a week. And that time was, at best, superficial. The family craved his attention, and he only doled it out as he saw fit. He devoted his time to career and golf. If anyone did not like it the way it was, they could leave. I don't think he ever realized what he had missed all those years.

Some men seem to think that it is all right to be engaged in every area but their family. They may be active at work, but they are disconnected at home. They may be dynamos on the sales team, but they cannot move from the television set long enough to eat dinner with the family on the weekend. Or they are active with *things,* not people. The yard, the workshop, the cars, the church activities all get lots of energy, but relationships just languish. They cannot understand why their families are so irritated with them or why their wives are angry all the time.

FAMILY BACKGROUND

What produces this type of man? One of the biggest factors is absent fathers. One hundred years ago our society was essentially rural. Families lived together, worked together, and survived together. Often Mother and Father worked in the fields while elderly relatives tended to the youngest children. Dad was a model of masculinity, and Mom was a model of femininity. Grandfather, grandmother, maiden aunts, or bachelor uncles were often a part of the family as well. There were other role models available too in a small farming community. Shopkeepers in the town, teachers, ministers, blacksmiths, doctors, lawyers, and neighbors all played a role in shaping a child's life from cradle to adulthood. From an early age kids were in the fields, in the barns, in the yard, tending to chores, helping their parents, neighbors, and friends. Young boys saw men and women work side by side in desperate as well as delightful times. They learned what it meant to be male working hour after hour alongside their dads, uncles, brothers, and neighbors. The community was connected; people had one another to fall back on in times of stress or crisis in a way that we do not see today.

With the industrial revolution, a new force began impinging on the family. No longer was the family unit also the economic unit. Now the male was *the* economic unit. He left the family each day to go into the city to earn the money necessary to care for his family. Soon families moved into the cities, and the woman had no economic role. Previously, besides contributing her labor on the farm, she usually raised chickens and sold the eggs, or made butter, cream, and other milk products for sale. In the city these avenues were closed to her. Now she centered her life on her children. Often grandparents and extended family were back at the farm, far away. There were few opportunities to share the burden with someone else. Fathers worked long hours at difficult, exhausting jobs in factories and foundries.

They came home tired and had little time to show a boy how to whittle, or play the banjo, or throw a baseball. Boys' lives began to center around the women in their homes. They felt estranged from dad, not knowing or understanding what he did at work. All they had to go on regarding how to be male was to observe Mom and do the opposite. This left most boys insecure about their masculinity and unaffirmed in their maleness.

The detached man has been underfathered and overmothered and is vulnerable to hidden emotional pain. He will renounce his masculine strength, at least in the home. He does not participate with the family because he has never seen a man participate. He cannot ask for what he needs directly and does not express his anger about unmet needs in a clear manner. He uses pained sighs, rolling his eyes, and pouting as his main ways to show his displeasure. He just wants to be left alone. And no one seems to get it. His wife and kids are furious with him, but he rarely understands why. He is unhappy and cannot see the source of his pain. When you go to his home he is either not there, in bed, or alone out on the back porch, away from family, immersed in a book or television show.

Mothers contribute to this pattern of development also. The route the woman takes in the marriage may be varied. Some women accept their passive, detached husbands and hide the anger and pain they feel at being shut out. They see life as consisting solely of providing for and nurturing the king in his castle. Sons learn that women should be like Mom, and they, too, become the passive despots when they marry.

Other women take a different route. They are angry, resentful, and therefore reject the husband and men in general. They stay in the marriage though, for the sake of the children or because of religion or economics. Bitter and hostile, the message conveyed is "Men are jerks. They want only one thing (sex), and they don't have the sense God gave a goose." This woman might degrade her husband in front of the children; henpeck, nitpick, criticize, and contradict him. Or she may be careful to never confront him directly but put him down and build herself up in front of the children. She takes over when she does not think he is doing something correctly, so he rarely attempts to contribute much to the family discussions or projects. Her son learns to hate himself and to be angry at women.

Still other mothers take a totally different approach. A woman may have married an idealist who went to a prestigious school. She loved him for his daring and somewhat rebellious dreams. However, he forsook his idealism and became a lawyer, doctor, or businessman. He became the typical absentee father and husband, and she was devastated. She had all these grandiose expectations of romance, intimacy, adventure, suffering for a cause—a life together in service to the ideal. Now all she has is drudgery, loneliness, deep disappointment, and anger. Her son becomes the recipient of all her transferred expectations. All her emotional energy focuses on him. His achievements give her life meaning. In this family, the son experiences the pressure to be the idealist his father failed to be. Overwhelmed, he quits life, albeit unconsciously. He often drops out of school and becomes detached, distant, withdrawn, and cool.

What does the lack of fathering and overmothering do to the detached man? They undermine his confidence in functioning as a male. Experiencing this pattern of parenting drives him to be overly assertive at work and to let achievement become his god. He begins to think and feel that if he is not an achiever, he is nothing. Often he becomes a driven workaholic. It also establishes a deep, underlying need for approval and acceptance from other men. This need leads to an unstable self-confidence. All this insecurity takes an emotional toll. It takes enormous energy to look good on the outside all day when you are eaten up with insecurity. No wonder he is exhausted when he comes home at night.

Workaholism is a common affliction of the detached man. He can justify his neglect of his family if he has a hard job with tremendous demands. For him, it is easier to work than to relate on an intimate basis. Even when the job involves people, there is a difference between relating, however intensely, to an employee or coworker, and to a spouse or a family member. It is easier to put up with stress with a coworker because you do not have to go to bed with that person later.

A workaholic is, of course, someone who works too much. Yet he is much more than that. A workaholic is a person whose focus on work is so intense and extensive that it begins to harm one or more of the following areas of his life: physical, mental, social, emotional, or spiritual. Work is a God-given opportunity for growth and stewardship. Even prior to the Fall in the Garden of Eden, God had commanded Adam and Eve to work tending the garden and "subduing the earth." Work was made more difficult by sin and by the curse God put on the ground as a result of it, but the ability to work and create is part of our being created in the image of God. God works and so should we.

However, work was never meant to take God's place in our lives as the source and defense of our lives. God alone is the source of meaning and strength. Cain, one of Adam and Eve's sons, made the mistake of thinking that he could please God and meet his demands for righteousness through the works of his hands. Cain's unwillingness to submit to God's leadership and bring the prescribed blood sacrifice led to his jealous rage during which he killed his brother, Abel. Was Cain the first workaholic? Maybe; he certainly placed such importance on his work, and his ego was so tied to it, that he ended up murdering his brother.

Work has always been the most common excuse for men to detach. It appears so honorable, so manly and responsible. If the detached man disconnected through a hobby like stamp collecting, taking hours away from the family, he would be viewed as inadequate or irresponsible. But when the excuse is work, he is applauded. No matter how much grief he causes his family, there is a certain nobility attributed to the man who works long hours to make a living. He makes a living, but he ruins a lot of lives.

CHARACTERISTICS OF
THE DETACHED MAN

These men are easy to spot. They have career-itis. Doing, achieving, obtaining are top priority to the detached workaholic, rather than being; that is, being a human being or just simply being there. It is important to realize this fact because he will use people and things to achieve what he wants, and he would just as soon use you as anyone else. Unless, of course, he does not deem you smart enough or sophisticated enough, and then he will just have an affair with you instead. He rides roughshod over others in the competition he calls life. How he treats others is a good sign of how he will treat you. These detached workaholics put people into categories: winners and losers. Winners are evaluated in terms of their power, influence, position, rank, money, or fame. If you don't continue to fit the image he is looking for in a woman, he will drop you like a hot potato. Or he will let you put him through graduate school, and then, once the career is set, he will find someone who fits that stage of life better than you do. He will wine you and dine you in the beginning, attempting to win you just as he wins any prize. He will be suave, sophisticated, debonair. He will do just about anything except connect his heart with your soul.

WHAT KIND OF WOMAN DOES THE DETACHED MAN WANT?

He looks for a woman who will support him emotionally and socially, and, above all, make him look good. Early in his career he looks for a combination "Gal Friday"/Ivana Trump. That way he has a social secretary and a beauty on his arm. Or he will look for a woman who is (or could be) as successful as he is. Then it appears that he has won another deal or made a great acquisition with the merger of your lives. He expects his woman to be there for him but does not return the favor. Even if she has a highly successful career herself, his only interest in it is to use it as a springboard to leverage more success for himself and/or to make himself look good. No matter how important her job may be, it must take second place to his at all times. While he is happy to have her distracted and busy, so as not to be nagging him for personal time, he still expects her to drop everything and be available as the perfect hostess, date, traveling companion, and trophy.

The woman who looks good but is emotionally weak or sick has special appeal to him. During the dating process he will be attracted to her looks, but he will be hooked on her neurosis. He will believe that her weakness will keep her dependent on him and tolerant of most anything he will do. He will believe that she can handle detachment and that her demands on him will be few. He is looking for someone with very low expectations.

WHY DOES SHE FALL FOR HIM?

At first she is attracted to his seeming charm and charisma, his wealth or potential to bring in good money, his devotion to hard work. He looks, acts, and feels like a man of accomplishment or of promise. That he is a relational moron has little impact on her. She thinks: *He's young, just starting out. It will be different once we're established.* She may feel flattered that such a dedicated man has time for her. What she does not realize is that once the prize (marrying her) is achieved, he will lose interest and move on to more important matters. His after-marriage persona is so different from the person she loves, it fills her with disappointment and often pushes her into a deep postmatrimonial depression. She will look for any way out of the relationship, sometimes even suicide.

RELATING TO THE DETACHED MAN

If you are single, you must examine what you want in life and decide if being second to a man's career is it. You may have been raised by a dad who was rarely there and so this feels normal, but it is not healthy. You may see fame or fortune as a satisfying reward for his unbalanced life. Is money really that important? Realize that it cannot compare to a man who knows you, loves you, and is as committed to your needs as he is to his own. If your attachment cannot be broken, at least take your time and see if through premarital counseling he can come to see some of the defects in his patterns of detachment and achievement.

What if you are married to a detached man? Pragmatically, don't expect much. The more you expect, the more you will be disappointed.

It will be easy to become cynical and bitter yourself, however, so guard against it. Aim for realism, not perfection. Acceptance is a crucial quality to cultivate in yourself. Grace is a concept the family of a workaholic needs as well. We all have character defects. It is easy to dwell on how the other person has wounded or neglected *us,* without realizing that we, too, have faults. Be sure you express to him your knowledge of your own shortcomings. Let him know that he has nothing to prove to you—that you accept him as he is.

How do we cultivate a loving attitude toward someone who is less than lovable? By being a servant rather than acting like a servant; that is, by developing a servant's attitude, a servant's heart. Real servant-hood is more than just going through the motions. Jesus Himself showed us the way in John 13. In this passage, He stooped (literally) and washed the disciples' feet. He humbled Himself and did the task that none of them had thought to do for Him. How could He do this selfless act of love? Yes, He is God, but the Scriptures give us the key. John 13:3–5 states:

> Jesus, knowing that the Father had given all things into His hands, and that He had come forth from God, and was going back to God, rose from supper, and laid aside His garments; and taking a towel, He girded Himself about. Then He poured water into the basin, and began to wash the disciples' feet, and to wipe them with the towel with which He was girded. (NASB)

The disciples had just been arguing about who was the greatest among them. Jesus, in His actions, demonstrated a heart attitude that they lacked. They were filled with pride. He was full of humility. Does humility of heart mean we debase ourselves? No! It means we know who we really are! Verse 3 says that Jesus "[knew] that the Father had given all things into His hands, and that He had come forth from God, and was going back to God." You see, Jesus knew who He was, from whence His authority came, and where He was going. With security like that, He could then be humble. He had nothing to lose because He already knew that who He was did not depend on what He did.

He was God's beloved Son. He had been given all authority. He was going back to the Father.

Humility comes to us when we are so full of the love of God the Father, so sure of our worth and place in Him, that we have no need of pride to puff up or defend or brag. We have no need to humiliate, degrade, or upbraid the other person. Humility is the product of looking up to God and away from ourselves, gaining an eternal perspective. Humility comes to us when we confess our own faults, rather than those of the other person. It is so easy to complain, murmur, and grumble about how another has let us down. We need to remember our own failures and misdeeds and use them as building blocks for humility, since they can remind us of our utter dependence on God. Humility comes as we trust God and humble ourselves under His mighty hand, casting all our cares on Him as we wait for Him to lift us up at the proper time (1 Peter 5:6–7).

Another crucial factor in developing a loving heart toward a less than lovable individual is the "old nature" or, as the King James Version calls it, "the flesh." This idea does not refer mainly to our sexual or sensual desires, though certainly it is used that way as well. Our flesh or old nature consists of the habits of mind and propensities of personality that make up our "human nature." When we rely on our own abilities rather than God's ability, we are operating in the old nature. The old nature is at war with the Spirit of God and does not want to please God. However, Romans 6:6 describes our old nature as being crucified with Christ so that sin might be done away with, and so that we no longer would be slaves to unrighteousness. Paul then goes on to admonish us to consider ourselves "dead to sin, but alive to God in Christ Jesus" (v. 11 NASB). To the Galatians, Paul also wrote: "I have been crucified with Christ; it is no longer I who live, but Christ lives in me; and the life which I now live in the flesh I live by faith in the Son of God, who loved me and gave Himself for me" (Gal. 2:20 NKJV).

Crucifixion of our old nature is something that the Lord did for us; we cannot do it. God did it in Christ for us (Rom. 6:3–10). We must, as an act of our will, submit ourselves to God, setting our minds on Him and His truth rather than on our own understanding (Col. 3:2;

Rom. 6:11–17; 8:5–13; 12:1–2; Prov. 3:5–6). We are to commit to God the work of His hands (Isa. 45:11) and trust in Him, not in our own imagination about how to handle things. As we delight ourselves in Him, He will give us the desires of our hearts; and He Himself will do it, as we commit our ways to Him (Ps. 37:3–5).

One way to cultivate a humble, gentle spirit when we are loving someone who is unlovely is to serve in an unrecognized or hidden way. How do you love someone in a hidden way? You pray for them (and don't make a point of it to them). You do kind, unasked-for things without expecting them to notice and without pointing out that you did them. You anonymously send them a gift or flowers or a box of their favorite candy. You quietly work on yourself regarding a trait you have that annoys them. You don't tell them you are going to stop doing it, you just stop. You build them up to others without their knowing it. (This statement, of course, means you do not tear them down without their knowing it either.)

It also means we let go of what Richard Foster calls the "everlasting burden of needing to manage others." How much of our activity is really aimed at trying to control others rather than serve them? Trying to get our own way can be such a burden. Attempting to change a detached workaholic is like trying to move a mountain with a toothpick as leverage. It is such a difficult thing to be right all the time. We release ourselves from much bondage when we just "let go and let God." When we stop trespassing on someone else's sovereignty, we learn how free we can be. Robin Norwood says that "helping is the sunny side of control." Are we really ready to let go? We may be right about the detached man's obligation to us and to our children. We may be right about his neglect of his health and spiritual life. However, being right does not give us any right to control. We must still let him go and let God deal with him, while trying to stay as healthy and sane as we can ourselves. Ultimately, we have to trust and let go.

We know that some women are in situations that can and will get better. We also know that there are those who have no hope for a different life. We believe in doing all possible to help the situation. Find what help is available to you so that you try to encourage change rather than nag and complain for it. Being an encouragement to him is not easy, but it frees him to become the man, or more like the man, he was created to be.

LIFE WITH THE DETACHED WORKAHOLIC

As attentive as he is during the courtship, he becomes more and more detached after the merger. At first, all was moonlight and roses, now you are lucky if you get a peck on the cheek before he falls off to sleep in the den. Before, he was all passion and sensuality, but as time wears on, he becomes less and less interested in sex. What used to be intense lovemaking turns into a clinical experience that is somewhat reluctantly and hastily attended to at the end of a long day. He is just as happy to let you do the work, because his pleasure is all that really matters to him. As in other areas of life, he likes to control things in the bedroom, and if he can turn you down, especially when you are very interested, he wins again.

Some of these men appear to be missionaries for a great cause. They seem so dedicated; so intent on saving the world; so focused on finding a cure for cancer; so committed to landing that rocket on some distant planet; all for the good of the human race, of course. It becomes hard to argue with them about the lack of intimacy, the lack of time for the relationship. After all, their work is "important" (implication: You are not). This is especially difficult for the Christian woman who is married to a detached workaholic who is also a professing Christian, since he will often use God, the Bible, his "calling," a vision from God, etc., to justify his time away, his exhaustion, and his lack of intimacy. He may be a genuinely pleasant person in many ways; he is just so obsessed with his call that he is oblivious to the cost you and the family are paying. He holds no ill will toward you or the children. Rather, he is just too absorbed and enthralled to notice you.

As mentioned earlier, workaholic detachment is a form of idolatry. Something other than God is put in God's place. Perhaps the focus is on doing something *for* God, or achieving some great thing *for* the kingdom, but the focus is misplaced on *doing*, not *being* in relationship. If you are married to one of these men, you know he is always tuned in to accept messages: beepers, cell phones, answering machines, and voice mail are his twenty-first-century friends. However, he rarely has time to stop and hear messages from God because he is so busy that quiet, solitude, and contemplation have all faded away. He may claim that all he wants is some "peace and quiet" at home, but, in reality, quiet—genuine solitude—frightens him. Being alone gives us the opportunity to sense who we are in relation to God, ourselves, and others. It gives us time to be in nature, to see ourselves in perspective. The detached workaholic rarely gives himself the chance. What with fax machines in cars, laptop computers, cell phones, and beepers, even when on "vacation" this driven man is preoccupied with the outer world.

Spiritually, the workaholic is usually works-oriented in his theology. That is, he believes, at least subconsciously, that he must earn God's approval and merit His blessing. While on one hand he is grandiose enough to imagine that the world cannot get along without him, on the other he believes that he must merit or earn the approbation of God. In a way, that notion is just as grandiose, for how can anyone earn God's approval? None of us are that perfect! Grace is a concept that the detached workaholic finds disconcerting, if not totally foreign. The idea of grace means one has to let go of control; that one's position is not dependent on doing; that one is powerless. All of those ideas are frightening to the detached workaholic. He tends to be at the same time tense, depressed, aggressive, stubborn, with low self-esteem, and yet act quite superior, perfectionistic, unyielding, narcissistic, audacious, and rebellious. Hence he is quite lonely. He is grasping at achievement, power, fame, and human glory, and in the end he finds his life slipping through his fingers. He has replaced his relationship with Christ and others with activity. He is holding on to everything he can, determined not to let go of anything, especially control. Jesus looks at life a little differently than this man. Jesus said, "For whoever wishes to save his life shall lose it; but whoever loses his life for My sake shall find it. For what will a man be profited, if he gains the whole world, and forfeits his soul? Or what will a man give in exchange for his soul?" (Matt. 16:25–26 NASB).

With so much focus on performance and work and so little connection with others, the detached workaholic is also burned out. He is exhausted mentally, physically, and emotionally. Though usually successful, he is still stressed. One root of burnout is bitterness and the inability to forgive. Not one of us can get through life without some injustice or unfair opposition coming our way. Everyone has been betrayed at some time by a colleague or a friend. No one is immune to hurt, and, hence, not one of us is immune to bitterness. Resentment is an odd feeling; it is directed at others, yet the harm it causes is primarily against us. One thing workaholics need to learn is to have a forgiving attitude. Instead of focusing on others' weaknesses, failures, and bungling, they need to learn to forgive and be gracious. This attitude is difficult for them to cultivate because they do not give any grace to themselves. It is a troublesome thing to attempt to give someone else what one has never received.

WHAT COULD THE DETACHED
MAN DO TO CHANGE?

What changes would be necessary for the detached man to connect with himself, others, and God? While there would be many, here are a few that stand out:

1. *Connect with himself.* He has been cut off from himself, his feelings, his thoughts, and his genuine desires for too long. He needs to reconnect with his emotional nature, his spiritual side, his human side. He needs to find acceptance from God, self, and others based on grace, not works. Learning to identify what he feels that leads him to believe he is second rate or inferior to others will help him find out why someone as competent as he is would not feel adequately equipped for life.

2. *Examine the roles his mom and dad played in shaping his expectations of life and marriage.* How is he like them? How is he living in reaction to them? If everything he is doing is in relation to them and a reaction against them, he must resolve his bitterness toward them so he can be free of their influence. We can only become free

from old familial patterns when we stop denying them and start accepting how we have adapted our behaviors to them.

3. *Develop the habit of being proactive, not passive.* This habit implies that he will take steps like these: renounce passive-aggressive behaviors, and become responsible in relationships. See relationships as an opportunity to succeed that will enhance other successes. Set relationship goals and work toward them. Schedule quality time with his spouse and quiet time with his God. Rather than allow life to just happen to him, he can become an active participant. The area of work must be balanced with relationships, and that can only be accomplished through time away from work.

4. *Find out what being male means to him.* See how his conclusions might differ from those of his father, grandfather, or uncles. He can look into how his relationship with his father might be controlling his life. Is he driven professionally because he never earned his approval? What influence could that have on his difficulty connecting? How did his father connect with others? Has his influence led him to believe that all men are distant and disconnected? Did his lack of relationships leave him without a model of how to relate to others? He can easily find ways to learn other aspects of being a man, such as by using books, tapes, and attending seminars for men, or being mentored by a godly older man.

5. *Be willing to cut his losses.* Just as it is hard to admit you have made a bad stock purchase and sell it at a loss, it is also hard for him to admit that the role of manhood he has chosen and invested his whole life in is wrong. Rather than waste all his life on a career, he can start over now, admitting to those he loves that he has made a huge mistake and intends to rectify it over time.

SNAPSHOT SUMMARY OF
THE DETACHED MAN

CLUES TO HELP YOU SPOT HIM

1. Appears emotionally retarded in relationships.

2. Talks about things, not feelings.

3. Active at work but passive at home.

4. Often uses work as an escape.

5. Most things in his life take on a mechanical and predictable feeling.

THE WOMAN TO WHOM HE IS ATTRACTED

1. Is used to being in relationships with detached, mechanical men.

2. Has low expectations and few demands.

3. Is often neurotic and unbalanced.

4. Is frantic, distracted, and busy; leaves him alone.

5. Is a "Gal Friday" type who will take care of everything at home. May also be a glamour girl to enhance his image.

THE WOMAN WHO FALLS FOR HIM

1. Likes the initial attention that comes at a safe distance. The attention flatters and the distance is comfortable.

2. His career-mindedness makes her feel secure.

3. Believes his statements about the temporary nature of his workload.

4. Thinks he will be a good provider for the family she wants.

5. Believes with all her heart that once he gets to know her heart, he will change and put her first.

WHAT YOU CAN DO

1. Realize that you accepted him as he was before you married him, so don't expect him to ever be much different.

2. The more you accept him as he is, the freer he will be to become what you need.

3. Point out any- and everything positive you can find in him. Praise him rather than ridicule him.

4. Find some small area you think he might alter and encourage him in that direction.

5. Forgive him daily, and refuse to let bitterness build up that will only serve to strengthen the disconnection.

WHAT HE COULD DO TO CHANGE

1. Start to ask people questions that will connect him to them.

2. Through counseling, discover how his parents have affected his patterns in relationships.

3. Become as active at home as he is in his work and accomplishments.

4. Start to see relationships as well as his work as part of his responsibilities.

5. Through a men's Bible study, discover God's acceptance of him, so he can develop an intimate, personal love relationship with God.

CHAPTER 2

THE CONTROL FREAK

Are you living with someone who tries to control every aspect of your life? Do you feel that you have been lost in his struggle to have complete and total control over you and everything else in his life? In the beginning, did you see and feel strength in him when he seemed to exert so much control over those around him, including you? Now has that controlling desire trapped you in a relationship that constrains you and fills you with fear? It is ironic that you would feel fear because, if the control freak in your life is like the ones we know, it is fear that drives his desire to control. Take a look at a man named Jim and see if he reminds you of anyone you know.

Jim never understood just how afraid he was. If you looked at him, you would never have guessed that his whole life was being ruined by fears he had never acknowledged, fears he never saw. He was afraid of being left behind, abandoned, left alone in the world, just as his mom had been when Dad left her for another woman and another life. That also left him feeling abandoned, rejected, and unloved by his father.

Being put down, ridiculed, and feeling second class were some other things of which Jim was afraid. His father had made him feel "no good" and told him that he was "doomed for failure." (As hard as it is to imagine, these are common words used by parents. They doom their children with these harsh prophecies, which are often fulfilled by the damage the very words cause.) These words haunted Jim, branding his soul, causing him to work hard to make sure they never came true. By working hard, he had succeeded in almost everything he tried, except being a person. So his father's words had planted the seeds of failure in a very bright boy, and Jim was a failure where it really counted: in being a loving human being connected to others.

On the foundation of his father's abuse and neglect, Jim developed into a control freak, one of those people who want to be in control of everything. If he could not control you, he did not want you around. He kept a tight ship at work, pinching pennies and hiring at the lowest wages he could. He especially liked to hire people who had been fired just before they came to him. That way, they had a special sense of gratitude. He would not allow failure. Jim believed that expectations combined with structure and control helped his employees do their jobs well. What he did not realize was that they all hated him and were too afraid of him to leave, too afraid to fail on their own. Jim's goal of never being abandoned seemed to be working. Rare was the person who left, but those who stayed were not really there with him or for him.

At home, it was not much different. Instead of a homey atmosphere, it was like living in a sanitized museum. Everything was in its place at all times, and everyone did as Jim desired. His wife hated his sermons on being a "good, submissive wife," and his kids despised him for trying to control every area of their lives. Since Jim saw himself as God's representative in the home, any rebellion against or disagreement with him was taken as rebellion against God. Jim did not realize that his true gods were order and control. He worshiped them and gave his life for them. They were the things that made him feel secure and whole in the midst of his craziness. All of this insanity made home a pretty tense place for everyone except Jim.

Yes, Jim was in control all right. He was one scared little man who used control to prevent any of his fears from ever coming true. He and his family were perfect examples of what happens when a controlling man tries to take control of everything and someone allows him to do so.

DO YOU KNOW SOMEONE WHO . . .

Controllers come in a number of styles and intensities. Yet they do have some common features. Do you know someone who

1. others say is a "control freak"?

2. is critical, negative, and even mean, most of the time?

3. is easily irritated, often over small things?

4. tends to be stubborn?

5. uses statements that sound something like: "It's my way or the highway"?

6. likes established ways of doing things, and rarely deviates?

7. is sure to tell you if he does not agree with you or does not like something you are doing?

8. is black or white, all or nothing in his thinking?

9. is close-minded; other options are not considered except superficially when he wants to look open-minded; is uncomfortable with ideas that are different from his own?

10. tends to be imperative, demanding, and intense?

11. emphasizes "doing things right" rather than relationships?

12. is usually very disciplined, to a fault?

13. sets very high standards for himself and others?

14. seems driven in everything he does?

15. gets irritated and angry when other people screw up?

16. takes other people's failures as personal insults?

17. is uncomfortable with emotions—his and yours?

18. holds the need to dominate, to be in control, to have the last word as more important than relationships or any other concern?

19. is rather resentful and, perhaps, bitter?

20. probably is a lot more insecure than he looks?

21. values people based on how similar they are to him?

22. attracts a strange group of compliant people at work and in friendships?

Chances are that if someone you know has most of these characteristics, he is a controller. If he knew you were reading this book, especially this chapter, he would confiscate it. Some controllers would burn it in the fireplace as you watched. If you are reading this as if it is forbidden material, we think you may need to spend extra time in this chapter.

IMAGES OF CONTROL FREAKS

Movies and television have presented us with a variety of controlling characters, some portrayed in a humorous light and some in a horrific light. Humorous examples of controllers would certainly include the old movie *Life with Father,* starring William Powell and Jimmy Lydon, or the television series *All in the Family* with Archie Bunker; or even the father in the famous story and film *The Sound of Music.* Less than humorous and even frightening versions can be seen in the old classic *Gaslight,* where a man tries to drive his wife insane so as to take over her estate; or in the modern film *Sleeping with the Enemy,* starring Julia Roberts.

In the real world, these men obtain their sense of identity and strength from the control they exert over others, especially women. In their younger years they bully their way through life using intimidation to enforce compliance. The control freak inspects his girlfriend's clothes before taking her out, making sure that she looks great for him but not so appealing that others would think she is available. As a father he may even teach his daughter about sex, victimizing her in incest through the teen years.

As a husband, he may spend foolishly on a big item for himself while refusing enough money for groceries and clothes for the rest of the family. If he is a churchgoing man, he will use the Bible as a source for his brand of leadership, which allows him to always have his say and always have his way. He may demand his wife be thin to make him look good, or he may help her stay fat so she feels inferior while he feels safe from her being stolen away. His rituals and attention to the details of his children's lives may drive them to anorexia or drugs. When those closest to him are away from him, they are off looking for some source of relief from the tyranny he imposes on them. This type of sick controlling makes for a very small and contrived life, void of risk and adventure and full of miserable people who have not found the courage to break out of the mold.

MARRIAGE AND THE CONTROL FREAK

When he marries, this type of man often decides he wants an isolated home outside the city, with lots of acreage. (This is *not* to say that every man who likes a country home with acres of land is a Control Freak, however.) If he lives in town, a fence around the property and a big gate at the entrance sure feel good to him. One woman reported that when they got married, he wanted to move out into the country, but she said no because she realized he was trying to isolate her, and she knew she needed other people. She was a bright woman and countered each of his attempts to control. She related that if she had not done so, she would have lost her mind because he was always willing to take whatever control she would allow him to have. She credits reading *Boundaries* by John Townsend and Henry Cloud with having saved her life.

Others are not as bright or strong, and they pay a huge price for it. One young woman was literally held hostage in her trailer home in a rural district of Kentucky. She had three very young children, no car, no money, and no telephone. Her husband would go to work in their only vehicle, a pickup, and then at various times of the day sneak back and watch to make sure no one came to see her or to pick her up. He regularly beat her and threatened to burn the house down if she ever left. One man kept his wife held hostage in her rural home by taking all of her clothes (except her nightgown) out of the house!

You might think that these women were stupid to have married these jerks in the first place. Often it is ignorance and insecurity that lead to a sick marriage like this. Yet, many times the control freak is so in control that he presents a completely different front before marriage. It is only afterward that the reality of who he is comes to light. Before marriage these men were seemingly nonchalant about domestic affairs. Suddenly, upon the wedding ring landing on his finger, he becomes not only interested, but the expert. Not that he does the work, mind you, but rather, he tells *you* how and when and what ought to be going on. He has lots of rules for the woman and the kids, and often stereotyped roles males and females are to play. Certain work is "man's work" and other work is "for women." If she had only known it might have been different, but often marriage to the control freak is a sick game of bait and switch that leads to a life of regret and pain for the woman.

As far as kids are concerned, he prefers boys. I (Steve) went to a baby's baptism where one of these men performed the service. He held our friends' little boy up in the air and spouted, "It is always a special time when a boy is born into a family." The father, of like mind, nodded proudly as the rest of us looked at one another in shock, shaking our heads while trying to get the smirks off our faces.

This type of father is strict, rough, and sports-minded with the sons. If he has daughters, he tends to spoil them and overly control them. Over time, he may become more rigid and more tyrannical. New ideas and change are threatening. He likes the status quo. He tends to be jealous even when there is no reason to be jealous. He sees other men as predators and feels very protective of "his women."

Controllers rarely show any doubt about anything, even when

they don't know anything about the subject. And if you are not convinced they are "together" at first meeting, you soon will be, for it will not be long until they are teaching *you* the correctness of *their* ways of doing things! They come across as the world's experts on everything. Controllers may have never changed a diaper in their lives, but they are *sure* you are doing it incorrectly! Often, they become obsessed with housekeeping. One woman reported that she knew something was wrong when, on the honeymoon, her husband yelled and screamed at her because she got the bath mat wet as she got out of the shower. He could not believe that she was unaware of the way drying was supposed to be done. You dry off in the shower, then, before stepping out, you stick your foot out the door, dry it, then place it on the mat. Then you shift your weight to that foot and repeat the procedure with the other foot, guaranteeing that the mat will remain dry. But all of this must occur only after the shower walls have been squeegeed to prevent lime and mold buildup. He claimed that she should have known this. He accused her of being inconsiderate. Welcome to "Reality Marriage" with a control freak. However long the engagement, it obviously was not quite long enough.

Not all controllers yell. This arrogant attitude may be expressed in a haughty, bossy manner or as a "benevolent" fatherly approach, both of which are demeaning and reflect an attitude of superiority. Diversity is sin to the control freak. He wants consistency, and he wants it all consistent with him.

One woman reported that her controller husband even controlled the type of stainless-steel flatware he ate with by raging if he did not get the set he liked. To him a three-pronged fork was no fork at all. A four-pronger was the only fork he would use. Dinner was a nightmare for this family, since besides worrying about silverware, the dad would routinely pick a fight with one of the kids, criticizing one thing or the other, until the child was in tears. Being happy or laughing or expressing an opinion different from Dad's was not allowed either. He was extremely threatened if his wife and the kids did not constantly mirror him. In fact, he even tried to insist that the wife vote as he did, or "it will cancel out my vote." This same woman tried to take racquetball lessons at the local YMCA, but he refused to give her permission because, he said, "Then you will be separate from me." She shook her head in disbelief!

Emotionless controllers insist on being informed about the minute details of what everyone in the household is doing, but never call home to let others know their schedule because then they would be letting someone else control them! Other people's needs are usually not considered, and, if they are, they are seen as a threat.

DISTORTING SCRIPTURE FOR CONTROL

As mentioned earlier, some men who are controlling justify their behavior with the belief that a man has the divine right to control everything and everyone in the house. They see women as things to be controlled, much like children. They believe that God has given them the right to "take dominion" (à la the creation story in Gen. 1:26–28) over women and the world. One woman told us that her husband justified his controlling ways by telling her early in the marriage: "The Bible says, 'The two shall become one' and that means you *have to do* everything *my* way." This kind of sick Scripture interpretation is all too common and casts a very distorted reflection of who God really is and how He expects us to relate to and respect one another. Allow us to take a little time to clarify this issue since it is often a severe problem for the Christian man who is also a control freak.

It was never God's intention for humans to take dominion over one another, whether a master over a slave or a husband over a wife. The Genesis passage refers to dominion over the fish, birds, and creeping things, not other humans. Only after Adam and Eve sinned and were removed from the garden and the subsequent flood, did God institute human government, via His covenant with Noah (Gen. 9:1–19). Usually, however, most controllers just like being in control, and their use or misuse of Scripture is only one more weapon in their arsenal rather than a sincere belief in God's Word. Many women and children have been abused and "taken it" based on some distorted interpretation of a Bible verse ripped out of context. Rather than provide light and guidance to heal, the Word is twisted and used to hurt.

A common passage used to exert control over a woman is Ephesians 5:21–26. In this passage of Scripture, verse 24 says, "Wives should submit to their husbands in everything" (NIV). These words have been used to cause much misery and cast the Christian faith in a very unhealthy light.

The problem is that this passage is taken out of context. It is one phrase lifted from an entire passage. When you understand the principles of the entire passage, this phrase about submission is liberating, not controlling. The first part of the passage starts off with the central message that is being communicated. Verse 21 reads, "Submit to one another out of reverence for Christ" (NIV). There is to be a *mutual* submission of husband and wife to each other. They should do this as a way of honoring Christ. No one is to lord it over another; they are to submit to and serve each other. This is how relationships work best, and here the Scripture levels the playing field between men and women. Each submits to the other. That is the message of this passage.

Women have gotten a bum rap on this. When I (Steve) read this I feel the demand is on me to do what I often don't want to do: that is, sacrifice all of who I am so my wife can be all of who she can be. I feel direction to submit to her rather than try to control her. And I believe that if I do my part in loving her the way Christ loved the church, she will respond with respect and mutual submission. But even if she does not, I am fulfilled in knowing I am doing what God wants me to do and that is to serve her sacrificially rather than control her superficially.

Here is an example of how it works for us. Sandy and I had been having some difficulty, and we were drifting apart. I use the term "drifting" very loosely. Actually, Sandy asked me one day if I would like to live somewhere else. My response was one of total amazement. I responded, "We love living here. Why would you want to move?" She replied, "I'm not talking about you and me, I'm talking about you. I want you to live somewhere else." I mustered up the international male sound for finally getting the message: "Oohhh."

I needed to get help to keep the marriage together and get us back to where we needed to be. I started going to a counselor, and together we looked at what I could do to make things better. One of the things that surfaced was the fact that I have a very quick wit. I have a comment for everything, most of which have some attempt at humor in them. The counselor suggested that perhaps these quips should be shelved when I am at home and that I should commit to supporting Sandy over the next couple of years with only positive reinforcement. "If she has a problem, trust God to have someone else tell her about it." Wow, that was quite a challenge for me. I had to not only submit to her needs, but to keep quiet and be a totally positive support. So what were the results? About eighteen months later I heard her tell someone that I was 100 percent different. I also had some friends who had not seen me in a while tell me that I was happier, freer, and more at peace with myself. The results were there because I did what I had to do to win my wife back: submitting to her needs and her agenda.

I (Steve) recently counseled a wonderful young couple who got off to a very shaky start because of the husband's expectations of the wife to do everything his way. Any man who thinks this passage gives him the right to boss around a woman, or have his way in everything, needs to read this passage over and over until the truth and grace and balance of it finally sink in. The fact is, two people submitting and sacrificing for each other is the only formula I know that leads to a successful relationship. It is no surprise to me that that formula would be found in the Bible. It is also not surprising that a controlling man would distort the meaning to fit his agenda.

TYPES OF CONTROL FREAKS

LIFE WITH A ROBOT

If you live with a man who is controlling, you know that he is just as interested in staying in control of himself as he is of you. Self-control means not reacting emotionally or even showing emotion, unless it would result in greater control. That was the way Dan was. Dan, a man who had not cried in five years (since his mother's death), described himself as "an unemotional man." He did not feel his emotions, so he thought he did not have any. Many men make this mistake. The reality is that all of us are emotional beings. All human beings (and other animals as well) have the capacity for emotion unless they are severely brain damaged. Dan, like many men, had emotions all right, but they were crammed down deep inside of him, somewhere where he would never notice them if he could help it. Dan controlled his expression of feelings out of fear. Not only was he controlling to those around him, but he demanded of himself a stoic self-defense that required no one know how he felt, unless he could articulate it without displaying his feelings. Naturally, if you do anything that taps into his deeply submerged feelings, and there is a threat that they might surface, then you have to stop doing whatever you are doing. He will see to it that all threats to his facade are dealt with severely and quickly.

Controlling men such as Dan, afraid of emotion, become like robots: the strong, silent type. John Wayne, Gary Cooper–type actors come to mind. These controllers are not content to control behaviors. No, they want to control feelings, too: theirs and yours. They see themselves as making the world better and justify their tactics by stating that they are "only trying to help" or "I'm just trying to make you a better person." They try desperately not to think about how they feel and try valiantly to stop others from stimulating any emotion. Emotions are extremely threatening to these men, though they usually feel justified if they do get angry and explode. Black-and-white thinkers of the "all or nothing" school of thought, their tolerance of uncertainty is minimal. Their usual reaction to everyone else in the family being upset or uncertain is a condescending, "above it all" attitude. "I just cannot understand what everyone is so worked up about."

One man's standard response when confronted with hurt or anger by his wife was, "Well, let me think about that, and we can discuss it later." An otherwise intelligent businessman, he seemed to lose his gray matter when he came home. His excuse (besides needing some time to mount a defense for his lack of care or connection) is that he "is not an emotional person," stated, of course, in a passionless, infuriating monotone.

To these robot men, any sense of feeling threatens their control. When something is disturbing to them, they often claim not to have any feelings at all. But the feelings are there. And sooner or later, in one form or another, they will be expressed. Feelings are never buried dead, they are buried alive. Eventually, they will find their way to the surface. It may be in a fit of rage or in a sudden illness, but they will get up there and force themselves to be dealt with.

VIOLENT CONTROLLERS

Violent controllers have a lot in common with the angry men mentioned in the last chapter. They do not take responsibility for their own feelings or behaviors; rather, they insist that their wives made them do it. They assert that they "would never have done it if their wives had not provoked them." They see their violence as simply an automatic and understandable (hence, irresistible) response to someone else's "doing something wrong." It is just one of many ways to ensure compliance with the way things ought to be.

One woman, engaged in a shouting match with her controlling husband, eventually became the recipient of his violence when he slammed the car door on her leg. He justified it by saying she had driven him to it. It almost broke her leg and did cut and severely bruise it. When she read an article in the paper by Dr. Laura Schlessinger about following the "4 R's of repentance with sincerity" she clipped it out and gave it to him. Later she found it stuffed in her Bible, with the following note scribbled on it: "Dr. Laura has Lots [sic] of good views and advice. But what is your point for wanting me to read the article? Do you expect something?" He later told her that he expected her to apologize for calling the police on him, and that he did not need to apologize to her because her "verbal abuse" justified his slamming the door on her. Good for her for calling the police. You may have to as well if you live with a controller whose anger is increasing as you try new ways to slip from underneath his oppression.

Some violent controllers have never actually hit their wives, but they make it clear through gestures, by throwing objects, by destroying property, or by hurting a woman's pets, that *she* is the next victim if she does not shape up. Intimidation is the controller's middle name. While his threats may seem at times to be a bluff, the woman never knows if *this* time he will cross the line. That way he maintains control without necessarily laying a hand on her. Other violent controllers know where to hit a woman so it will not show and how to deliver blows or shoves in such a way as to not leave marks. Some will threaten to kill the woman, her children, or her pets if she goes to the police about the beatings.

VERBAL ABUSERS

Some controllers use verbal abuse to get their way. Verbal abuse is a wound that can haunt a person for years. Physical bruises heal; bones mend; but verbal attacks can ring in your ears forever. One woman had put up with foul language and degrading remarks for years. Not knowing what else to do, she finally wrote the elders of her church begging for help. The following are excerpts from her letter:

> I must name the most serious problem for what it is—verbal abuse. It has taken years to get to this point of admitting that [my husband] is abusive, so please do not take this lightly . . . The first time he called me a "b——h" was when [child's name] was a few months old. I don't really want to write these next things down . . . I am in tears just thinking about doing this.

> Many times he has told me to "Shut the —— up." This is usually when he is fussing at (abusing) one of the kids and I try to step in.

> He has told me that I am a "G— d—— wicked, evil b——h!" He says, "You're mentally ill . . . You had no upbringing, no discipline, so you don't even know what discipline is." The discipline issue comes up when I disagree with him yelling at and berating the kids.

> . . . he'll say, "Go to h——! I hope you burn in hell forever!" If he thinks I am being self-righteous he'll call me "[first name] Jesus Christ [her last name]."

Sadly, one of the reasons she approached the elders of the church was because her husband was a leader in that church. The elders handled it appropriately, but when they confronted him about these behaviors, he decided it was time to go to another church! He wanted to wield "authority" in his home, but he did not want to submit to it!

Can you imagine the pain inside a man who talks to his wife like that and beats her down with the cruelest and most vile words? We can only imagine the horrific life he has had that brought him to this level of inhumanity to another.

MALE CHAUVINIST CONTROLLERS

Male chauvinist controllers are men who believe that women are inherently inferior to men. They may or may not base this belief on some religious doctrine. (It is important to note as well that not all men who believe in the "traditional role" for women in the home and/or the church are necessarily controllers, nor do they all see women as inherently inferior to men.) The men we are talking about, however, see their rights stemming from the fact of their maleness and may or may not bolster this assertion of power with religious beliefs.

I (Meg) was on a talk show in Chicago when a trucker called up and tried to say that because men dominated women in every culture on earth, then that domination was what was supposed to be. When I mentioned that murder happened in every culture, too, but that its prevalence did not make it proper, the caller said, "Oh, but that's different." Men who want control will use any justification they can find to ensure their place of dominance.

Male chauvinist controllers often have a "life is like pie" mentality; that is, they believe there is only so much love, attention, power, sex, and money to go around, so you must contend with everyone to get as much as you can for yourself. They are very jealous and see their families as possessions. Their control, while oppressive to their families, is viewed as protective by them. They believe they are unappreciated for the sacrifice and dedication they have that motivates them to attend to so many details.

One kind, gentle woman reported that her husband would rage at her if a man she knew from a class at church would greet her on Sunday morning, or if her best friend's husband (whom she had known for years) kissed her on the cheek upon greeting her. Another man would not let his wife answer the phone because "you never know who might be calling." I (Steve) know of this because I have witnessed how he screened every call my wife made to his wife. This, his third wife, seems to thrive under his control. She never complains or resists, never confides in my wife that there is a problem. Finally, my wife gave up on the friendship. She felt that it was just too weird to be part of his system of control.

MOTIVATIONAL DYNAMICS

What is going on with the control freak on a motivational level? What motivates a person to be so self-focused that he has to control everything around him? The things that he tries to appear to possess are the things he is without. It is no surprise that insecurity and fear of rejection are at the root of most, but not all, controlling behaviors. Since this type of man is so common and so destructive, we want to spend some time looking at examples of the foundational problems of his need to be in control.

Rick Joyner comments on the foundation of fear and rejection in his book *There Were Two Trees in the Garden:*

> When fear controls us, every perception is distorted. Until there is restoration of union with God, a person is utterly alone. You may have relationships with others but true union is not possible until the perfect love of God has cast out all your fears. To the fearful the world is a threat and life is a battle to gain control. When the fearful gain control of a situation the result is oppression. Fear causes over-reactions [sic] to real or perceived threats to one's position . . . The lust for power is fueled by the insecurity of a man; his drive for control is often a defense mechanism to protect him from rejection. But power over others will never allay fears; it will only increase them.[1]

While it may appear simplistic, for the control freak, love is the problem and love is the answer. Not experiencing unconditional love from parents leads to difficulties, if not impossibilities, in experiencing God's love. Until he can grasp the depths of God's love, he will live in fear and fight the insecurities that drive him. His control of others is a form of the conditional love he experienced early on. He became a victim of it and then a carrier of this loveless condition of fear.

As astounding as it might seem, God really does love us unconditionally and created human beings to be in relationship with Himself. He also created us to be in relationship with one another. We are created with these relationship needs, and when they are not met, loneliness and isolation become the dark swamp from which our deep problems emerge. The whole creation groans for the fulfillment of this plan of relationship. In other words, just by looking around we can see in nature the relationships that exist and the drive for connection. We can see it in elephants who support the grieving mother of a dead calf. We see it in monkeys as they play with and groom one another. As creations made in God's image, we need to be in healthy relationships of mutual respect and unconditional love, not lopsided arrangements where all is controlled, all is sickly predictable. In the absence of love and relationship, in the presence of insecurity and fear, the control freak compensates with obsessive control to "feel" connection and "feel" commitment. This lonely man fights against rejection, not realizing that those who have been destroyed by his control reject him, even though they are still around him.

CHARACTERISTICS OF THE CONTROL FREAK

In summary then, what clues do you have that a man is a controller? Here are a few:

1. *Emphasizes doing things "right" rather than the relationship.* His way of working does not take into account the feelings of others. He is totally focused on how things ought to be done rather than how to relate to others or how he is perceived by others.

2. *Gets irritated or angry when you make an error or do something your way instead of his way.* What would be seen as a careless error by someone else is seen as a major affront or attack by him. He rages because he does not think you respect him enough to do something the right way. So you spend a great deal of your time on edge,

hoping you don't do the wrong thing at the wrong time. These and other conditions he has established for the relationship leave you feeling that his love for you is very thin.

3. *Is critical most of the time.* He cannot see his own faults, only yours. He may use sarcasm or humor on occasion, but he is always onto something that someone, especially you, needs to do better. The children hate to bring their friends over because when he is in one of his critical states of mind, he will likely humiliate the kids in front of their friends, just as he has humiliated you in front of others. He is a huge mass of negativity and brings others down when he is looking at them to find the flaws and point them out.

4. *Is close-minded; not open to new or different ways, especially yours; has established ways of doing things and will not vary.* Order and control are his gods, and sameness is his security blanket. He will go to great lengths to point out how ridiculous some of your suggestions are, even though you know they make excellent sense. He does not want you to think that there will be any "making this stuff up" allowed along the way. Innovation is up to him, not you. His family and his traditions are paramount to him. To him, his parents and grandparents had it right on how to get along in this world, and everyone else just does not get it.

5. *Uses intimidation to force others to do things his way.* At times this may be subtle, but at other times he is quite forceful in his insistence. He may threaten to take things away from you as if you were his child. He may threaten to embarrass you or even hurt you. The more desperate he is the more force he will use. If you have given in easily to his intimidation, he has learned that it works. It is not easy to reverse the pattern, but it can be done. He has to learn that intimidation causes a problem for him, not someone else.

WHAT KIND OF WOMAN DOES THE CONTROL FREAK WANT?

The control freak tends to be attracted to women who feel insecure and unsure of themselves so he can more easily portray himself as strong, confident, and together.

He wants a woman who is loyal (like a Girl Scout or a dog) and completely devoted to him before *anything* else. The control freak needs a woman who will not walk out, and he will even test her perseverance during the dating process. He is best at reeling her in when she has few friends; he will alienate what friends she does have. The less attached she is to her family the easier it is for him to develop in her an undying loyalty to him.

Women who are willing to be controlled are desired by the control freak. This opens the door to all types of women who will change under his demands. A stubborn or strong woman who stands up for herself is repugnant to him. He will flee her and search out someone who bends under his unreasonable pressure. Remember that there are controllers out there, but they only win because they are allowed to do so.

Rather than look for a woman who is insecure, male chauvinist controllers seek a woman who knows what she is doing in marrying him and who is skilled and willing enough to satisfy his every desire. He wants a woman who is competent in meeting his needs. He wants a woman who is willing to prove her loyalty to him and to be devoted to him as his private possession (though he may not be so crass as to put it quite that bluntly). He wants a woman who at least resists his physical advances enough to prove she won't give away what is rightly his after they are married. His attention is often strongly sexual, and he makes the first move. He likes to ogle women. The woman is to receive, submit, surrender, allow, acquiesce, relinquish, and accept. He is to initiate, dominate, control, demand, and pursue. He sees women as sexual objects available for his pleasure. Anything sexual that he wants to do should be acceptable to her. As another form of control, he may have developed keen skills as a lover. This only serves to strengthen the trap in which he has placed his wife.

This type of controller does not like "his woman" to work, but if she must, then she had better earn less than he does and have a job with few men around. And, of course, her money is really *his* money, not "our" money. He feels more comfortable being the only provider and tends to let the wife know how lucky she is to "get to stay home and do nothing." He is apt to joke and say, "Yeah, just keep 'em barefoot and pregnant." I (Steve) worked for a man who used to say to anyone who would listen, "When I am reincarnated I want to come back as a Newport Beach housewife. They have it made."

WHY DOES SHE FALL FOR HIM?

Why do women fall for these controlling men? Perhaps the more appropriate question is, Why did you fall for him? What happened that led you to this kind of man? Here are some thoughts that may be helpful as you explore your motivations or the motivation of another to be attracted and attached to a control freak.

1. Some women want to be controlled! They want to have someone else in charge so they do not have to grow up and make their own mistakes. They like being the child-victim. It allows them to feel sorry for themselves. They have felt so out of control in earlier life that it seemed like a relief when someone else took over. But when they start to mature, they discover that what was once attractive is now the biggest challenge to developing a fulfilling life.

One woman admitted that she realized she had to choose between letting her husband control her every move (literally), as if she were a child, and growing up and taking the heat for her own life choices. She was honest enough to admit that sometimes being controlled wasn't so bad, because painful choices did not have to be made and then she could blame *him* for all the problems.

2. Other women may be so used to living with a controlling parent that moving on to a controlling spouse feels normal! These women have grown up without an identity separate from a man. They look for a man to define and dominate them. When he steps in with his take-charge attitude, this woman melts in his arms. This is not a conscious attraction, but often we blindly fall into relationships that are similar to the problems we have experienced at home. We may feel threatened by someone who allows us total freedom if we have been constrained in our youth. The very thing we should be fleeing, we fall back into because, in a strange way, it feels comfortable. Because we are so used to the feelings, we mistake them for normal or good.

3. She may have mistaken his perfectionism for efficiency and thought that he only tried to control *things,* not people. The controlling perfectionist seems to have life so together. He appears to be on top of so many things, able to manage so much at one time. For those of us who are a bit scattered and disorganized, these people seem like a tower of strength that could easily complement and compensate for our weaknesses. We are drawn to their sense of mastery and the perception that they are much better put together than we are. In the end, we discover the sickness of his ways and that without the control, he feels weak, small, and insignificant.

RELATING TO THE CONTROL FREAK

All of us act in a controlling manner once in a while. All of us can identify somewhat with the anxiety the controller feels about inadequacy and his fears of abandonment. Yet even if you are able to empathize, living with someone who is controlling is very difficult. How can you cope?

One important principle of living with controllers was brought to Meg's attention by a colleague, Dr. Ed Smith from Campbellsville, Kentucky. He is fond of saying: "There are really no such people as controllers, only those who allow themselves to be controlled." While Dr. Smith would never deny that abuse does exist and that there are people who try to control others, he is emphasizing that *we do not have to allow ourselves to be perpetual victims.* We may have been sucked into the vortex of the controllers' behaviors. We may have learned early in life not to resist inappropriate actions on the part of others. We may have been terrorized into senseless obedience to cruel parents, teachers, or spouses. Yet, at some point, at some juncture, we become accountable to ourselves, to those who love us, and to God to take responsibility and STOP the abuse. We can creatively cope and, in the case of control through abuse, get away from the abuser. We may have been victimized, but we do not have to remain as victims. We can find a way to cope and to overcome.

Les Parrott, in his book *High Maintenance Relationships,* makes some good suggestions on how to cope creatively with controllers. We have included some of his thoughts with our own embellishments. To cope with controllers:

1. *Acknowledge when they are right.* Sometimes the frustrating thing about the controller is that he *is* right, at least partially. When he is, acknowledge that point and compliment him. This will usually defuse a great deal of tension.

2. *Focus positively on who they* are, *not just what they do or do not do.* Controllers are very performance-oriented and tend to see their own worth as tied directly to their "successes." They usually have not learned to see any good in themselves beyond what they can do or achieve.

3. *Look for "the log in your own eye" first.* Jesus knew our tendency to point the finger at others without examining ourselves first. Our friend or spouse *may indeed be controlling,* but we have all erred and failed in one way or another, and it never hurts to have humility as a covering.

4. *Remember, his behavior is really not about you.* It may be directed toward you, but it is about him and his anxiety and fears. Do not blame yourself when he gets upset, and do not take responsibility for his actions.

5. *Do not try to fix it or "make it better" when he is upset.* That behavior on your part will just give him more rope with which to hang you. Let him sit in his anxiety or rage. Do not own it. If *you* are too anxious watching him go nuts, leave temporarily. Go to a movie, go to a friend's home, or to the local mall. Just do it.

6. *Stay calm.* Nothing fuels the controller's rage more than hysteria on your part. Do not let yourself sink to his level.

7. *Look for the good even if it is a small thing.* For example, you might say: "Well, I cannot agree with your plan of action regarding the children, but your concern means a lot to me. It

is good to know you care so deeply about their discipline. Let's see what we can negotiate that works for both of us."

8. *Look behind the behavior to the feeling.* What is his need? Is he trying to quell anxiety about feeling inferior, inadequate, unnoticed, powerless? Is there a way to meet his need for reassurance and support without compromising your values or needs?

9. *Avoid a confrontation if you can.* For example, if he makes a snide remark about you in front of the kids, you might say something like:"Oh, so *that* is what you think!" or "Oh, so *you* think I . . ." Said with a quiet yet surprised tone, these statements put the problem back on him and his perceptions. After making the remark, just continue calmly doing what you were doing.

10. *Do not expect a rational discussion right at the moment.* His worldview is different from yours. Accept it. His goal in these interactions is to control and dominate. He wants to win. Yours may be to have mutual understanding and problem solving. No matter how sincerely you explain your goal and desires to him, he will continue to see things from a "power over" position. If you are to have a rational talk, it will probably be later.

11. *Offer a one-down (humble) suggestion as a way to defuse his intensity.* For example, "This may not be the way we end up doing the deck, but maybe we could look at my idea to see if there is anything worthwhile in it?" This gives him a chance to "win" because he is being gracious enough to look at your admittedly unlikely idea! So even if he agrees to go with your plan, he still *feels* like a winner. Later he may even say, "Well, you know how women are. Always have some bright idea or something. Well, I decided to let the little woman have a go at designing the deck. And guess what? I think I can make her little plan work. Just needs my expertise, is all." Sometimes it helps to let someone save face.

12. *Do not be intimidated.* While some confrontations can be avoided, not all can be. Stand your ground when you must. When you do give in, however, remember that the kids already know what kind of man he is. So your acknowledging his need to control is no surprise to them. Acknowledging his problem will defuse the tension for you and the children when you do have to give in to him. You will not win all the battles. Some are not worth winning anyway.

13. *Do not expect to have the last word.* You can maintain your boundaries by saying something like: "Okay, we will do it your way. However, I will not listen to you until you can calmly and respectfully explain to me your rationale." This allows him to "win" if necessary, but puts limits on his behavior.

14. *If he is proved wrong, especially in front of others, let him save face by your not saying, "I told you so!"* If he is willing to express it at all, listen to his pain or disappointment empathically. Defeat for the controller is often the first step toward healing. So don't waste it by rubbing it in.[2]

WHAT COULD THE CONTROL FREAK DO TO CHANGE?

It is most difficult for the control freak to change because the very act of change necessitates loss of control. Even attending a counseling session is a threat to his control. He will usually go to see if he can win the counselor over to his side. If he feels he is really in control of the sessions, he will continue. If not, he will usually drop out.

In some cases, the controlling man begins to see what he has created and to sense what he really is inside. Some decide that they want something better. Someone somewhere gives him hope that he can live without being in charge of everything. When that happens he can begin the process of gradual change. It is a change that leads him away from *control* of others into *connection* with others.

Here are some steps he can take to change:

1. *Surrender to God, who really is in control.* This way, he can ask God to heal him and help him with his insecurity and fear of rejection.

2. *Let go of his performance orientation, which causes him to be demanding of self and others.* This involves accepting the grace and unconditional love of God and then sharing that with others. He cannot give away what he does not have. In his relationship with God, which must be paramount, he can experience forgiveness, acceptance, and a second chance.

3. *Turn away from the desire to have power over others, by submitting himself to God and practicing giving, not receiving.* He must make a conscious effort to meet others' needs. This may require making lists of things he can do for others. This does not come naturally for him, and it will take much practice before his obsession with self is replaced with a focus on others.

4. *Look for his own flaws first rather than focusing on others' failures.* He must learn to see the good, the effort, the attempt, instead of the bad, the mistakes, and the failures in himself and in others. He also needs to look for the log in his own eye before he points out the speck in someone else's eye. If he becomes committed to change and to doing the work that is needed, he will be so busy working on himself that he will not have much time to identify all that is wrong with others.

5. *Connect with people who need help or are in trouble.* He can develop humility by asking God to humble him and then going out there and doing the things for others that no one else wants to do. He will learn learn from the lowly, the broken, the undesirable. It will help him to develop some level of ministry to others in need.

6. *Wake up every morning and start with a prayer, asking God to be in control and committing to God to give back control when it is inappropriately wrestled away.*

7. *End each day with jotting down times in a notebook when he was controlling.* Then he can examine how the situation could be handled next time. He also should take note when he stepped back and did not control others when it would have been easy to do so.

8. *Make amends to anyone who has been hurt by his controlling*

nature in the past. He needs to be sure they know he was wrong and is working on change. This will help him live and feel forgiven.

CONCLUSION

If you are in a relationship with a control freak, and if he is in control, you are obviously out of control. Your life is not your own, and your misery is greater than most will ever know. Move beyond denial and accept the reality of him and your relationship. Look within to discover what has led you to respond to him the way you have. Look to God for courage to change those patterns. Look to a good counselor to help you develop new ways of responding. You probably feel very trapped, but you are not. You have choices to make, and the most important one of all is the choice to heal.

SNAPSHOT SUMMARY OF
THE CONTROL FREAK

CLUES TO HELP YOU SPOT HIM

1. Doing things right is more important than relationship.

2. Becomes irritated and angry when you mess up.

3. Is critical of others most of the time.

4. Is close-minded, established in ways and will not vary.

5. Uses intimidation to force others to do it his way.

THE WOMAN TO WHOM HE IS ATTRACTED

1. Is insecure, unsure of herself.

2. Is confident only in her role of meeting his needs.

3. Is loyal and devoted.

4. Is willing to be possessed and controlled.

5. Is mousy and weak.

THE WOMAN WHO FALLS FOR HIM

1. Wants to be controlled so she won't have to grow up and make her own mistakes.

2. Is used to living with a controlling parent, especially the father.

3. Mistakes perfectionism for efficiency and proficiency.

4. Believes he controls situations and things, not people.

5. Compensates for insecurity with his seeming confidence.

WHAT YOU CAN DO

1. Acknowledge when he is right.

2. Praise him for who he is, not what he does.

3. Remember that the problem is about him, not you, no matter what he says.

4. Stay calm and avoid confrontation if possible.

5. Refuse to react, and don't try to fix things when he is upset.

WHAT HE COULD DO TO CHANGE

1. Develop his relationship with God to heal insecurity and fear of rejection.

2. Let go of performance orientation and become less demanding of self and others.

3. Turn away from a desire to have power over others and use what power he has to help others.

4. Examine his own flaws while looking for the good in others.

5. Explore how feeling out of control as a child scared him into wanting to be overly controlling as an adult.

CHAPTER 3

MR. WONDERFUL

It is difficult to understand why some women are attracted to certain men who are severely sick. The problems these men carry are so obvious and so destructive that it amazes everyone, even you, if you are one of those women. Some men are just downright objectionable from the start, and anyone growing closer to them is obviously either sick themselves or easily deceived. In contrast to these glaringly bad men, there are some men who seem easy to love—at least at first. It is easier to see how someone could be attracted to a guy who is suave, charming, romantic, and so utterly fascinating that he seems just too good to be true. That is exactly how you might describe Larry, an example of Mr. Wonderful, who turns out to be anything but wonderful.

Larry is the kind of guy who appears to flow through life. He is smooth in his talk and mannerisms. Some people are attracted to Larry like moths to the flame. While you may not be able to figure out if he is for real or not, you will most likely enjoy the way he treats you. Larry grew up in the South, where men are shown how to be gentlemen, where manners and the Bible are taught hand in hand. He has a slight drawl, which he exaggerates whenever it suits his cause. While not overweight, he is a large man who seems to fill up a room when he walks in. Only the best suits, custom shirts, silk ties, and designer shoes will do for Larry. He always looks as if he just stepped out of a fashion ad, though not trendy. With him there is never a hair out of place, shoes are always shiny, shirt pressed, tie straight. He comes across as relaxed, totally at home with himself. A former football player in high school, he still has an imposing build, even at fifty years old. His voice is deep and commanding. He expects people to listen to him, and if they don't he is not above intimidation to make sure they do. Larry did well in business, and it is obvious. He makes sure you know it. He's been in sales all his adult life, a profession that began while he was in high school, selling Bibles door to door.

If you looked back into Larry's early years, you would detect some odd experiences that shaped Larry into the man he is today. Larry does not realize these things were important, but they were. Larry maintains that he had a happy childhood and never once was afraid, not once. He claims to not remember much about his childhood, except that it was good. He says that even when his dad beat him cruelly, it was okay because ". . . I probably deserved every beating I ever got." His dad was a hardworking tradesman, who was also talented in design and mechanical things. Larry saw him as frugal, a "waste not, want not" sort of fellow, who was very conscious of the small things, such as lights being turned off when not in use in the house. (Larry's second wife reported that he seemed to have followed in his dad's footsteps, in that while he was so generous with others in public, he was a penny-pincher in private. He wasted nothing at home while he lavished upon himself the best clothes and the best cars. Whether because of a lack of funds or merely his dad's frugality, Larry reports that he never had a new bike to ride, and he has been making up for it ever since in the cars he drives and the money he stashes away in case things go bad.)

Larry's only sibling, Linda, was six years younger, so, in a way, they were each only children. Larry sees Linda as more even-tempered than himself but also more introverted. He claims that everyone likes her because she is genuine, reliable, and sensible. He sees himself as the hardest worker, the most intelligent, the one who got the best grades, the strongest, most powerful, and most spontaneous in the family. He views himself as less rebellious and more conforming than his sister, but also more idealistic and less easily hurt.

Larry's personal relationships have been tumultuous. He has been married three times, and all three wives left when their Mr. Wonderful turned into Mr. Cruelty. What started as arrogance led to neglect and emotional abuse. His third just walked out the door one day with only the clothes on her back. She did not want to waste another moment of her time on him and his problems. Larry claims his first wife, Susie, was a slob and that they had nothing in common. He had three children with her and denies that he was mean or condescending or neglectful. He met his second wife, Matty, while married to Susie, though he told Matty at the time that they were getting a divorce. Matty learned later that this was untrue and that while he was sweeping her off her feet claiming to be divorced, he was still married to Susie. He insisted that Matty move in with him (because, of course, he was not yet really divorced) and she did so, against her Christian values, because she was afraid of losing him. (Men like Larry can talk you into almost anything.) He insisted that they tell no one of their arrangement.

After divorcing Susie, Larry finally made Matty his wife. During the course of their ten-year marriage, however, he became verbally and emotionally abusive to Matty and also was hurtful to their son, Scotty. He competed with the boy and could never let the child win. He would yell at Scotty when he was hurt or cried, and only participated in his son's activities if it was convenient. He met his third wife, Laura, while in counseling with Matty about their troubled marriage. He initiated a separation, saying he just needed some time, but started seeing Laura on the sly. She thought he was the most honorable and righteous man she had ever met. (Ironically, she was seeing the same therapist Larry and his wife were seeing, and kept reporting how she had met this wonderful Christian man who was totally misunderstood and mistreated by his witch of a wife!)

Like many men of his ilk, Larry loves to impress people with his generosity and wealth. He is closefisted with his family, but his mistresses have always had the best. He drives a BMW and lovingly massages it with a chamois every day. He uses money as a way to manipulate others and is very disdainful of anyone who has less money than he does. He has a great therapist but looks down on counselors, since they would never make any decent money. He gives to his church but wants someone (at least, the pastor) to thank him personally for it. His tendency is to use someone insofar as it benefits him, and then he finds a reason to discard them. His children thoroughly dislike him, and he is alienated from his family of origin. Larry is one of the men we call "Wonderful Guys," but below the surface, despite his charm, Larry is anything but wonderful.

WHAT MR. WONDERFUL IS REALLY ALL ABOUT

Everyone probably has known a Mr. Wonderful in their lifetime. He is such a good conversationalist, knowing something about just about everything; in the beginning he may even come across like a genius. He certainly sounds brilliant on most any topic that arises. This is the guy who thinks he is "God's gift to the universe" in the areas of looks and brainpower. He won't tell you that, and you probably won't pick up on the fact that he thinks that at first. He is just that smooth. Whether he is truly more talented, smarter, more artistic, or more anything is debatable, but he expresses a confidence that makes you believe it is true.

It seems that this man has what it takes. Since he has been treated specially by so many, the rules do not apply to him. He gets special prerogatives, privileges, special rights. Other people cannot park in handicapped spaces, but he believes he can because he has important business to conduct. It has been that way all his life. Other people in the gated community have to park their boats at the marina, but he can leave his in the driveway because he's too busy to drive all the way over there. Other people have to bring library books back on time, but not him—he isn't done with them yet. He can lose his temper in public (or in private) because he is right, and smarter, richer, and more connected than other people. He can get rowdy and intoxicated because he's paying for the meal. He can be tyrannical because he makes the money. His sense of entitlement is clear. But none of that comes through until his charm and wit have lured you to him and he is in control of you and the relationship. Only then does the creep in him start to come out. Then the facade of Mr. Wonderful is shattered. But it is too late. His victim has been secured long before that.

Mr. Wonderful is self-centered, self-absorbed, narcissistic. His favorite song might be "I Did It My Way!" A flamboyant fellow, he comes across with strong flavor, lots of character. He tends to overwhelm others with his charm. He is so very convincing that his weak areas are hard to recognize at first. He seems so wonderful, so extraordinary. He says exactly what you want to hear. Perhaps it is what you have longed to hear for years. It is as if he has emotional radar and can discern your weakness and knows how to say what will soothe you when you are down. He does this by being attentive to you and picking up clues from what you say and how you react.

His emotional age is somewhere between one and six years. He has no concept of boundaries. Everything belongs to him, or ought to. Since he regularly uses magical thinking, he believes that he can get away with anything. Other people have to be held accountable, but he can look innocent, bite his lower lip, and every sin is forgotten. A demanding sort of man, Mr. Wonderful requires an inordinate amount of attention. He is uncomfortable if he is out of the spotlight for very long. He fears losing control. He is always doing something, or at least thinking about doing something—always something grand or impressive, of course.

Mr. Wonderful's reaction to criticism is very predictable. He acts outraged that someone would dare question him or his ideas. He tries to humiliate the critic, pointing out what he perceives as their weaknesses or faults, thus shifting the focus from himself. He may feel shame, but if so, it is often unexpressed. In relation to others, Mr. Wonderful is exploitative. He takes advantage of others for his personal gain. He uses people and then discards them, all the while proclaiming himself a great humanitarian. Grandiosity is another characteristic that others who can be objective are sure to notice. He has an exaggerated sense of his own importance, seeing himself as unique and special. He even sees his problems as unique; for example, he will take the following attitude with his doctor: "Well, Doctor, I don't know if you can help me or not. I have a call into the Mayo Clinic . . ."

Often Mr. Wonderful is preoccupied with fantasies of unlimited success, fame, brilliance, power, adoration, beauty, or ideal love. He constantly needs to be reassured of his wonderful qualities, and if you do not remind him, he will remind himself. He can be inordinately jealous if a colleague or family member gets some attention or gets more attention than he does. Mr. Wonderful is unable to empathize with the plight or feelings of anyone else. Every relationship is seen only in the light of how it affects him. He has no desire to understand others and sees their feelings and needs as silly or stupid. His motives are entirely self-oriented. The paradigms through which he views the world are necessarily narrow, since they only take himself into account. He tends to be reactive to the world rather than proactive. He focuses on what is out of his control rather than that which is in his control. He focuses on others as the cause of his problems rather than himself. His stance toward others is closed, defensive, and rigid. His integrity is in question, though he tends to see himself as a person of the highest ethical character.

How does he compensate for this lack of character? He sees those who are attracted to him, his list of accomplishments, and his accumulation of things and believes they could only be a reward from God or the result of the work of one with character. Often, Christian men will use Scripture as a source of authority; they misquote it to achieve dominance or control over another.

Mr. Wonderful sees other people or outside forces as being responsible for his actions. He is not responsible; others make him act the way he does. For example: "I wouldn't have to scold you in front of my family if you did not act so stupid." His manner is defensive and arbitrary since he has replaced cooperation with fear. Others comply, not out of mutuality or cooperation, but out of fear of humiliation, shame, ridicule, or even physical harm. "I wouldn't have hit her if she had only . . ." Mr. Wonderful is driven by the wind, by feelings—his and other people's; by circumstances; and by environmental stimuli.

CHARACTERISTICS OF MR. WONDERFUL

If you were trying to pick out a "Mr. Wonderful" in the midst of some good guys, you would notice that he goes to extremes. Joe gives us some good examples of the extremes of Mr. Wonderful. He converted an old railway station into his home. He had previously lived in an old schoolhouse that he had remodeled himself. Like other Wonderful Guys, Joe's approach seemed to have just the right touch of genius, pizzazz, or eccentricity about it. Whatever he does is calculated, whether choosing to wear cutoffs and Docksiders with no socks or to drive an old MG convertible. While other people are content to have an ordinary office, Joe wanted one that was special. So he chose the old warehouse overlooking the lake. He put in new picture windows, installed huge reproductions of antique ceiling fans, and finished the ceiling to look like old green tin pressed with Victorian designs. Just the right furnishings—some antiques, some modern—finished off the look. He could often be seen staring out the window as if posing for a photo, even if he did not know anyone was looking at him.

Some people think he is affectatious, but the women in his life find him captivating—at least at first. He is gregarious and could probably charm the socks off Mr. Clinton's cat! People like listening to him, and he enjoys talking. So it is a perfect arrangement. He gets all the attention he yearns for, and the other people, especially the women, feel grateful that they got to spend time with him. Those who work more closely with Joe, however, find him explosive and given to rages. He is not above being verbally abusive if it suits his purposes. He uses his anger to humiliate and control others. He pouts, fumes, fusses, rages, and may even become violent. He never gives in or cooperates. Similar to the control freak, it's "his way or the highway." Winning and having power over others are the main purposes of his existence. Unable to admit his own fears, Joe uses intimidation as his interpersonal style.

He is like the ultimate contender. He must win every contest. He has a "That's the way I am" attitude, with "Like me or lump me" as his motto.

Below are five identifying descriptions of Mr. Wonderful:

1. *Mr. Wonderfuls are too good to be true.* They do have a dark side, you just haven't seen it yet. You may never see it until whatever he wants from you is taken. He may want your virginity or just sex. He might want your money or someone to take care of him. He may also just want you to assure him that someone loves him, then once assured, he will leave you for someone else.

2. *Mr. Wonderfuls tend to go to extremes in taste, possessions, places to live, opinions, causes to which they are devoted.* They act like experts on wine, coffee, even bottled water. They own things that at least give the appearance of taste and class. If they have an automobile that is a few years old they will also have a good excuse for why they don't have the latest model. If they cannot afford a nice house they will find a great condominium. If they cannot buy a house they will spend an unreasonable amount of money on an apartment so they can look good. They have an opinion on everything, and it seems that they have spent a lot of time ensuring that most everyone will either disagree with them or not understand their position, thinking they are really out there on the edge.

3. *Despite the charm and seeming devotion to you, the main goal is always "power over," not mutuality.* All of his wonderful characteristics are used as a trap. That is why he is not truly wonderful. He may feel in control when you consent to sex. It could come from the amount of time he is able to siphon off your schedule. Your money in his account would also be a symbol to him that he is achieving his objectives. He uses all of these things to beat down the feelings he has about himself. Most of these feelings center around his realization that he is not so very wonderful at all, so he will do anything to assure himself that he is wonderful.

4. *He can con the fuzz off a peach, is very smooth, and can talk his way out of anything.* At first you will be astounded, but then it will start to make you feel uncomfortable. You will observe him getting

stopped and not getting a ticket from a police officer. You will see him do irresponsible things, like forgetting to pay the bills, and then watch him catch up without paying a penalty because he convinced the creditors he did the best he could in paying. Because of his charm people will amazingly want to make exceptions for him. He has learned over the years what works and what does not.

5. *He tends to be self-centered, self-absorbed, narcissistic, and grandiose.* He has some great stories. And they are all about him, and they make him look very good. If he has his way, he will have you wondering how you could have landed a date with such a wonderful man. You will think he is great and justify all the self-adulation because you think he deserves it. He will do things for you that will make you think he is kind and generous, but all of those things will soon stop because they are nothing more than bait in his trap.

WHAT TYPE OF WOMAN FALLS FOR MR. WONDERFUL?

None of these characteristics seem very wonderful upon reflection. What type of person would find such a man attractive? Women who are attracted to Mr. Wonderfuls are as varied as they are. While not all Mr. Wonderfuls are wealthy, many are, or at least live as if they are. Some are actually on the verge of bankruptcy, but you would never know it to hear them talk. Some women who are attracted to wealth, power, and position often team up with Mr. Wonderful. Some of these women are as smart and as crafty as he. Others are naive, poorly educated, and easily swayed. Some go into the relationship knowing what they are getting but decide to ignore it because the power and/or money is the main attraction. Others do not catch on for a number of years to the con their Mr. Wonderful has pulled. They may suspect that things are not all they seem to be but choose to deny or look the other way.

Some Mr. Wonderfuls are the "misunderstood genius" types who appeal to women who like the underdog. The student activist or political radical would fit this description. Women who are into their own rebelliousness and need to feel special by association are attracted to these men. At least at first, the women who go for these men are easily fooled; if not about his money, certainly about his genius and specialness. They are attracted to his confidence, the self-assurance with which he handles himself. Perhaps insecure or less experienced, they enjoy following along, at least in the beginning. As wives, they buy into the notion that he has "special needs" and are more forgiving of any unfaithfulness or flirtations than they might have been with someone else. Sexually, they are willing to let him do the initiating (he would not like it any other way). The woman he pairs up with allows him to push her for more surrender, sexually and emotionally. He wants to make her feel certain emotions and sensations, make her give herself more fully to him. He wants control and she lets him have it (even if in her own mind she thinks his sex games are silly).

Other women do not think they are smart enough or sexy enough or successful enough on their own. This is the kind of woman who is so thrilled to have a chance with a man like him that she puts up with emotional manipulation and sexual experimentation that would otherwise be distasteful to her. One woman totally changed her personal style to please her Mr. Wonderful. Prior to the relationship, she had been a traditional, stay-at-home mom who liked denim jumpers, Grasshopper shoes, T-shirts, patchwork-quilt skirts, and blue chambray blouses. Flannel nighties and socks were her late evening apparel. She wore her hair long, tied back with a ribbon that coordinated with her outfit. Not one to wear much makeup, she primarily relied on lipstick and a bit of blush to round out her brief, morning beauty routine. Upon divorcing her first husband and finding Mr. Wonderful, she started wearing lots more makeup, had her hair fashionably coiffed, and began letting him pick out her clothes. He would take her shopping at Saks and other upscale stores. His taste ran along the more sophisticated, designer-look lines. He liked sexy lingerie, not flannel pj's. He wanted a woman who looked glamorous and alluring. So this woman became what he wanted. She confided to her therapist that though she detested "the look" he had designed for her, she felt it was a small price to pay for the chance to be his wife. Although bright and college educated, this woman could not see herself as able to manage on her own, and she thought anything she had to do to keep him was okay.

If you are one of those women who have changed their look for someone they thought worthy of stealing their identity, don't feel bad; just determine to never do it again. You are in very good company. My wife (Steve's, of course) is one of the strongest women you will ever meet. She is very responsible and has, to the nth degree, better judgment than I do. Knowing that now, I asked her what she ever saw in me, and she said I had potential. Boy was she ever an optimist because I was fairly messed up when we dated. Coming from Texas and working in a conservative men's clothing store through college, I loved women in traditional clothes. So I bought her things I liked, and then she bought things she thought I would like, and before she knew it she looked a lot like all the other women I had dated in Texas before moving to California. But she was nothing like anyone I had dated. What I loved about her was her sparkle and independence. Her freedom and strength drew me to her. It was tragic that we both fell into my trap of trying to re-create her in my own image.

If you met my wife I think you would love her and you would see just how creative and artistic she is. After being with her thirty minutes or less, you would wonder how she ever could have agreed to wear traditional clothes to make me feel comfortable. But she did. So if you have fallen for the same scheme of a man taking away who you are so he can manipulate you into what he wants, don't feel bad; just don't let it happen again.

RELATING TO MR. WONDERFUL

Can you confront him and hope for change? If you confront him, he may change for a while but will most likely revert back as soon as you let down your guard. He may seem accepting of the criticism, or he might use his temper and wit to cut you down to size for daring to uncover his weakness. If doing so in private fails, he will do it in public.

His goal at all times is to appear to be in control, appear to have power, and appear to win. Looking like a winner is the most important thing to him. Never forget that fact.

His patterns were developed long before he met you, so don't count on being able to change him. If anything changes it is apt to be you. He changes the rules just when you think you've figured it all out. He seems to create new problems for you to solve, just to make you crazy. The relationship tends to get worse as it goes on. You begin to doubt your intelligence and lose all confidence in yourself. Your Mr. Wonderful is all too happy to reinforce this view, as he has said all along that you were inferior. You get depressed and withdraw from your support systems. You change. He doesn't.

As mentioned earlier, he is reactive and does not take kindly to being criticized. He eventually will seek solace from someone else, as he will see you and your criticisms as being too wearing. Believe it or not, he often uses the line: "My wife does not understand me." (How's that for someone who is supposed to be so smart? Maybe the amazing thing is that some women actually fall for it.) He wants a babe on his arm as he ages because he is preoccupied with ideal love and beauty. If anyone has a midlife crisis, it is Mr. Wonderful. He has one big time. All of this, while not wanting a divorce, just a separation or "some space."

Over the years, as he feels more like a failure and a fraud, Mr. Wonderful begins to demand more and more control over you and your circumstances. He implies in his tirades that you do not deserve him and that you are lucky he keeps you around. He resents any growth or autonomy on your part. You begin to be worn out. You may become physically ill and/or depressed. One woman began to have multiple car accidents because she was so depressed; she kept falling asleep at the wheel. After three close calls she decided she needed counseling. The perversity of this type of relationship is that the wife has to decide how much she is willing to put up with to have financial security. She has to give up her dreams of oneness, since he will most likely be too self-absorbed to be truly one with anyone except himself. He may have fooled around, but his mistresses always discovered that the affair Mr. Wonderful likes most is the one he has with himself.

One of the most important things you have to do in dealing with a Mr. Wonderful is to face reality. As with other situations involving someone else, remember: *You cannot change him.* Living with him means that you must learn to expect his cycles of ups and downs so that you will not feel cheated. Notice how your moods change with his cycles and crises. Gain control of yourself. Create a life for yourself. Above all, do not slide into the little girl or slave-girl model of relationship. That is a sure path to no respect or attention from him. Play along with his pretentiousness. Give him as good as he gives. If he is Antony, you be Cleopatra. If he is Lord of the Manor, you be a Grand Lady. If he is the Bishop, you be the Bishop's Wife.

Much of what you see in this man stems from troubled relationships with his parents. There is a good chance that their love for him and for each other was mostly sizzle and little substance. That has come to characterize his way of dealing with others and interacting with the world. What he needs is not enabling or babying. He needs reparenting with strength, balance, and healthy love. He needs acceptance for who he is, not approval for what he does. He needs to learn alternatives to his lifestyle and alternatives to style without substance. If you can get him to go to counseling, there is tremendous potential for him to grow. If he will not even do that for you, you should be prepared for an increasingly difficult relationship. Be sure your support is in place so that you not only survive but also conquer.

If you have not married him already but hope to do so, plan the ceremony many, many months hence. Demand that he go to premarital counseling with you. In the right situation, with a great counselor, he can come to see himself and desire to change. However, this outcome is very rare. If you do follow through with the marriage, you may not have children because he will not want the focus of attention on anything other than himself. If he does want children they will be treated like little trophies. You can almost be guaranteed he will not be available to help you with them. You need to consider all of that going into the marriage. More than anything, take your time, go slowly, and do nothing until you see good character start to emerge in him.

If, after reading all this material, you are still stuck on this man and his many contradictions, you must look inside yourself as honestly as possible. Ask yourself why you are so committed to marrying him. Work on your irrational beliefs. Women attracted to Mr. Wonderful are usually codependent, hate conflict, and are willing to put up with a lot of junk just to have a man around. They may see themselves as okay or adequate, but easily succumb to his assertion that he is smarter, wiser, and better than they are. Put your security in the Lord. Do not let his manipulations intimidate you. The Lord will never desert you, so don't give up. You cannot change him, but you can, with God's help, become a stronger, wiser, happier person. Do not let fears run your life any longer. Jesus is your protector. Seek Him and His courage minute by minute. Rest in the Lord and the power of His might. Take up your spiritual armor (Eph. 6) and stand firm against the fears Satan would throw at you through your man. Ask the Lord to fill you with the Holy Spirit and give you boldness for His sake. Do not let cowardice or weakness overcome you. If you fear abandonment, seek Jesus until nothing will ever frighten you again. If you fear rejection, seek the Lord's affirmation from Scripture. See how He views you. Take a God's-eye view of the situation. Change your perspective. You may need counseling and special prayer to overcome lifelong habits of oversubmissiveness or fears. There is nothing wrong with seeking help. That is why God made us to relate to one another in the body of Christ.

WHAT COULD MR. WONDERFUL
DO TO CHANGE?

If a Mr. Wonderful decided that he indeed had a problem (which it is doubtful he would do), what would he need to do to change? He would at least need to do the following:

1. *Learn to see the world from other people's points of view.* This

shift in perspective will be difficult, since he has had his view and only his view in sight for so long. His sense of superiority to others will have to go, and this, too, will be difficult. You cannot truly take another's view of things when you are seeing yourself as one up on them. So humility will be necessary here. But he can do it.

Sometimes there are life-changing moments that cause Mr. Wonderful to question how he is living and look for alternatives. Most of the time these are moments of desperation. He may sense the detachment, the superficiality and start to ask questions of others and listen to their answers. His desire to be an expert in everything and look stupid in nothing may lead him to study other people. At first he may do it for his own gain, but in doing it he may find that not everyone thinks like him or is motivated by the same things that motivate him. If he will start learning about the lives of others, he may like the way it makes him feel when he has connected authentically.

2. *Stop seeing himself as the master of the universe.* It might even help if he could get one of those small action figures that depict the "Master of the Universe" and put it on his desk, just to remind himself to get off the throne. He probably has many talents and has been given many opportunities. It may have given him some pleasure to believe he has developed all of these himself, but if he could see it another way, it would actually benefit him more. Who he is, is not due to his own efforts but to God's love and provision for him, and if he could see that, he might relax into God's love rather than feeling unworthy of it. Many a business genius, fashion model, or athlete has discovered just how out of their hands their lives are with one twist of a market, increase in age, or career-ending injury. Mr. Wonderful's wonderful things are only there because God allowed them to be or wanted them to be. They may still be there only because God is patiently waiting for him to wake up.

I (Steve) was riding back from a seminar with a gentleman who said that I was much more successful than he was. It struck me as strange for two reasons. One, this man was Charlie Hedges, who has written a book entitled *Getting the Right Things Right.* Far better than any book I have written, it communicates four life-changing principles that everyone should plan their lives around. That alone made him more successful than I am. He had started his own business, supported his family for years, and had been able to spend about twice as much time with his family as I had. For that I considered him most successful. I also told him that I believe he is a much better communicator than I am, who uses richer words and brighter examples to hold his audience than I do. All of that made me feel that he had misjudged his own success.

The other thing that caused me to think on this so much is the fact that I honestly, with no false humility, can tell you I am a failure in many ways who stumbled into some successful projects. I felt as if every paycheck, every book published, every clinic, and every seminar that changed lives was a cosmic accident. I used to think some of the good stuff happened because some angel misunderstood the assignment, that maybe God wasn't watching and it slipped by Him. But I don't feel that way anymore. And how I feel is the same way Mr. Wonderful can feel about himself.

Now I believe that whatever success I have had was intended by God. I see every talent, every successful project as a gift from the God of the universe, who really, truly does love me for who I am. I know that I could not have made happen some of the things that have happened if God had not knocked down the barriers that would have led to failure. Rather than feeling as if I am the master of the universe, I now feel even better knowing that the real Master of the universe loves me and is not too big to do some of the small things in my life that have given me the greatest pleasures. If you are patient, your Mr. Wonderful may come to these life-changing realizations also. He may discover that his life and success hang by a slender thread and that each day God does not snip that thread is a gift to be humbly proud of.

3. *Repent of arrogant self-interest and become humble enough to profit from criticism.* This will be scary for someone who has blinded himself to the reality of who he really is. But if he can come to see his flaws and defects as no greater than the flaws and mistakes of others,

he might be willing to accept them, work on them, and repent from some of the seamier ways he has adopted.

He also needs to be in a long-term relationship of accountability so he has the time to develop character. Being accountable to someone who is not able to be conned by him will be crucial. It is so easy for men to hide from one another. There is so much to talk about other than what is really important. But when two men commit to honestly help each other grow, character that was never there can be built.

4. *Develop his spiritual life so his security and identity come from an abiding sense of God's love for him rather than from his own achievements.* Too many men believe and act as though it's all up to them. What a relief to discover that all accomplishments and successes are designed or allowed by God. Calling upon God's strength rather than living in fear because he knows he doesn't have enough power is a much easier way to live. It is also much easier on everyone around him. God's strength is far better than your own charms and wit.

5. *Connect with those less fortunate and give them the benefit of what God has given him.* The loss of love for others starts when he disconnects from others, especially those he believes to be inferior. He can find love again by reconnecting with others and discovering their value. He will realize what he has missed in an "all for me" world by focusing on the needs of others. Find a need and fill it. Find a wounded person and help them heal. Find someone who is down and help lift them up. Rather than use God to get what he wants, he should use what God has given him to help others find what they need.

CONCLUSION

In the beginning, Mr. Wonderful attracts you, reels you in, and seems almost too good to be true. The problem is he *is* too good to be true. He seems so romantic, so self-assured, so tender. Wait long enough and your Mr. Wonderful will be revealed as the impostor he is; someone who is willing to manipulate and control you in any manner that prevents you from discerning how weak and dependent he really is. If you are married to a Mr. Wonderful, get help for yourself. Sometimes, doing that will lead to his eventually getting help, too.

SNAPSHOT SUMMARY OF MR. WONDERFUL

CLUES TO HELP YOU SPOT HIM

1. You feel as if he is just too good to be true.

2. He goes to extremes to impress you and to be involved in every area of your life.

3. It feels as though he is consuming more and more of your time, directing more of what you do as if he wants to have more and more power over you.

4. You observe him being able to talk his way out of things like traffic tickets and talk his way into places like full restaurants.

5. You come to realize that he is self-centered, self-absorbed, and most of what he says about himself is grandiose.

THE WOMAN TO WHOM HE IS ATTRACTED

1. Is beautiful but naive.

2. Has confidence only in her desire to meet his needs.

3. Passively accepts abuse.

4. Has a history of neglect and abandonment.

5. Has codependency needs met through him.

THE WOMAN WHO FALLS FOR HIM

1. Is attracted to his charm and wittiness.

2. Loves the attention and his gentlemanly nature.

3. Is codependent.

4. Would rather be attached to something sick than not attached at all.

5. Is unwilling to look beneath the facade he has constructed of himself.

WHAT YOU CAN DO

1. Remember, you cannot change him.

2. Set boundaries on things you are not willing to put up with, and enforce consequences that expose who he really is.

3. Realize his Jekyll-Hyde cycles have nothing to do with you or your behavior, even though he will try to get you to believe that.

4. Create your own interesting life full of friends and activities you love.

5. Put trust in God to provide you with what he cannot.

WHAT HE COULD DO TO CHANGE

1. Step outside himself and try to see life from the point of view of others.

2. Stop seeing himself as the master of the universe and begin to trust the real Master of the universe to help him and meet his needs. Attend a Bible study for men to develop a greater understanding of God's character.

3. Be willing to accept feedback from others and establish accountability relationships that are safe enough for him to reveal who he really is. A counselor can assist him in building character.

4. Find security in God's love rather than his own performance or others' approval.

5. Reconnect with people by serving others, especially those less fortunate than him.

CHAPTER 4

THE COWARDLY LION

Let me (Steve) write this introduction solo. I'll bring Meg back in for the really good stuff. The reason I am on my own here is that this chapter concerns one of those men who rise to the top of the list of things men would not want to be. To be characterized as a coward is one of the hardest labels to face. Sadly for me, I relate to this man much too closely. In the past, I found that I could not, would not, stand up to peer pressure. I cowardly went along with the crowd. Drinking and promiscuity are a part of my past because I was too cowardly to stand up to peer pressure. I would not say no when I needed to or yes when I should have. Within me were fears that overpowered my faith and led to horrible consequences throughout my life.

There were relationships that lasted too long because I was afraid to leave or afraid I would look bad if I let go. There were people I should have confronted but did not, even when it affected the welfare of my family. Perhaps the worst example of my cowardice happened when my girlfriend got pregnant. I arranged for an abortion in secrecy rather than face the consequences of my behavior. I cannot speak for others in their experience with abortion, but for me it generated tremendous guilt and shame. More than eighty ulcers caused great pain and almost took my life. Like most cowards, I often paid a huge price later rather than paying a smaller price earlier.

On the outside, you might see a fairly competent, confident guy, but on the inside is cowardice. I wish that character defect was all in the past. I would love to tell you I took care of it. But to this day, there remain the shadows of a coward where courage should be. Those shadows are not as long or as dark as they once were, but they are with me wherever I go.

COWARDICE

Cowardice is not something about which we like to think. No one wants to think he or she is a coward. To be sure, we have all done cowardly things in our lifetimes, but none of us would want to think of ourselves as having a pattern or habit of cowardly behavior.

Besides, when we think of terrible sins or faults people could have, cowardice is not at the top of the list in most people's minds. Things like adultery, murder, rape: *Those* things seem to be the bad sins. Yet Revelation 21:8 states: "But for the *cowardly* and unbelieving and abominable and murderers and immoral persons and sorcerers and idolaters and all liars, their part will be in the lake that burns with fire and brimstone, which is the second death" (NASB, emphasis added). Seems like a pretty intense consequence for something so seemingly minor, doesn't it?

So what is cowardice anyway? *The Merriam-Webster Home and Office Dictionary* defines it as "one who lacks courage or shows shameful fear or timidity." In the same section it defines *courage* as "the ability to conquer fear or despair." In the New Testament, the Greek word *deiliao* is translated as "timid, to be cowardly, to be fearful, to be afraid"; it is never used in a good sense. Two familiar passages in which this term is used are Matthew 8:26 and Mark 5:40. Jesus and the disciples are in a boat when a storm comes up suddenly. Jesus asks them why they are so *deiloi* (cowardly or timid). John 14:27 states, "Peace I leave with you; My peace I give to you; not as the world gives, do I give to you. Let not your heart be troubled, nor let it be fearful" (*deilia*). Second Timothy 1:7 quotes Paul's letter to Timothy in which he tells him that God has not given us a spirit of cowardice or timidity. Somehow, the idea of *timidity* seems less reprehensible than *cowardice*; yet *deiliao* can be translated as either term. There is always a sense of shame associated with cowardice. Brave people are admired, lionized, even worshiped. Tales passed down from generation to generation are usually about the great heroes whose valiant deeds immortalized them for all time. They are the dauntless, the bold, the noble, the lionhearted.

The Bible gives many examples of people who were at one time or another cowards. David's hiding his adultery by having Uriah killed was an act of cowardice. Abraham's telling a neighboring king that Sarah, his beautiful wife, was really his sister, because he was afraid the king would kill him to take her, was another cowardly act, and he did it twice! Certainly, Nicodemus's sneaking out at night to see Jesus was a result of being cowardly (John 3). Luke 19:20–21 tells the story of the servant who hid his master's money away in the ground because he was afraid, knowing that his master was an exacting man, rather than at least putting it in the bank and gaining interest. John Mark ran away naked from the Garden of Gethsemane rather than be taken in by the Romans with Jesus that night. Peter acted cowardly by denying Christ. Judas's betrayal and later suicide were cowardly as well. Yes, if you want a long list of cowards, you can find it in the Bible!

Modern examples come to mind as well: the men on the *Titanic* who masqueraded as women in order to get on a lifeboat; Susan Smith, who murdered her children rather than risk losing her boyfriend—these are a couple that come to mind. But most cowards and what they do never make headlines. They go about their lives doing what is convenient, never taking a stand for anything other than their own protection and comfort.

Some examples of the cowardly lion come to us in the lives of friends, family, or clients: the father who let the older brother beat his younger sister, and who answered when confronted: "Well, she probably deserved it"; or the man who lets his son beat his wife on a regular basis and never says a word; or the father who allows his wife to verbally or physically abuse their children but is too afraid of her anger to intervene; or the father who lets their three-year-old run the household because he doesn't want to cross him and hurt his feelings; or the dad who lets his son run wild because he is afraid of his son's anger if he disciplines him.

The cowardly lion goes along with shady business deals because he is afraid if he speaks up or walks away, he will be ridiculed or unable to find a job. He allows employees to be mistreated rather than take a stand for what is fair and right. He is void of both assertiveness and leadership. He is the consummate sheep at the mercy of whoever is at the head of the flock.

The cowardly lion continues to go to the same church his parents attended even though its teachings are flawed and the messages are more to beat the sheep than to feed the sheep. Yet he will not leave and risk people thinking poorly about him. He never speaks up for himself. He never confronts anyone for the sake of his family. He feels inferior and only survives because he is numb to the demeaning treatment he receives from so many people. He often marries someone else who is just as cowardly as he. Sometimes they live out as much of their lives as possible within the confines of their own home. They can become two trapped agoraphobics with little more stimulation than the background drone of a television.

Sometimes the cowardice is less than obvious. Sometimes it is only noticed in retrospect long after the damage has been done. Marvin is a case in point. Marv was a very intelligent fellow. Despite less than supportive parents, he went off to college and did well. He had given his life to Christ while in high school and was liked by both adults and peers. He received two scholarships to study abroad while in college and, despite many obstacles, finally got his degree. In some ways, he had indeed been courageous. He had faced poverty and got an education anyway. He had faced poor living conditions and made the best of them. When rejected, as we all are at some point, he went on and made new friends. He seemed destined to rise above the problems that enveloped the members of his family of origin.

Marv married and found new challenges to stretch him. He got a master's degree and became an insurance appraiser. He worked hard, and yet there was a hidden flaw. Under his success there was an immense volcano of unresolved fear. When he was young two family members and a close friend all died tragically within a year of one another. This had led the young Marv to believe that God was going to get him, too. Marv became more and more anxious and depressed. When he grew older he began to medicate himself with alcohol. Alcohol led to cocaine, and cocaine led to the destruction of everything he held dear. What was his cowardice? What timidity led to his destruction? He later admitted that it all fell apart because he was not willing to face the emotional pain and the fears around the tragedies in his life. He was too afraid to get help though it was readily available to him. Marv lost everything: his marriage, his home, his friends, his family—all because he would not face the pain inside himself. He let fear destroy him. All of this even though he loved the Lord. His cowardice was costly, as is anyone's.

A coward who retreats into alcohol will drive onto his yard, fall out of the car door, pass out in the driveway, and lie there all night until he is sober enough to wake up and discover what he has done. As the shades of the neighbors are pried ever so slightly open, he picks himself up, drives the car into the garage, and hides in his home. He may suffer this humiliation over and over, but he is too much of a coward to go to an AA meeting. If he did that, he would be admitting he had a problem. People might reject him. He might look bad if people found out. So the coward hides behind poisons of all kinds: people, places, and potions that help relieve the fear that he could remove if he would only face the pain within.

Some people are cowards in their relationships. One dear man, whom we'll call Sam, calls himself a "recovering wimp." Short, balding, soft-spoken, Sam is the kind of person most people overlook. One limb was disabled because of a birth trauma and was never corrected. Naturally shy, this disfigurement, though slight, caused him great emotional pain. He was sure everyone noticed it and went to great lengths to conceal it. Sam had been raised in a strict religious home and felt that he was always under somebody's critical glare. Unable to participate in sports, he threw himself into his studies. Yet he found he had to study twice as hard as the next fellow to get good grades. This fact (which later in life was attributed to a learning disability) damaged his fragile self-esteem as well. He pressed on, however, and finished college with a fine degree and landed a secure job at a large company. While successful at work, Sam was not so happy at home. He had married a nice young woman, and soon they had a houseful of children. She was an efficient, careful homemaker, though, due to her own background, an unaffectionate spouse and mother. She was often distant to Sam, acting afraid of him, and he never confronted the problem or tried to help her. He swallowed his disappointment and never brought up the problem, fearing that if he did, she would leave him or reject him even further.

His wife was actually well-meaning and did love him, but they could never find a sexual rhythm that suited them both. He grew more and more distant and disappointed and more and more passive. He became depressed and resentful. Hurt by his rejection and isolation, she withdrew more, and they became estranged. Sam just could not bring himself to confront the truth about himself and his relationship. Only when he became suicidal did he realize that he needed help. Counseling for him became the lifeline that transformed him from the cowardly lion to the mouse that roared. He involved his wife in his counseling, and the results have been quite dramatic. He has measurably improved his marriage and his friendships, developed a ministry in his church, and, though still plagued periodically with depression, has the tools he needs to confront it when it rears its ugly head. He has reduced his fears from a hovering vulture to a mosquito he can swat away. He is an example of the hope that is there for the cowardly lion.

Chameleons are another type of subtle cowards. These people change their colors with the surrounding milieu. If everyone in the crowd drinks, then this fellow drinks; if everyone is crazy for rap music, he is crazy for rap; if everyone is praising Jesus, so is he. Having no courage of his own convictions, he latches onto what others are doing as the way to have an identity. Don is a chameleon. Active on the debate team, he wants to fit in with the intellectual crowd. He can debate with the best of them. Although he has a personal friendship with Jesus Christ and claims Jesus is his Lord, he never speaks up in a debate if Christ's name or Christianity is derided in the process. On trips with the debate team he remains silent when others tell dirty jokes, not having the guts to tell them how demeaning those jokes are to both men and women. When he is at the college-career group at church, he makes a big deal about always having his Bible, but he hides it when he is away from church friends. One day a debate teammate found his small New Testament sticking out of his travel bag. Don blushed and said it belonged to his girlfriend, who had left it in his car. At work on his co-op job, Don changes again. Now he is Mr. Business—all professional and above it all. He models his behavior after his manager, a sort of no-nonsense type of guy, but one who does not mind shafting someone if it is in his own interest. Don has done some of his manager's dirty work in this regard, all with a wink and a knowing look. After all, he has to make it, doesn't he? Jesus will understand.

Men are especially vulnerable to being afraid of their emotions. Programmed from an early age to stuff feelings, men often do not even know how they feel, much less know how to express the feelings. Men can be cowards when it comes to feelings. They are many times afraid to share feelings of fear, weakness, anxiety, or pain. Men are told that they are to be the strong ones, the ones with all the answers. Admitting they do not know something is a male cultural no-no. Men are cowards at times when it comes to affection, especially with their sons, fathers, brothers, and one another. Homophobia is so strong that many men have never been touched by their own fathers. One good thing that has come out of movements like Promise Keepers is that men are beginning to break down some of the emotional and physical barriers that have kept them apart.

Cowardly lions have caused despair and destruction throughout history. Cowards allowed Jews to be killed by going along with orders they knew were not right. Cowards allowed free black people of Africa to be stuck in the hold of a ship for ninety days, lying in filth. If they became sick they were thrown overboard and eaten by sharks. If they survived they faced a life of demeaning work and torture. Cowards allowed this. Cowards allowed racism to rule for years, and injustices to minorities are allowed to continue by cowards. Cowards allow little babies to be killed even before they breathe their first breath.

Walt is another example of a cowardly lion. He was only eight years old when his daddy died suddenly in his early forties. He does not remember much about his dad at all. Actually, Walt does not remember anything personal very well. A successful computer programmer, he has excelled in every company he has worked for. He is smart, competent, and well liked. He tends to be somewhat superficial though; for example, all he ever talks about is his work or his love of chess. Although a deeply committed Christian, Walt cannot seem to engage with his family or take a meaningful stand on personal issues. When asked in counseling about events his wife remembers with great pain, his only response is "I don't recall."

When asked how he feels now or felt in the past regarding something about which others would have been enraged, Walt's only response was a soft-spoken "I don't know." For example, when his daughter was in high school, one of the school coaches began "hitting on" her. Mom found out and went to Walt about it. He literally had no response. He just stared blankly ahead as if nothing had happened. Now he does not recall the event but says it must have happened, he just cannot remember it. His family reports that his favorite line, which they want to put on his tombstone, is "No sweat." It is no wonder his wife complains of feeling unprotected, and the kids believe Walt "does not care" about them or their feelings. He told his therapist that "things just don't bother me."

Walt became a coward quite accidentally. When his father died, he just shut down. He made an inner vow never to feel or react to anything ever again. And he has kept that same defense mechanism going for more than sixty years. Not dealing with a childhood vow has made Walt a prisoner of cowardice. He has unintentionally abdicated his role of protector of his family. He barely lets himself understand what "the problem is"; in fact, he keeps asking his wife and therapist why the family is so upset with him. He just doesn't get it. Natural fear and pain in childhood grew into a bondage of cowardice of which he is only dimly aware. His family experiences it daily, but he lives on in oblivion. In the absence of his own strength, he needs God's. He may be too afraid to ever ask for it.

WHAT IS GOING ON HERE?

What makes men act in a cowardly manner? In the Matthew 8 and Mark 5 passages mentioned earlier, Jesus attributed the disciples' cowardice to a disconnection with God and a lack of faith. It is interesting that in the list of sins in Revelation 21:8, *cowardly* and *unbelieving* are listed together. Perhaps this is coincidence, but perhaps not. In Paul's second letter to Timothy (NASB), chapter 1, verse 7, he said: "For God has not given us a spirit of timidity [cowardice], but of power and love and discipline [sound judgment]." He linked his remarks to Timothy's sincere faith (v. 5) and says, "For this reason [because of your sincere faith] I remind you to kindle afresh the gift of God which is in you through the laying on of my hands. For God has not given us . . ." (vv. 6–7). Paul knew Timothy's weakness: a tendency to be intimidated and to act in a cowardly manner. The gifts of God are always linked to the Holy Spirit, and here Paul was reminding Timothy that God gave him the spiritual gift he needed to overcome his fears. God's Spirit is one of power, love, and sound judgment. Timothy did not have to be fearful of anything or distrustful of his judgment, despite his youth, when, through his sincere faith, he stirred up that gift God had given him. He had the sound judgment and power of God Himself available to him.

Jesus linked the Holy Spirit's presence with a lack of cowardice in the John 14 passage mentioned earlier. In this discourse, Jesus was preparing His disciples for the fact that He was going to die, rise again, and go to the Father. He knew they would be afraid. He said to them:

> These things I have spoken to you, while abiding with you. But the Helper, the Holy Spirit, whom the Father will send in My name, He will teach you all things, and bring to your remembrance all that I said to you. Peace I leave with you; My peace I give to you; not as the world gives, do I give to you. Let not your heart be troubled, nor let it be fearful [cowardly]. (John 14:25–27 NASB)

Luke 21:14–15 and Mark 13:11 also link the Holy Spirit with not being afraid. Jesus in these two passages was telling His disciples that when they were persecuted for His sake, not to worry about what to say because the Holy Spirit would give them what to say at that time. Jesus knew we would face moments, as the disciples did, when we would have to decide whether to face up to the challenge, trust Him, and act faithfully. He was trying to give us the key: reliance on the Holy Spirit, not ourselves.

Romans 8:15 links fear to the spirit or attitude of slavery we had before we knew Christ: "For you have not received a spirit of slavery leading to fear again, but you have received a spirit [the Spirit] of adoption as sons by which we cry out, 'Abba! Father!'" (NASB).

In the Roman world, you could disinherit your natural-born children, but it was forbidden to disinherit someone you had adopted. So being adopted was a more secure status than being born a natural child. Before Christ, we were strangers and aliens, but now we are of the family (Eph. 2:19). We are adopted into His family through faith in Christ. Slaves are insecure, never knowing if they will be sold, killed, or treated kindly. Children are related intimately to the Father. They can cry out "Daddy" with no fear of rebuke. They can be secure in who they are. They do not have to be chameleons.

Why do people act in a cowardly manner? The Scripture makes it clear that it is because of a lack of faith in Jesus Himself; a lack of reliance on the power of the Holy Spirit and the gifts He has given us; and because of insecurity, which comes because we do not understand our status as children, not slaves, in God's household. Yes, there may be old wounds from the past, learned behaviors from childhood, intimidating circumstances or people, but God's truth is still true. The answer does not come from within ourselves. It comes from Him— from beholding Him (2 Cor. 3:18).

Peter, for all his failings, was a man of faith. He was the only disciple who jumped out of the boat when he saw Jesus walking on the water. He sank only when he looked at the waves instead of at Jesus. He failed and acted cowardly when he denied Christ, but he did not go hang himself as Judas had done. He hung in there with the other believers, despite his shame. He did not run and hide from Jesus when He rose from the dead. He took up Jesus' challenge to feed His sheep and became one of the men who turned the world upside down.

A cowardly lion is a man who does not believe God loves him enough to take care of him. Because he feels that he must survive on his own, he lives in fear of decisions and makes each one to preserve the world he has created to protect himself. If his love relationship with God were strong, he could step out front and lead. He would not care if standing up for something wonderful caused him to lose something unnecessary. If he ever fixes his relationship with God, he can develop courage. If he does not, he will always be a victim of the crowd and at the mercy of what everyone else wants to do.

CHARACTERISTICS OF THE COWARDLY LION

1. *Cowards remain silent when they ought to speak.* Brave people are no less afraid than cowards, they are just so passionate about the truth that they will not be silent. The coward allows wrongs to continue, even to his own family, rather than confront someone. If his child is feeling mistreated at school, he will not be the one to handle it. If he were to see his pastor with a woman other than his wife, he would say nothing. He does not need a whistle at work because he would never blow it if he knew something unethical was going on. He would remain huddled beneath his lean-to of silence to protect himself from rejection.

2. *Cowards think of themselves first, others last.* Covering their own backs is more important than standing for what is right. "Take care of numero uno" is their motto. If he is in a compromising position and needs to make a decision, his thinking pattern will automatically run down a list of analytical questions: What would be best for me? What would be easiest for me? How could I get out of this without objecting to anything anyone is doing? Isn't this really a lot less important than people think it is? How can I protect myself in this situation?

3. *Cowards tend to be more fearful than resentful and passive.* They do not like the way they live but do not have the drive to change it.

There is no courage, so there is no motivation to be any more than they are. Lacking power, they are resentful of others who are strong. They wish they could be like them, but to do so would involve risk—something cowards want to avoid at all costs. Any expression of emotion is done so passively that it appears to be of little consequence. They go along with orders or the crowd, but all the time they are wishing those in charge would fail. They resent their power and assertiveness.

4. *Some cowards are chameleons, very changeable, inconsistent.* They flow with the flow. They are so anxious to fit in, they will do almost anything. They can be so "open-minded" that their brains fall out. They have no backbone, so they function as if they were on a little raft in a deep ocean with huge waves. They are tossed back and forth. They change their opinions to fit what is popular or accepted. They do not even like to order first in a restaurant. They like to order last so they can pick something someone else has chosen.

5. *Cowards have probably not fully accessed the power of God, through the Holy Spirit, in their everyday life.* They may be religious but deny the power available to them. They do not believe that God is a personal God who loves them. They fear God will destroy them. Rather than allow God to strengthen them, they run from God and act as though God does not exist, is not there, or is angry at the cowardly lion.

WHAT KIND OF WOMAN DOES THE COWARDLY LION WANT?

The cowardly lion looks for a woman who is much like him. She is most likely wracked by fears and insecurities just as he is. Other men will often seek out a woman who can either take care of them or compensate for their weaknesses, but the cowardly lion is repulsed by any sense of strength. Their relationships are often quite sad because, unlike others, they do not complement each other; they increase each other's weaknesses. If he is less than outgoing, he is often apt to look for the wallflower. If he is a chameleon, he will veer away from any woman who expresses a clear knowledge of her convictions and a willingness to stick to them. His wimpy nature only feels comfortable with someone who is even weaker and more afraid than he is.

Some cowards do appear accomplished, but this type will not seek out another who is accomplished. He will want to be assured that she will not overshadow him with competence. If he is the coward who acts like a bully, he will look for a timid woman who will acquiesce to his demands, flatter him, and not ask anything of him. She will need to be as much a doormat as he, but she will never complain that she is treated unfairly.

The one slight exception to this is the coward who marries money. He will not marry a strong woman with family money, but he will marry someone who has money if she has also had a horrible life and is left without a strong sense of herself and her needs. He will love the money because it will allay his fears of failure and of not being able to provide for himself. While her money may make it look as if he has married someone strong, looking closer will reveal that although wealthy, she is also quite scared.

WHY DOES SHE FALL FOR HIM?

Some women will be attracted to him because his weakness makes them feel strong. These women like to be powerful and strong and feel superior to the man in their life. The problem and frustration for them is that he will not be attracted to them. The powerful woman is too threatening. She is his biggest fear. He is afraid she will draw him in and then abandon him, or that he will be totally consumed by her. So while his weakness may appeal to her, she will not appeal to him. She may spend years trying to win him over, but the relationship will just drag on, lead nowhere, and waste her time.

As is obvious by now, a cowardly woman will most likely be attracted to him because he poses no threat to her world. These women are afraid, as he is, and thus see his cowardice as attractive and comfortable. They rationalize that his timidity is really caution and good sense. If he puts up a facade of power, she will be able to see the coward underneath, and that will make him the man of her dreams. She will adjust to his ever-changing needs and desires. She will adapt to his opinions, wherever they land. She is lost; the two of them are an authentic example of the blind leading the blind.

RELATING TO THE COWARDLY LION

What do you do if you are involved with a cowardly lion? Certainly, if you are not married yet, do reconsider. Look at what attracted him. Discover why weakness is so appealing to you. Find out if his lack of strength makes you feel strong or comfortable. If it makes you feel strong, explore why you need to be in the one-up position in a relationship. If it makes you feel comfortable, then there is a good chance you are a cowardly lioness and you have some work to do on your own fears.

If you are married, you can ask God to increase your faith; to increase your reliance on the Holy Spirit; to increase your sense of security in who you are in God's family. The more you focus on Jesus and learn to fall in love with Him, the less power other forces have over you. Just because your spouse is a coward does not mean you are doomed.

Examine your situation. Most likely your husband's cowardice is not putting you or your children at risk. But could he be afraid to confront you when *you* are abusive to your children? He may not be protecting you and them *from yourself.* If that rings true with you, get some help. There is also a chance that he is not protecting you and the children from someone else in the family who might be physically or emotionally abusive. If so, what resources do you have? Is the risk great enough to warrant separation? Do what needs to be done to protect yourself and the kids.

Ask yourself some tough questions. Is your husband afraid of *you?* Sometimes women can be just as intimidating and aggressive as men. Other times, the husband is not reacting to you per se, but to old relationships that scared him. You may be as sweet and gentle as a newborn lamb, or you may be sarcastic, cruel, mean-spirited, or nasty. Only you and the Lord know the truth. You cannot change your husband into Braveheart, but, with the power of the Holy Spirit, you can change your behaviors if necessary. Men feel more intimidated by women than they like to admit, or than women realize. Most women do not know the terror it strikes in a man's heart when he hears his wife say, "Honey, we need to *talk*." Women think, *What is there to be afraid of? All I want to do is* talk. And the man thinks, *That's what I am afraid of.* Not that women should stop asking to communicate, but it might help if they realized how scary that request is to most men. Learning what certain words trigger in the one you love can be a way of opening rather than shutting off communication.

What if you *are* open, kind, loving, and all that, and he still acts as if you are going to eat him alive? Well, try talking about it with him. Point out your safe behaviors and the discrepancy in how he reacts to them. Urge him to get some professional help. Pray for him. Don't take responsibility for his fears. Help him see them as coming from within himself. When he breaks out of the cowardly behavior, praise him profusely. Recognize how hard it is to change. Encourage him (note the word *en-courage*). Everyone does better with praise than with criticism. Don't throw examples of brave, courageous men and women in front of him. That will only make him feel more inferior. He has some work on his heart to be done first.

Get involved with a support group and counseling for you, and encourage him to do the same. And on Sunday morning, be sure you do all you can to have both of you sitting in a church that understands both God's power and His grace. Inspiration is a powerful tool in strengthening our courage muscles. Faith can change a heart, even one that does not even seem to exist.

WHAT COULD THE COWARDLY LION DO TO CHANGE?

What does a man do if he is tired of being a cowardly lion? Well, we know he cannot just go to Oz and get a medal from the Wizard. Popeye's spinach won't help, nor does eating Wheaties make him a champion, despite the commercials. The following are guidelines:

1. *Begin with his relationship with God.* If this can be mended, he

can live without fear. He must seek the Lord and His strength. The key to overcoming intimidation is to seek the Lord with sincere faith and use the gifts He has given. God has not given us a spirit of fear, but of love, power, and a sound mind (1 Tim. 1:2–7). Accepting Christ's peace through the ministry of the Holy Spirit will remind us of all He has said to us (John 14:26–27). The power of the Spirit is key to overcoming fear. He will recognize his position as a child of God's household once he has given himself to Christ and trusts Him with his life. Insecurity comes when we forget who we really are to God: His children. We *can* do all things through Christ who strengthens us (Phil. 4:13), but only when we recognize our authority in Christ Jesus. Because the cowardly lion's situation has come about due to a lack of faith, finding a way back to God and His Son will lay the foundation for a future without fear.

2. *Examine the source of his fears with a competent counselor.* He is not cowardly for no reason at all and should find out what that reason is. In my case (Steve), I felt inadequate because of growing up with two older, competitive brothers. I did not trust God to help me, so I felt I had to do it all on my own. I lost so much because my relationship with Him was broken. Being accepted by Him was not enough; I wanted to be accepted by the world. Later, when I lost a wonderful girlfriend, rather than see it as a result of my godless life, I saw it as proof that I could not trust God. This perspective was not easy for me to abandon. It took time and a lot of work with a counselor. A cowardly lion needs to spend time with someone he can trust in order to look at his fears, where they have led him, and how he can change them with God's help.

3. *Read, listen to tapes, and take a class on assertiveness.* Assertiveness training is really courage work. It will help him discover how to express himself and his needs, feelings, and beliefs. It will help him overcome fears of rejection and discover the satisfaction of expressing himself honestly. Many cowards have found a new way of living through this kind of training. It should be a part of his plan to move out of patterns from his past.

4. *Practice taking risks, despite fears and doubts.* Most of what we

fear never happens anyway. Confidence comes from experience. Stepping out and risking lead to both success and failure. We find that the failures are less horrible and the successes more delightful than we had imagined. The next time he has the chance to fall back into his old pattern, he can consider the worst outcome possible if he does the risky thing, and see that he can survive that outcome. He might consider how unlikely it is and how probable another outcome would be, one much more pleasant. Taking the risk will help him to discover that risk does not mean disaster, failure, or rejection. It is merely discomfort that goes away.

I (Steve) fly a lot and am used to it. I have a couple of friends who are terrified by it. First, they don't understand some of the principles of flight. If the plane ride gets bumpy, they think they will crash; I think of it like a boat hitting waves on the water. Second, they do not consider the worst outcome and accept that they can live with it. The worst is that they would die, and for a Christian that is okay. In my case, yes, I would miss my wife and be sad I did not get to see my little girl grow up, but I can handle death because I know that when I die I will be in heaven. If I didn't know that, every time I walked onto a plane I would be terrified of an unpredictable outcome.

5. *Open up with others about his fears.* One of the tough things about being a coward is that you don't want anyone to notice. So not only do you live with your fears, but you live with the fear of being found out. When I (Steve) speak in front of a large audience and try to act as if I am not afraid, my mouth gets dry and my voice is strained and I mispronounce words. I will make some joke about it, like "Don't be alarmed if my voice cracks, sweat comes pouring off of my forehead, and I shake like we are experiencing an earthquake. Don't be afraid because it is just a sign that I am scared to death of talking to this many people." Then on the way home if I ask my wife if she thought I looked nervous, she will most likely say, "No, not at all. Why? Were you?" And this is after I have admitted to the fear.

The cowardly lion will be amazed at how much easier his life will be when he stops trying to hide his fears and is just open and honest about them. He can start with his best friend, wife, or girlfriend, and move on to ever-expanding circles. One day he will sense that his fears have almost disappeared and he really doesn't have much to be afraid of.

SNAPSHOT SUMMARY OF
THE COWARDLY LION

CLUES TO HELP YOU SPOT HIM

1. Is silent when most would speak up.

2. Is always making sure he is taken care of and safe before considering you.

3. Is much more full of fear than resentment in his passive nature.

4. Quickly changes his opinions to match whomever he is talking to or if it makes him feel secure. However, when you appear strong in your opinions, he tends to back away from you.

5. His faith in God is very weak.

THE WOMAN TO WHOM HE IS ATTRACTED

1. Is as much like him as possible.

2. Is willing to cower alongside him as the world passes by.

3. Has money and can take care of him, but is not someone who has earned it due to personal strength and character.

4. A mousy woman who will make few or no demands on him and his routine.

5. Has very few goals and low expectations, and most likely feels like an outcast from society.

THE WOMAN WHO FALLS FOR HIM

1. May confuse his cowardly ways with caution and caring.

2. May find his weakness attractive if she has needs to control someone. (He will not stick around when he senses this.)

3. Feels comfortable with his ways, which were normal to her family of origin.

4. Enjoys the freedom of his low expectations of her.

5. Lives in a very small world; she does not see her potential beyond someone who will ensure sameness in life.

WHAT YOU CAN DO

1. Explore why you are so attracted to him, whether out of a need to control or a need to be free of risk.

2. Develop your faith in God so that your own fears are not driving you to him.

3. If married to him, avoid the temptation to try to change him with books by his bedside and other not-so-subtle hints.

4. Seek out some healthy couples through a healthy church and find ways to spend time with them.

5. At a minimum, be in church on Sundays—hopefully, with him. But if not, be there yourself.

WHAT HE COULD DO TO CHANGE

1. Explore his relationship with God and discover the source of his lack of faith. Seek out a minister, prayer partner, and a men's Bible study.

2. Explore the sources of his fears with a counselor.

3. Read books, listen to tapes, and take classes on assertiveness.

4. Start taking small risks and see how it feels to move out of the norm in small steps.

5. Open up to others about hidden fears. This will reduce his fear of being found out.

CHAPTER 5

THE ANGRY MAN

There is just something about an angry man that attracts women like bees to flowers. Rarely is the angry man alone. He usually has a broad field from which to pick his mate and most likely victim. He has power that some cannot resist. He takes control, and the weak, smelling a familiar scent of male domination from the past, allow him to conquer. He is a man of action, and those who are dormant sense that he could awaken them to life. They fall into his arms hoping for a strong savior and instead find a cruel warden of a prison called home.

Why would anyone find anything attractive about a man who is driven by internal rage? Once grabbed too hard or spun around to ensure proper attention, it would seem logical to move on. Isn't life too short for a woman to want to spend it with a man who punishes, lashes out, and expects it all to go away with a tearful "I'm sorry"? Sadly, angry men are full of opportunities for relationships. Part of the reason is the confusion over what a man should be. Magnifying the confusion is the misunderstanding that surrounds the expected roles of a man and a woman. An even larger part of the problem centers on the deadly emotion of anger.

ANGER IN OUR CULTURE

Our culture gives contradictory messages about anger. We are supposed to "get a grip" and "hang in there." "Don't get mad, get even."

"Living well is the best revenge." "Love your enemy." "Forgive and forget." "Get over it!" "Let go of resentments." "Question authority." "Anarchy is the only way!" "Kill the ump." We see slogans on bumper stickers. We get advice from friends and fellow workers. It is all very confusing.

Everyone with any sense decries the violence on television, in the movies, on our streets. Despite this concern, many people let their kids play the most violent, degrading, horrific video games imaginable. Sports stars are still given million-dollar advertising contracts despite beating their girlfriends, choking their coach, biting off part of an opponent's ear. Anger in civil service jobs has gotten so bad that the phenomenon of outraged postal workers shooting fellow workers and managers has provided us with new slang: "going postal." In the film *Falling Down*, Michael Douglas plays a repressed, uptight "geek" who decompensates in a traffic jam and goes on a bloody rampage. "I'm not going to take it anymore!" seems to be the rationale for all types of violence, even children killing fellow schoolmates over junior high girlfriends or imagined persecution.

The examples of anger on the evening news is seemingly endless. Few will forget the tragedy of Columbine High School, where two angry young men took the lives of twelve students and a teacher and then turned the guns on themselves. And what about elder abuse? Older adults are being cared for by family members and young adult caregivers as never before. Gang warfare, drive-by shootings, child abuse, on and on. Our newspapers are filled with it every day. It is a sign of the times, a sardonic but insightful glimpse of what we have become as a society.

UNDERSTANDING ANGER

Men are angry. Women are angry. Children are angry. In the Christian community, however, we shy away from the topic of anger. We try to pretend that good people do not get angry. Anger isn't "nice," and so we push it away or euphemize it with words such as *frustrated, annoyed,* or *irritated.* The Bible does not shy away from the topic, however. There are 445 references to anger in the Scriptures.

Ephesians 4:26–27 is perhaps the most familiar. Paul admonished us: "*Be angry,* and yet *do not sin;* do not let the sun go down on your anger, and do not give the devil an opportunity" (NASB, emphasis added). He referenced Psalm 4:4, which uses the phrase "tremble [with anger], and do not sin . . ." (NASB). How can we sin with our anger? We sin either by holding the anger inside destructively or by expressing it outwardly in a hurtful or evil manner. Anger and how we handle it can make all the difference in our relationships.

ANGER VS. DEPRESSION

Women and men encounter differing messages from society regarding anger. Women are told that it is unladylike to be angry, so their anger is expressed more often as being emotionally hurt. Being hurt is a *feminine* thing, we are told, *weak* and fittingly female. Perhaps that is why the rate for clinical depression is so much higher for women than men. Women learn to be depressed, not angry.

Men are in an odd position, however. On one side, they are to be strong, stable, impervious to stress and strain. Nothing is to perturb them. Somehow the pain and turmoil we all are feeling are supposed to just go right through them. If a man is unable to rise above the stresses of life, he feels shame. He is not much of a man, in his own eyes or in the eyes of others. Thus, he cannot acknowledge hurts and pain. He cannot acknowledge or even notice if he is depressed. So men tend to get angry. Anger is an emotion with which they are more comfortable. Anger is tough and rough. It's a manly emotion (probably the only one men are allowed to have without being drunk or involved in a sports activity). Visions of "The Incredible Hulk" rising in anger against injustice cannot help but be in the back of most male baby boomers' minds. Anger feels like a macho thing. Or if they are the more passive type, they use their "superior masculine logic" (i.e., suppression of emotion) to cancel out their anger. They reason their opponents to death, with a condescending smile. They express their anger by *not* doing things, rather than actively acting out. They "forget" to do what they promised, or they "just don't have time" to follow through on commitments.

ANGRY, VIOLENT MEN

Such angry men are profoundly lonely, terrified of abandonment, and emotionally dependent. They fear being anything but hypermasculine and often are sexually addicted, aggressive, physically and emotionally abusive, ruthless, unfeeling, uncaring, and reckless.[1]

John Friel wrote about men whom he calls "Offender–Little Boys." These are men who are destructively powerful on the outside, but pitifully weak, vulnerable, and afraid on the inside. Friel sees three types of OLBs:[2]

1. *Tough Guys.* These men are overtly abusive to women. They are macho, tough, rough specimens. These are the men who, when hauled into court for battery or murder, sob and cry about how much they loved the woman they hurt or killed. These men do not know how to love—they only need. They are afraid of abandonment; afraid of not having a mommy to take care of them. Inside they are filled with shame and fear. The idea of having to take responsibility for themselves and not having a woman to take care of them is terrifying to Tough Guys. This is how a man can kill a woman and believe he has done it for her own good! Since she has moved from his "protection," he cannot allow her to wander freely. Thus, a man can justify killing a woman and think she is to blame. "She led me to do it" or "I had no choice" or "She deserved it." These men are able to kill and proclaim their innocence (and even believe in their innocence). "She pushed me to the brink" or "It wasn't really me" or "The demon inside me did it." These Tough Guys feel entitled to everything, even a person's life. They may even kill "just to teach her a lesson."

2. *Smart Guys.* These fellows are suave, sophisticated, debonair. They overwhelm and dominate with their intense verbal skills and their superior intellect. Logic, analysis, and verbal repartee are their mainstays, yet their underlying rage is clear to all with whom they interact closely. By using these tools and, above all, by suppressing emotion, the Smart Guy can persuade you that you really do love caviar (when you actually loathe it) or that it really is okay for him to have an affair with your sister, since she is family. This guy can con-

vince you the lamp shade made him drink and that an adulterer does love his wife. He is the ultimate con. The angry Smart Guy is often the man who emotionally abuses a woman—always thinking, always plotting and manipulating her thoughts, behaviors, and feelings, or at least attempting to do so. On the surface he looks as if he has it all together, but inside he has a seething disdain for women. If he is religious, he will also spiritually abuse, using religious dogma or distortions of the truth to bind a woman to him rather than set her free.

3. *Seductive Guys.* Very scared inside, these guys are extremely dangerous. These men have graduated from Smart Guys to Really Smart Guys. They can schmooze the fuzz off a peach. These guys are sexually addicted and can con their way into a woman's heart with a blink of an eye. We all can probably think of someone we know who is illustrative of this type of man. You can find them almost anywhere you look, on television, and in ordinary walks of life. The Seductive Guy is the one with the nice, soft voice, who loves to talk about his feelings—to the right woman, of course. He has a touching, boyish quality about him that is very appealing to certain women. Seductive Guys can cry at the drop of a hat, the perfect embellishment to their con. They can thrust out that lower lip and seem oh, so sensitive. They seem to be able to genuinely feel your pain. Inside they are deeply lonely little boys, who learned to believe that the only nurturing they deserve is through their genitals. A Seductive Guy finds his self-esteem in the number of people he can use as he tries to get back at women for all the hurt Mom and Dad caused him. His anger is going to make women pay. For men like these, people are merely objects, and love is a tool or control and a method of nurturing the sick little man inside.

All of these men are playing at being men. They have not learned who they are or what being a man is all about. Desperately disconnected, they often go from relationship to relationship, looking for the perfect woman. When they do not find her, they become more and more angry. More and more dangerous. More and more desperate.

Angry, violent men make crucial processing errors; that is, they make errors in how they process what happens and how they tell themselves what to do.[3] These errors include:

1. *Maintaining a belief system that includes a good-bad split of the world.* They develop a cognitive scheme that produces a collection of negative beliefs about women. They tend to see women as either goddesses or witches, madonnas or whores.

2. *Denying, dissociating, and protecting from feelings.* Violent, angry men don't want to be aware of their beliefs about their dependency on women and their fears of abandonment. So they use violence to control those around them, thus avoiding their fears. When this strategy fails, they do an about-face. To keep the woman from leaving, and hence evoking his abandonment fears, the man does the opposite of what he usually does. He gets religion; he acts contrite; he makes an apology. When he turns to religion, the woman believes he has changed, and he may even think he has changed. He says all the right things, using a brand-new vocabulary of spiritual lingo. Some do experience a true conversion, but most are involved in another form of manipulation, trying to gain back control. Within weeks, abused women are back with these guys, hoping that this time it will be different.

Often the woman, too, has sought religious counsel and support, and may have experienced a spiritual awakening herself. Ironically, this experience of a new commitment to God may make her even more vulnerable to his con. She knows her own renewal is genuine and so expects his to be as well. Sadly, what she discovers is that even an authentic commitment-renewal on the part of herself, or her husband, does not instantly change one's habitual patterns of behavior, nor magically give one an instant character transplant. Maturity and character changes only happen with time and the work of the Spirit in a person's life.

Recently, I (Steve) was involved with a couple who were obtaining counseling through the church. The church had a wonderful lay counseling ministry except for one major flaw. The counselors had not been trained to identify when they were over their heads, when they needed to refer out their people because the problem was too deep or complicated.

I became involved when the woman of the troubled couple asked my advice. She wanted to know if the lay counselor was on the right track with her and her husband. The husband was obviously an angry man full of control needs beyond what most people could imagine.

She had moved out of their home to initiate change in him, and it had worked. He had gone on a retreat and made a new commitment to his marriage and to change.

The counselor had told her to honor his efforts, to move back in as a way to support the changes he was making. My advice was quite different from that. I hate to go against a counselor's advice, but this was a horrible mistake. She should have been encouraged to do nothing. Wait, talk, discuss, and see if over time the changes were real. Then she could move back in and have the life she wanted.

The difficulty with this case was that she had made a renewed commitment to the Lord, and he had done the same. He was sincere in thinking that he was a changed man. I believe he thought his troubles were over and that the old patterns that had caused them so many problems were behind them. Sadly, it takes a lot more than a decision to make a difference in a lifestyle and in ways of relating in marriage. Sincerity should not be the barometer of the decision. The changes that are seen and the actions that are taken over time are the things that matter most.

3. *Hypervigilance.* The third processing error is that the man notices small things and exaggerates their importance, for example: "That man said 'Hello' to you! Are you having an affair?" or "You did not say 'Good morning' to me, so do you hate me now?" or "You're talking to your sister more. What are you doing? Planning to divorce me?" This man is so sick and so scared that he saps the life out of those around him. Rather than look within, he looks at every detail of "his" woman. She becomes his obsession. If he stops focusing on her, he starts to sense his own isolation, the void in his soul, and the relentless criticism from his mother. Rather than leading him to get help, these feelings push him deeper into his obsession to control.

CHARACTERISTICS OF THE ANGRY MAN

How do you identify a potentially violent, angry man? We actually know a great deal about men who tend to be violent. Read the signs and see if you are related to or in a relationship with an angry man. The angry, violent type:

1. Tends to be jealous.

2. Competes with other men; compares himself unmercifully to other men; is insecure.

3. Sees women as extensions of himself, necessary to complete his image as a real man. He actually wears women like jewelry or some other possession.

4. Blames others for his problems, especially his wife: Her mistakes, her vulnerability, her body come to represent all the things he is angry with in the world.

5. Keeps his emotions under wraps at all times, except when angry.

6. Needs to appear the "boss" or the one "in charge" in relationships, especially those with women and children.

7. Rarely comes across as relaxed, blissful, or even happily content.

8. Amazes or shocks others (and often, himself) with outbursts of anger.

9. Is envious of other men and their achievements; is resentful of what others have.

10. Likes order, regimentation, and running on schedule. May even seem obsessively perfectionistic.

11. Is a careful, sharp dresser; his drawers are neat and tidy, closets in perfect order; wants everything in the home to be in its proper place at all times. Often criticizes his wife for not being neat enough.

12. Likes sports with other men, but usually does not like women to be on the team.

13. Reattaches quickly if the marriage ends, since having a woman

on his arm is an important sign of his masculinity, and he needs a woman to protect him from his fear of abandonment.

14. Believes all the money is his, especially if he is the primary breadwinner. Thinks women should take the beatings, since they take the money. Rarely encourages the woman to work or praises her achievements if she has a career outside the home.

15. Hates to admit weakness of any kind; may ignore physical health problems because it would be weak to need a doctor. Any offers of help on a project are taken as insults because he thinks you are saying he is too stupid or weak or incompetent to do it himself. Cannot take criticism at all, even if couched in the most nonthreatening manner.

16. Gets furious if the woman "steps out of line." Has preconceived ideas of what a woman's place is and becomes enraged if she dares to step over into an area he thinks is not within her purview.

17. Sees sex as the answer to any domestic problem. Believes that all women need is a good man in bed, and everything will be okay. (And if that does not work, a "good slap" will.)

18. May threaten to hurt you, your children, your pets, your belongings. (These threats may be nonverbal, such as tossing a hunting knife in the air while arguing with you.)

WHAT LEADS A WOMAN TO FALL FOR AN ANGRY MAN?

Why do women fall for these men anyway? Surely, no one would intentionally choose someone who is so angry and, thus, a difficult person with whom to live. Here are some ideas as to why a woman may fall so hard for an angry man:

1. She may mistake his anger for strength. Her dad may have been

so detached that any show of emotion is a welcome sign. She may think he is braver than Dad; able to "stand up" to others, etc.

2. She may be used to living with a father who is angry, whether passively or violently. It is not what she wants, but what she is used to experiencing.

3. She may have an old pile of inner anger herself and is looking to be able to vent in the relationship. His anger or passive aggression gives her the outlet she is needing for her own rage.

4. She may feel special to be the focus of so much of his energy and attention, especially if her father was a detached, uninvolved man. Negative attention is better than none, remember.

5. She may think that she deserves to be treated angrily or violently. While it seems odd that someone would think she deserves such treatment, often the woman is filled with guilt and shame (real or imagined), and unconsciously feels she needs to be punished. Some people believe that because they *feel* guilty, it means they *are* guilty, and thus need punishment.

RELATING TO THE ANGRY MAN

What if you are in a relationship with such a man? Do you have options? Are you destined to live out a life of misery? We don't think so. Not everyone will change, but many can and will. If you live in denial, you can be 100 percent sure there is no hope for a better life. If you have the courage to accept the reality of who he is and how you got into a relationship with him, the information below will give you some hope, perhaps the best hope for a better life and for him to become a better man.

If you are in this type of relationship, like many women, you may be convincing yourself that his jealousy is not sick, it is just an indication of how much he loves you. You may be feeling a sense of power that a man like him could be so enraged with you. You may be getting the most attention you have ever received in your life. It may seem flattering that he wants to know your every move. You may be in denial: still refusing to call a spade, a spade. You may not yet understand that his love is only for himself and that you and the children are just props. It is very frightening to face all of these facts about violent men, especially if you know someone who fits the profile. Questions race through your mind: *Am I safe? Will he be angry if I stand up to him? What in the world can I do? I have young children. We've been married thirty years. Isn't it a bit late now to do something?*

You may, on the other hand, be done with denial. You see the picture all too clearly. You are embarrassed and humiliated at allowing yourself to be treated so poorly all this time. You are sick of living in the pressure cooker of his critical scrutiny and the threat that his rage may erupt at any moment. You may see your sons as beginning to exhibit the same types of behaviors and attitudes toward you as their father. Your daughters may be receiving the same degrading abuse you have received for so long. If you have had enough, here are some suggestions:

1. *If you are not married to him yet, do not move any closer to him or to marriage.* It will not get better when you are married, guaranteed. It will only get worse. Do not fall for the idea that once the ring is on your finger he will feel secure and settle down. Sadly, once he has married you he will feel that he completely owns you, and his attempts to control will only intensify. Move out of the relationship until this guy has gotten help—a lot of help! Or, better yet, find someone who does not meet these criteria. You will want to get some help yourself to find out why you would be attracted to such a man and why you need to be married so badly that you would consider such a person to be marriage material.

If you are determined to continue the relationship, then let him know what troubles you. Request that he seek counseling for those problems. If he loves you, he will. If he does not, he will move on to someone else or attempt to make you feel like the source of the problem. If he will not get help before you are married, he will not get help afterward.

2. *Realize that you will not be able to change him.* You did not cause his behavior, and you cannot fix it. If there is a fix in your future, it will come from your getting help and his getting help. Through that combination, he might actually change. But nothing you

will do on your own will change him. You are in a battle for your life, your marriage, and for the stability of your kids. Those are all valuable enough to require help from a third party.

3. *If he threatens to hit you, act as if he did hit you.* Why wait until the blow is actually struck? The threat is intended to be a mental and emotional blow. Sometimes the threat actually carries more force than the fist. Why wait to be hit or allow yourself to be manipulated by threats? The first threat is the time to treat the problem as if it were capital murder. Ask him to leave and not come back until he has learned to manage his anger. If he will not leave, *you* should find a way to leave. If he loves you, he will do whatever he has to do to get you back in the house.

These may seem like drastic measures over a little threat, but they are not. Since he has so many signs of an angry man, and this is just one of the most obvious ones, it is important that you get help and demand he get help before the problem escalates and you get hooked too deeply into it. Above all else, realize that you are seeing the tip of the iceberg of his threatening behavior.

4. *Recognize his pattern of confessing but never genuinely getting the kind of help he needs.* Begging for forgiveness is not change. He may even go for some type of treatment but continue to blame you for the problem. He may accept a separation and say he recognizes his unloving behaviors, yet at the same time say that if only *you* were different he would not have reacted so badly. None of this behavior is true remorse.

You must break this cycle with the courage to take action. You must stop listening to what he says and only look at what he does. His words are lies, and his actions are destructive. Wishful thinking will not change that. What often does change it is your changing and his learning that the old rules no longer apply. If his self-pitying apologies stop getting the result he wants, he may desire or be forced to move on to some other mode. That mode could involve a healthy change. If you continue to listen to what he says, it will never happen.

5. *If he has hit you or hurt you or your children, do not stay.* Leave immediately. Get help. Do not remain where he can get at you. Do not believe he will change without treatment and separation. Go whether

you have money, a car, or clothes. Run, do not walk. *Do not go back.* He needs to have you around so he can hit you and so avoid his fear of abandonment. The best thing you can do for him is to stay away. As long as he has you around, he will not have to face himself and his terror of abandonment. Not going back does not mean you have to get a divorce. It means staying safe and, if need be, living apart until he has truly gotten help and changed. For many women, especially those who are Christians, this move is very tough. They have a hard time seeing that there are circumstances where staying is the "bad" thing to do, and leaving is the "good" thing to do.*

Staying results in greater sickness and sinful results for the entire family. Leaving becomes the only hope for initiating change. Some pastors may tell you to stay and submit to the abuse. If you are influenced by that type of teaching, you need to ask yourself why you would accept such a distortion of the truth. Some ministers who teach this actually believe it is the right thing to do. They believe it allows God to use the situation to make you more godly. They believe to do otherwise is dishonoring of God. God can do all of that without your staying around to be hit or placing your children in danger. Unfortunately, there are some ministers who are just like your husband, and you are not getting an unbiased opinion. No one should ever subject themselves to physical harm. Your job is to get yourself and your children to safety. No matter what the price, no matter what the sacrifice, you must get away.

You must not let any excuse be good enough to prevent you from taking action. Money, security, loneliness, and many other issues will glue you to the current situation. Don't allow them to do so. Your depression may sap you of your drive to find alternatives. They are there if you will look for them. If you cannot look for them, ask for

---

*If he threatens you or hurts you and/or your children, find a way to leave. Most large cities have an organization like "Women Helping Women." Call your local YMCA, the police department, the United Way office, or the alcoholism council in your area. They will be able to help point you toward help. Some cities even run "safe houses" for battered women and children.

Be sure to take photos of bruises and serious injuries, and seek medical help immediately. Never lie to emergency room workers. If necessary get a restraining order against him.

Christian counseling is available in many cities. Call 1-800-NEW-LIFE, and our team will direct you to the level of care most appropriate for you, through New Life Clinics or another agency.

help from a friend, a minister, or a counseling professional. Ask them to help you save your family.

6. *Learn not to be a victim.* Examine your own motives. Do you have a secret belief that you deserve to be hit? Do you think you will never find anyone better? Women are taught to be submissive and somewhat masochistic in our society. Are you overly apologetic? Do you blame yourself for his behaviors? Do you set him up so you will get what you think you deserve? Take self-defense training. Get into therapy. Learn how to set limits. Learn how to handle your own anger. Get back in touch with your gifts and strengths. Do some things you're good at. Set up situations where you get some positive feedback. Hang out with people who really do love you and treat you with respect.

When Christ came to earth, He treated women with great respect and understanding. He showed His healing power and His willingness to forgive. He took away the excuses that might have existed for a woman to be a victim. See yourself as He saw women. See yourself as someone who is worthy of the effort it will take for you to stop playing the role of a victim and start creating a life of meaning and worth. You must start to see yourself as you are, not as others have seen you or as they have treated you. You are worth the effort to move from being a victim to living a victorious life free of abuse.

7. *Develop your spiritual life.* Reconnect with your childhood faith if that was meaningful to you. If not, find a church that honors Christ and His Word and promotes healthy relationships. Devote yourself to prayer: not in order to manipulate God into changing your husband, but to change yourself so you can make it without him. He may or may not change; it is okay to pray that he will, but you may still have to stay away from him so he won't lapse into his female-dependent ways. Make Jesus Christ the love of your life, the husband of your heart, and the father of your children. Then no matter what happens with your man, you will be okay.

An angry man creates a life of hell around him. Those living in that hell often get used to the heat rather than run from it. These angry brutes are blind to how small they are, how dependent they have become, and how sick they are making everyone around them. Their anger may have been taught them by an angry father or gathered day by day in the absence of any strong, healthy male influence. These men have been known to channel their anger into great causes and achieve great things, even while they stuck with their sickness. But when these men have no constructive outlet for the rage, they choose weakness to receive their tirades and attacks. Their anger wants a person like you to be there, ready to respond in a way that assures their weakness that they have strength. When you stop being there, then and only then is there hope for the development of real strength and healing.

PASSIVE-AGGRESSIVE MEN

Some men do not appear angry, but under their meek outer shell, the anger is there. Ruth was married to one, and she was miserable. She was miserable in her marriage and miserable because she thought she had no right to be miserable. Her husband never hit her. He never said an angry word; rarely did a negative word come out of his mouth. He didn't even criticize her. He was a good provider and spent a lot of time with the children. "Who wouldn't be thankful to have a husband like him?" she asked herself continually. Day after day she rolled that question around in her mind. *What is wrong with me that I am not happy to have such a husband?* also tumbled and bumped its way into her thoughts. He appeared to be the perfect, responsible husband. Why was she so miserable?

Finally, Ruth went to get some Christian counseling through her church. The counselor probed and prodded, and soon Ruth began to see that her husband and their relationship were more complicated than she had understood. She began to notice some other behaviors that had escaped her conscious awareness previously. Her husband was always late: late coming home, late getting them to church, late even for their big wedding anniversary celebration! The only time he was not late was when the kids had a soccer game or needed to be picked up at a friend's home or after school. When it involved the kids, he was very punctual.

Not only was he late getting to where she wanted him to be, but he also procrastinated over anything and everything she wanted him to do. He never had time or would forget or something always came up. Her projects always got neglected. If a project or event or chore involved something for the children, however, he was Johnny-on-the-spot. He would dive right in, work hard, and finish the job ahead of time. There wasn't anything he would not do for those kids. Yet the kids were feeling pretty miserable, too. And no one understood why.

He had this odd habit of managing to ruin the things that were really important, like the wedding pictures he left overnight on the radiator, aging them one hundred years in eight hours, or christening her new car with a "Big Gulp" Pepsi. Even the yard was not immune from his withering touch. One year it was brown from too much fertilizer; the next year it was brown from not enough water. If there was a breakable object within two feet, he was sure to find it. He never intentionally broke anything. Accidents just seemed to follow him around, especially when he was at home.

These were just a few of the irritations that Ruth began to uncover as she talked to her counselor. Maybe her husband was not so perfect after all. Maybe her misery had a source. She began to understand that she was married to an angry but passive man.

CHARACTERISTICS OF PASSIVE AGGRESSION

Do you know someone who has many of the following characteristics?

1. Appears compliant with almost every request but completes the assignment with grumbling remarks under his breath and sometimes openly sarcastic remarks.

2. Does not want anyone to set his agenda for him and wants to complete something only on his own schedule. Will resist any deadline imposed on him by others.

3. Is very manipulative. Will often have a huge smile on his face, but the anger is just underneath. Will use intimidation rather than rage to demand things be done his way.

4. Does not look like a rebel, but is always involved in doing things his way. He has his own code of behavior and will not be influenced by anyone else's demands on him. He feels entitled to control everything, especially his own life.

5. When told directly what to do, he comes the closest to losing it. Will often respond with irritation and then isolation.

6. Will apologize only as a manipulative move to gain control or get out of a situation. Has great difficulty in seeing and admitting his own mistakes.

7. Always finds a way to get others off their schedule. Will constantly forget things or create catastrophes that cause himself and others to be late.

8. Will make what appear to be very sincere promises to do something but finds a way to never get around to doing it. Seems to get some gratification when others are upset and powerless over his inaction.

9. Considers himself carefree, loose, and fun, and unable to grasp why someone would be hard on such a nice fellow as him. Expects you to just adjust to his carefree ways.

10. The seething anger beneath the surface comes from his sense of weakness and powerlessness. He feels like a victim who is being controlled, so he resists the best he can whenever he can. His self-esteem is extremely low, and this feeling is reinforced by the way others treat him. He is an outcast fighting his own internal battle to feel alive.

11. The simplest slight or challenge in conversation can start him seething in anger. He does not lash out, instead he sulks.

12. Is ready with an excuse for anything he did not do or anything he does not want to do. "I forgot" and "I can't right now" are two of his major coping phrases.

13. Procrastinates even when it is not in his best interest to put something off.

14. Often is attached to an overachiever who is able to work over and around his weaknesses; all the while he resents her doing so.

15. The focus is always on him and his moods. Others are not valued.

16. Usually viewed as never reaching his potential.

17. Either does not know or does not care how his behavior affects others.

If you know a man who has eight or more of these characteristics, you are definitely dealing with passive aggression (anger expressed passively). While most everyone is involved in these behaviors from time to time, the passive-aggressive man has a pattern of them.

CHILDHOOD FACTORS IN PASSIVE-AGGRESSIVE MEN

What type of family background tends to produce passive-aggressive men? There are a number of possible combinations of parents and atmospheres that reinforce passive-aggressive behavior. All of us act passive-aggressively sometimes. Yet certain family constellations can shape a boy into a passive-aggressive grown-up.[4]

Often Mom was young and energetic and expected a lot from herself and from others. She wanted to produce a child with a perfect life, so she scrutinized everything her child did. She was forever correcting him, not necessarily in a mean way, and in her own mind, "trying to help him be a better person." She would say things like: "Do it this way"; "Here, let *me* show you"; "No, you are holding it incorrectly. Do it like this." She felt she was helping him. He felt he was being controlled and manipulated.

Because she needed his perfection, her response to childish mistakes or behaviors was to take it personally. She thought he did those things on purpose to frustrate her. Normal childish behavior on his part was felt as betrayal by her. This only served to intensify her efforts to achieve total compliance in him.

The dad in this family tended to be a passive man who was content to take the overly controlling and demanding behavior of his wife. He kept busy with his own stuff and did not have much time for the boy. He did not become emotionally involved with his son and showed no interest in child rearing. After all, that is "women's work anyway." Most often he just went along with whatever Mom wanted done with the kids, giving passive support to her nagging and correcting. He modeled for his son the act of angry compliance. This type of compliance led to a disconnection among all three family members.

The son in this scenario set up his own internal standard of behavior to protect against the constant criticism. He rejected any standard set by the parents. Thus, even if they were not pleased with him, at least *he* felt pleased with himself. They never seemed pleased anyhow, and it was much easier to please himself. His parents became more and more frustrated and increased the pressure on him to conform. He thus got used to people responding negatively and just kept his anger about it underground. He would explode and rant and rave occasionally in order to intimidate and manipulate his parents, but generally kept his anger stuffed below the surface. He just acted it out in less obvious ways. He became more and more resistive; "forgetting," dawdling, doing things halfway, or promising to do things but never doing them. The parents, in turn, pushed more, and he resisted more.

A variation on this theme would be where the mom was even more critical and Dad was passive-aggressive. If the son is firstborn, he will become passive-aggressive, since Dad modeled this behavior. A later born son would most likely become a caretaker like Mom, feeling sorry for her; or he could team up with his older brother and the two of them could passive-aggressively drive both parents crazy.

In other families, both parents are too tired or too lazy to parent. The child becomes passive-aggressive because he is allowed to determine what he wants to do and when he wants to do it. He sets his own standards. Likewise, kids labeled "genius" will often become passive-aggressive because they are regarded as "special" and allowed to do as they please. Laissez-faire parenting styles lead to this outcome as well.

It is important to note that, in all of these scenarios, the common denominator is the *uninvolved father*. Today, with so many single-parent families and dads who are not involved in a meaningful way with their kids, it is scary to think of all the potential passive aggressives being cultivated under our noses. Violence is an increasing danger because passive aggressives often plot for revenge and then explode or destroy when they can no longer take the demands they view as unwarranted.

LIVING WITH A PASSIVE AGGRESSIVE

How do you cope with living with someone who is passive-aggressive? There are probably few things in the world more frustrating than living with or working with someone with these characteristics. Here are a few hints:

1. *See this situation as an opportunity to grow in patience and trust in the Lord.* People who attach to passive aggressives are usually caretaker-codependent types who like to have control, so the passive-aggressive person is especially irritating. "Letting go" and "letting God" are two recovery principles that are helpful. We are not able to change someone else anyway, so we might as well give it over to God and increase our own serenity.

2. *Decide to stop being angry with him.* This advice may sound impossible, but it is important not to give him the negative response he is used to receiving. A passive aggressive's behavior is so intrusive on your life that it is hard to imagine not being angry, yet, when you get mad, you give him the ammunition he is looking for to fight back. Also, the focus shifts to you and your feelings rather than his behavior. Hot tempers are rarely calmed by more anger, so it is in your best interest to get a grip. Every time you get mad, he feels the anger his mom generated toward him. Your pressure on him to change actually prevents change. Affirmation of who he is and what is good about him will go a long way in freeing him to move beyond his need to control by withholding.

3. *Do* not *ignore his behavior, however.* If you ignore it, you just

reinforce it. (Does it seem you can't win here?) In actuality the desired response is a firm, objective statement of the facts regarding what *you* will do, and/or what *you* need from him. For example:

- "When you are not going to be on time picking me up, please call so I can make other arrangements." (*Not:* "How could you be so inconsiderate as to let your wife wait an hour for you to pick her up?")

- "I am not going to sit here and be yelled at. When you are calm and want to discuss things with me, I will be on the deck." (*Not:* "You nasty so-and-so. How dare you scream at me when I do all the work around here and you can't remember what day it is?")

- "I know it is difficult for you to understand why I am angry. Being on time is not as important to you as it is to me. I understand that. However, it is not acceptable to me to arrive at church fifteen minutes after the service has started. So next week, if you are not ready when the rest of us are, we will go on ahead. That way none of us are stressed and we can all enjoy the service. We'll meet you afterward." (*Not:* "If you dawdle one more time on Sunday morning I think I'll scream. You know when church starts. Why can't you ever be on time? Sometimes I think you are the laziest jerk I have ever met.") Then the next Sunday, just calmly go your way, cheerfully telling him you will see him there.

4. *Develop a support system for yourself.* Sharing life with a passive aggressive is very stressful. You will need a healthy outlet for your frustrations. Take up a sport where you are able to work off some of your own anger at his behaviors, so you do not bring it into the relationship.

5. *Praise him when he does do something he promised to do or meets a standard not his own.* Everyone does better when praised rather than criticized.

6. *Try to accept that his standards are different from yours, and while yours may seem better, don't let yourself become self-righteous.*

Attempting to make him see the logic or "rightness" of your way of doing things is pointless. His parents tried for years, and they couldn't do it, so what makes you think you can? In a hundred years most of it won't matter anyway, so chill.

7. *Realize that he may not change.* This fact is difficult to face, but it is important to understand. You have to have a life and serenity whether he changes or not, so figure out how you can best do that.

WHAT COULD AN ANGRY, VIOLENT MAN DO TO CHANGE?

An angry, violent man does not always want to change, but if he does, here are some ideas as to what he could do to become whole:

1. *Change his belief system, which sees things (especially women) in a split manner: good-bad, black-white, all-nothing.*

2. *Stop denying, dissociating, and protecting himself from his feelings.* He must learn to handle anger without violence.

3. *Recognize his fear of abandonment and dependency on women.* Finding a personal relationship with God through Christ will resolve these painful feelings.

4. *Take responsibility for his own behavior and emotions, and stop blaming others for his troubles.*

5. *Accept help, invite critique, admit weakness and failure.* (*Note:* All of these things will be difficult for him to do without counseling.)

WHAT COULD A PASSIVE-AGGRESSIVE MAN DO TO CHANGE?

Here is what a passive-aggressive man would need to do in order to change:

1. *Recognize, accept, and be willing to adapt to standards of behaviors that are set by others, without resentment, hostility, or defensiveness.*

2. *Never promise something he will not do.* He must always do what he has promised.

3. *Get counseling to resolve his underfathering issues.*

4. *Work on not forgetting important dates, commitments, and promises.* He will have to eliminate procrastination.

5. *Develop his spiritual life, so he can experience God's love, reducing his insecurities and sources of anger.*

Whether your angry man is so obviously angry he erupts into violence, or is so passive that it is hard to notice his anger at first, *you* are not the source of his anger. You could not ever become good enough, smart enough, strong enough, or spiritual enough to ease his inner turmoil. His anger may come from having a controlling mom or a violent, rage-filled dad. Maybe he had no father or his father was passive, too. Whatever the source, he has chosen to hold on to it. His rage has become a large vat of rotting emotion, and nothing you do will drain the poison from his soul. He must get help for himself. He must begin to see the reality of who he is and the damage he is causing. He must learn to express his feelings appropriately, not in habitually damaging ways. He must come to terms with those who have hurt him and learn to forgive. He must learn to like and accept himself as imperfect and weak at times. A skilled counselor can help him find resolution to his problems, especially when the spiritual issues are addressed along with the other areas. Even if he has a total conversion experience, however, he must learn to take on the character of Christ, and that takes time to incorporate. This is not an instant process. In the meantime, you have to take care of yourself. You did not cause his problems, and you cannot fix them. However, with God's help, you can get through this desperate time in your life safely.

CONCLUSION

I (Steve) know the angry man just a little too well. I have been him, and it was a horrible time for me. In high school I had a darling girlfriend who was too strong for me to control. When I felt her slipping away, I slammed her against the lockers and held her there. Somehow I felt that the display of strength would endear her to me. That I would achieve compliance rather than revulsion. To her credit, we broke up.

There was another girl that I came close to marrying in college. Years later we discussed our relationship, and she let me know that much of it was full of fear. She wondered if I would have been violent and physically abusive if we had married. It was a dose of reality that within me were all the ingredients of an angry man. I could have been the abuser if I had not found help and hope through good counseling. But from my experience I know how horrible a person feels to be in a constant state of inner rage, not knowing when or how it will explode or whom you will hurt in addition to yourself.

Over the years many men have come my way who were full of anger and bitterness. Some were paranoid; they felt that others or the world at large was out to get them. The deeper their anger was submerged, the more paranoid they became. They acted as if they were at war with everyone, real and imagined. These paranoid men would always be mistrustful and accuse those around them of betrayal. The most faithful spouse was always suspected of having an affair. All that was wrong with themselves they projected onto another, refusing to see the defects in their own lives. They were sad and lonely, incapable of intimacy and overwhelmed by a fear of being hurt and rejected. Their bitter existence affected everyone around them, but they were blind to the misery they caused.

There have been other men who would be considered a borderline personality disorder. Perhaps they were deeply injured as a child through emotional, physical, or even sexual abuse. If their basic needs have not been met as a child, they spend a lifetime compensating for the loss. Those around them are demanded to walk on eggshells, always careful of what is said and done in the presence of the angry man. They see everything in black and white. Often a new acquaintance is seen as all good, all white, and the new star of the day. Soon that opinion changes. The star fades, and the one who was chosen is rejected when they turn out to be less than perfect. The lives of these men are cluttered with those who have been pulled in and then thrown out of the inner circle. When they dated, they said all the right things to get what they wanted and then moved on to someone else once the conquest was completed. Pain in others is the legacy of these men.

Angry men come in many shades of the two types we have presented here. One may be more paranoid than another. You might be in a relationship with an obsessive-compulsive man who is nice on the outside but expects so much of himself and his mate, is so rigid and controlling, that he lives in constant disappointment and anger. He may be loving only when his behavior expectations are met. But even then, his love is mechanical, thin, and fading. Other angry men are sociopaths. They feel justification where others would feel guilt.

Whatever shade of anger your man exibits, there is hope—if not for him, then for you. If the relationship is destroyed you can still be whole. It won't be easy and it won't be quick, but your best days can be ahead if you finally decide that enough is enough, that the abuse is over and respect will have to replace it. Your mind and spirit can be restored, and you can find new strength if you will trust God to help you move beyond your world of living in fear, waiting to be controlled, and falling victim to forceful manipulation. You can do it, and we hope that something written here will help you find the hope for a new way of living.

SNAPSHOT SUMMARY OF THE ANGRY MAN

CLUES TO HELP YOU SPOT HIM

1. Is passive or active, subtle or direct with rage.

2. Targets his rage on you.

3. Sees women as good-bad, madonna-whore, perfect-worthless.

4. Is uptight, obsessive, demanding, perfectionistic.

5. Rages when you have needs because he discounts others and their needs.

THE WOMAN TO WHOM HE IS ATTRACTED

1. Is a caretaker.

2. Is a people pleaser.

3. Is someone he thinks he can trap into taking the brunt of his anger.

4. Is someone who lets others dominate her.

5. Is apt to blame herself for any problems.

THE WOMAN WHO FALLS FOR HIM

1. May mistake anger for strength.

2. Is familiar with living with an angry person.

3. May need an excuse to vent her own anger.

4. Feels special being the focus of even negative emotions.

5. May feel that she deserves his rage.

WHAT YOU CAN DO

1. Realize you cannot change him.

2. Learn not to be a victim.

3. Develop your spiritual life; get support from others.

4. Handle your own anger.

5. Get away if he is violent.

WHAT HE COULD DO TO CHANGE

1. Stop seeing the world and people as all good or all bad.

2. Accept his feelings of anger and handle them without violence and abuse.

3. Explore and deal with his fear of abandonment.

4. Take responsibility for his own actions.

5. Seek out a counselor and listen for wisdom.

CHAPTER 6

THE MAMA'S BOY

Every woman knows that you need to be careful if your friends fix you up with a blind date who lives with his mother. Especially if he is over twenty-five years old and living with Mama "just until he finds his niche in life." If he is thirty-five and still living at home, we can conclude that living with Mama is his niche, and he's not trying to find anything. If he is forty-five years old and still living at home with Mama, and you are foolish enough to go out with him, be prepared to cut up his meat for him.

We have all known the type: nice guy, polite, kind, fastidious, often successful, but rather introverted. Some mama's boys have dated a lot, others have not. Some are openly attached to Mom, some do not appear so at first glance. Some mama's boys treat their moms well; others neglect them and take advantage of them. A woman could easily fall for a mama's boy who treats his mom well. He seems like such a good person, especially in the way he takes care of his mom. He'd have to make a good husband; after all, "Don't men usually treat their wives the way they treat their mothers?" He is so gentle and kind, even noble, in his service and devotion to Mom.

The beginning of your relationship with him seems so positive, so natural, so filled with potential. It is easy to get hooked on a man who loves and respects his mother so much. However, as time goes on, even before the wedding rings are exchanged, there are signs that only one woman can have priority in his life. At first, it may be just a change in plans because "Mama did not tell me she had a doctor's appointment." Or his mom may make a snide comment that hurts you, and, instead of comforting you and confronting her, he defends his mother. Warning signals go off in your head, but you may not pay attention at first because he seems so nice. It would be disappointing to notice how attached to Mama he really is and that he is likely to remain so at least until her death.

The clinical term for mama's boy is *Passive-Aggressive Personality,* which is the same as passive-dependent. He is overly dependent on his overly controlling mother. Somehow she did not take up the mission of producing an independent child. She was unwilling to free him from the nest. She never taught him to fly. This has placed him in a very difficult double bind. Subconsciously, he is very angry at his mother. At the same time, he deeply fears her rejection and dares not express his anger. As a result, the anger comes out in his behavior.

If he is like most mama's boys, he will spend the rest of his life punishing and mistreating substitute authority figures without even knowing it. That will definitely include you. If you are already married to one, you have heard all the things he always wanted to say to his mother. You have been treated with all the spite and coldness that he wanted to give his mother. Most likely, you hate her and him and your life with a man you thought was going to be a gentle giant.

His anger will also be expressed to others through his behavior, not his words, especially when those people are in authority or are important. This will manifest itself in being late for appointments with important people. He will miss a lot of planes. He will drive slow in the fast lane just to annoy other drivers. When his partner wants sex, he will be the one to have the headache. He will often work for companies that want control over almost every waking minute. Sometimes he will find his way into cultish religions that control him just as Mama did. What you see on the outside is devotion to his loving mother. What is on the inside is an angry, mixed-up man out to get back at someone other than Mama for the trap she put him in.

He is either the result of a "mother who smothers" or a "why bother? father." Most likely it is both. His father has either rejected him or just ignores him, while his mother drags him down with her grappling hooks of emotional incest and dependency.

AN EXAMPLE OF THE MAMA'S BOY

The twins were born into the family, it would seem, rather unexpectedly. Everyone knew that Martha and Bob did not really get along that well, and their daughter was twelve when the boys were born. No one got the idea that those twelve years were spent pining for more kids. They were an odd family. Bob was a high school history teacher. He was a veteran of World War II. The G.I. Bill had financed his education, along with support from his wife, who was a nurse. They had met, presumably, in the military, married upon discharge, and she worked until he finished school. Their first child, a daughter, was born in 1949. Both of them were from an Eastern European background, with rather severe, cold, and unemotional parents. His dad was dead, and he was devoted to his mom. Her dad was deceased as well, and her mom lived an hour and a half away. His mom was in the same town, down the street from where he taught school.

Bob's students reported that he was an odd duck, often jumping up on the desk to reenact battles from the war. To neighbors, he seemed a bit cool, though he occasionally smiled. Bob was hardworking, no one could doubt that. He had built their home in the country, brick by brick, himself. He was quite a craftsman and an avid gardener. Martha was a sour sort of woman who, for her part, rarely smiled. The neighbors all thought that one day they would find that she had shot herself and the kids just to spite her husband. No one really knew what was going on in the home except that they did not have friends, rarely socialized with neighbors, had strict, seemingly stupid rules for their kids, and everyone in the family seemed depressed.

When Jerry and Jerome were born, big sister Sally was thrilled. She was a bright, competitive girl who was given ballet and art lessons. Sally loved her brothers and helped take care of them. As they grew, the boys remained close to each other (they were identical twins), and though there were lots of kids their age in the neighborhood, they never really formed any close friendships. Reclusive like their parents, they seemed quiet, withdrawn, and somewhat depressed. While they did okay in school, they were not academic whiz kids like their sister or the kids next door. When they were about seven, their mom sued their dad for divorce. Everyone in the community was sad for Bob, but not overly surprised. The rancor of the divorce was evident in that as soon as it was final, Martha went out to the backyard and cut down dozens of ornamental fruit trees that Bob had planted and diligently and lovingly cared for over the years. Mom went back to work, and after the twins finished junior high, she moved the family to New Hampshire. Sally had completed college in nearby Maine and was working as a teacher. The boys went to vocational school for their high school experience. They continued at a community college for a year or two, still living at home with Mom. They rarely saw their dad, who had moved in with his mother when the divorce took place.

Twenty-five years later, neither has married, and, at last report, they still live with Mom in New Hampshire. The twins run a small business, support Mom, and take care of the family home. Their social life has not changed much since they were children. They are polite, smile appropriately, talk when spoken to but volunteer little. Sally went on to get a doctorate in something, was engaged once, but broke it off. She, too, is estranged from Dad but tries to keep up ties to the twins and Mom.

COMMITMENT AND THE MAMA'S BOY

Most women who have run into the mama's boy know that he has a problem with commitment. Oh, he may *marry* you. However, in biblical lingo, he will never "leave and cleave." He does not know how to leave his mother or move her out of the most prominent position in his life. Nor does he know how to grow closer to you, much less be genuinely intimate with you. Mama and her agenda and needs always seem to get in the way. In some way you are always in conflict with her through him. It is as if he is inviting you to slay the mama dragon while keeping you from reaching for the sword that could lop off her head. He wants you to save him from the beast he hates, but he cannot because he is fused to her, and protecting her feels like protecting himself.

Poor Mama's lawn is going to get mowed when she asks for it even if yours is knee-high. After all, you could mow the lawn for both of you. Or you could mow Mama's lawn, allowing him to maintain distance from her while still ensuring that her needs are met. In fact, one of his underlying desires is that you will become her caretaker and he will be free. If Mama's gutters need emptying, you could do it for her; if her fence needs mending, you could learn how to mend fences; if she needs to go to the hospital (who cares if you are having surgery the same day), you could take her and put off your surgery until after he is assured that Mama will survive. If Mama is lonely, her dedicated son must go there for lunch every day—unless you are willing to take on that chore also.

But the more you do for her, the more it threatens her allegiance to him. He cannot allow her to believe that anyone can do for her what he can, even though he is groaning to have the burden of her demands removed from him. He is trapped in a maze whose only path to healing is through pain, depression, separation, and the construction of a new world without the beloved Mama as the dominant force in life.

As he delivers the services she requires, you may tell yourself, "She'll be dead soon, and then I can have all his attention."

You may ask yourself, "How can I be so selfish as to want my husband to stay home with me and our kids or to take me out to lunch? His mama's all alone, and we've got him all the rest of the time. What's a few minutes on the weekend?"

Of course, a "few minutes" always turns into an hour, and "an hour or two" always turn into three, but who would be selfish enough to count? And how can you be so cruel as to ask her not to call every night? Even if it is during dinner, she is just lonely and wants to be sure to catch you at home. You talk to your mother, don't you? These are all your own rationalizations that guard you from the truth that neither you nor your children are the most important things in his life. And while you long for the day when her death frees him from her claws, it will not. Death will only usher in overwhelming guilt for him that he did not do more, and he will blame you for not being there for him when she "really" needed him. Her death will also produce dreadful feelings of abandonment within him. To him it is her way of doing to him what his father did many years ago.

There is another slight variation in type for the mama's boy. This one is the type that is all for a relationship until it comes to something serious where he would have to move out and leave Mom alone (or so he says). He loves you to death, wants to spend the weekend with you, takes you to romantic hideaways, swears eternal devotion; but when you mention "marriage," the ugly specter of MOM raises its head. "Oh, I can't move out *now*. She would die if I left her. She's so sickly, you *know* she'll not be here for long. Can't we wait?" "Well, why not move in with us? Mom wouldn't mind. She *loves* you. We'd have a great time. Just the three of us." "You know I love you. It's just that work is so demanding right now. I have those big projects to do. And then I did promise Mom I'd put a new roof on the house this summer. And she's already booked us on an AAA tour in October to New England. I don't see how . . ." With this type of mama's boy you will never have marital problems because he will never marry you. The terror that arises within him when he thinks he might have to care for another woman blocks all hopes of commitment. Your demands, along with his sense of inadequacy, will produce a myriad of excuses that will prevent marriage.

The central theme in the mama's boy's life is protection. He wants to protect her. He needs to protect himself from his doubts and fears. He must fend off any attack on his world and the way he has organized it. Most of all he wants to protect himself from the painful reality that he does not want to face. For most mama's boys these are the priorities. There are some exceptions to this. When a mama's boy has a big chunk of the eternal kid inside of him, he not only wants to protect, but he also wants to take. He wants to stay close to Mama while he uses another woman to fund the enterprise.

One mom reported that her thirty-five-year-old son was finally moving out. He had always lived at home, worked hard at his blue-collar job, and "had always been a good boy." He had rarely dated and was content to be at home with Mama most of the time. Now Mama was distressed because he was going to move in with (note: "move in with," not marry) a woman he barely knew, who was separated but not divorced. Mama had tried to dissuade him, saying, "But that's not how I raised you!" to no avail. He wilted in the face of her ridicule and left the house with his anger unexpressed and his seething rage just below the surface. At 7:00 P.M. he came home and queried: "Where's dinner?"

Mama was upset that, after all day with the girlfriend, he would come home and still expect her to fix him his dinner. She knew that the only way to prevent this episode from ever happening again was to punish him appropriately. Mama told him to fix his own dinner and that she had a headache and did not want any noise, so she did not want any television on in the house. On that night there would be quiet in the house so that he would not be distracted from evaluating his horrible mistakes of the day. She recommended he go somewhere else. Mama knew that a little rejection and separation from her would bring him back with a compliant attitude. She also knew that his girlfriend would not be able to control him as she had been able to control him.

If he did move in with "the other woman," he would be in for a shock. Used to Mama doing his laundry, packing his lunch, having a hot meal at 5:30 P.M., and cleaning up after him, he was about to find that life was going to be different. She knew that if he made the move it would not be long before he would be banging on her door, begging to come home again. And left behind would be a naive woman who would wonder what she could have done to meet his needs so that he would have stayed. She won't realize that his mama was a powerful magnet, more powerful than anything she could do to keep his attraction to her strong or to please him.

CHARACTERISTICS OF THE MAMA'S BOY

1. *There is a void of male behaviors, thoughts, feelings, and reactions that leaves him with a fragile foundation of masculinity.* He is

without the strength that allows tears to flow in joy and sadness while remaining in control of his emotions. He is missing the part of him that can be separate and alone without needing to medicate his feelings of loneliness with sex, drugs, work, money, food, or a relationship. While we would not want anyone to be defined by stereotypes, like the macho American persona, the mama's boy has no definition of his maleness. He does not understand what it means to be a man.

2. *There is often confusion over his gender identity and sexual urges.* Gender identity is whether he believes he is a man or a woman, deep inside. Sexual preference is whether he is attracted sexually to women or men or both. Lacking a strong father in his life, the mama's boy does not have a role model for masculinity. He is unsure of how to be a man. He may have been molested as a small boy but has never told anyone, or may not fully remember the experience. The smothering and control by his mother may have produced an alienation toward women. He may be unconsciously living in terror of being devoured by a female while he longs for the attention and unconditional love from a male that his father never provided.

3. *Since he is confused about his identity, he will go to extremes to prove that he is a man, strutting the behaviors that make him feel he is proving his maleness.* He often obsesses over his manliness, questioning it and comparing who he is to other men, wondering if they accept him as one of their own. He may be macho in the way he protects his mother. He may be the charming, gentle son who courts Mama and tries to make up for all she suffered with or without his dad. He may retreat and just exist, waiting for someone to come and "kiss" his frogness, so his princely self can emerge. He may be homophobic, due to his own conflicted sexual issues. As such, he may talk a good talk about sex and his exploits in the past, but he doesn't always live up to his self-made reputation. He is everyone's friend, escort at the ready, best bud, but nobody's close, intimate main flame. He may go through a series of sexual relationships, only to retreat when the woman starts to talk "happily ever after." All the while he is trying to figure out what being male is all about.

4. *His reputation is that of a country gentleman, an amazingly nice*

man with many social graces. Everyone wonders why "good old Jerry" is not married yet. He seems to be able to talk about his feelings but in reality is quite reserved and reveals little about what is really going on inside. His talk about feelings is just that—talk. Rarely is he able to clearly express his own emotions. He is essentially a pleaser. So if talking about feelings pleases you, he will do so. You may be drawn to him because of his desire to please you, but you will not be privy to the private world that exists within his head. A private world that scares even him.

5. *He is unaware that he is angry and unaware that it goes unexpressed.* He is the type who will give in and yield, and give in some more, and then his irritation will drive him to revert to his passive-aggressive mode. He cannot ask clearly for what he needs. Like his mom, he pouts, and he withdraws love, affection, and sex as a way to show his displeasure. He will roll his eyes and give deep, agonizing sighs to show his disapproval. If you assert that he is angry, he will withdraw from you until the threat you present passes. You threaten the way he has organized his inner world and compensated for too much mother and too little father. He does not want to endure the pain required to face the reality of his family past that has produced the severe conflicts he struggles with in the present.

6. *While he obsesses over men and masculinity, he is severely dependent on women.* Inside, he fears he cannot live without a woman. Women pick this up as a sense of neediness and helplessness. Outside, he protests that he does not need a woman or, maybe, even want one; inside, their approval is the reason for his existence. He vehemently denies he is dependent, especially on women, notably, his mother. He is filled with hurt, shame, and fear, but covers this with an outer shell that is hard to penetrate. Inside, he demands that women meet all his needs; outside, when they fail, he resists, usually passive-aggressively.

If you are married to a mama's boy, you already know it. If you are dating someone and you wonder about him, consider and answer the following questions:

1. Do all your friends (and his, too, if he has any) often wonder

aloud, "Good old so-and-so. I wonder when he is going to finally get married and get away from his mama." His reputation with his mother is renowned. He is defined by her and his attachment to her and their symbiotic relationship. In her presence he is not the same man that you know. In fact, in her presence he is not a man. He is the mama's boy.

2. Does he treat his mother almost too well? At first you are amazed at his respect for his mother. You long for someone to speak of you in the same terms he talks of her. It makes you feel as if you are with the first man who was ever able to understand what women need. But as you are around him more, the sweet smell of his love for his mother starts to sour. You start to feel uncomfortable with it. The thought may flash through your mind that rather than *love* his mother, he is *in love* with his mother.

Or on the opposite end of the spectrum, does he mooch off of her and take advantage of her? He says he loves her, but you see that this is tied into his deep dependency on her. He clearly uses her to do for him and provide for him things that he should have been doing and providing for himself years earlier.

3. Does he always seem to find a reason why *now* is not the right time to be with you, or to make a commitment, or to move out on his own? This man is the consummate excuse maker. The scary thing is, since he has been making them all of his life, he has perfected the art. You believe his excuses. They make sense to you, and when you explain them to your friends and they shudder in disbelief, you still defend him and his excuses. He may eventually want to marry you, if you convince him you can do as good a job for him as Mama has. Or, when she ages and he senses she won't be there for him, he may marry you to replace her. Most likely he will not marry you, but you won't know that until you have wasted some of the best years of your life. When you finally realize he will never marry you, you may feel it is too late for you, that you are too old, too unattractive for anyone else. Many of those feelings spring up in your heart because he has sown those seeds throughout the relationship.

4. Does he accuse you of selfishness and of being mean-spirited

when you complain that he does more for her than for you? She is his biggest blind spot. He has created a protective wall around her and his relationship with her. Any attempts to break down that wall are defended with all the resources he has. You become the target. You are accused of all the selfishness and sickness that rest at the bottom of his mother's soul. When you hear the venomous accusations he hurls at you, realize that he is saying to you what he cannot say to her. If you marry him you will hear those all your life.

5. Does he defend her even when she is wrong but refuses to see your hurt and pain when she offends you? This man has deified his mother. She is his false god who has his focus and controls his life. His idealization of her will not allow him to see where she is weak, sick, or ignorant. She is a jealous god, and in quiet moments with her he will hear all the negatives about you, but he will not be your defender. You are an object owned by him the way he is owned by his mother. Objects do not have feelings. He will think it is your responsibility to get over any problems you have or emotions he does not want to hear about.

WHAT KIND OF WOMAN DOES THE MAMA'S BOY WANT?

The mama's boy wants "a girl, just like the girl . . ." that married Daddy: That is, he wants a mom. He wants a woman who willingly takes second place in everything, behind his mother. He wants a woman who is independent and willing to bear all the weight of the relationship. She must have low expectations of him and high expectations of herself. And above all, she must be willing to put up with his passive-aggressive behavior.

A woman willing to take on the task of raising him as a childish adult and nursing him as an elderly boy cannot think too highly of herself. She is most likely in a performance-based relationship with one or both of her own parents and with God. She just does not feel that she can ever do enough to be worthy of love. He will sense this and use it to train you to perform for him. If you do well, he will tell you he loves you more than any woman he has ever met. That will be a lie, but you will believe it.

WHY DOES SHE FALL FOR HIM?

There may be any number of reasons someone falls for a mama's boy. Here are a few:

1. *The woman may be used to being used.* Perhaps she had a dad who was a mama's boy, and she watched that pattern growing up. To her, it seems normal. Or perhaps she had a brutal relationship in the past, and, to her, the "nice" way he treats his mom is appealing. She knows only to give everything she has to a man and expect little in return. To her, it is likely that he is no different from other men, perhaps just a little behind in his growing up. He is sick, but so is she— so it all feels natural, something to cling to rather than flee.

2. *She may feel powerful being the "mom" or primary caretaker.* If she has been in a performance-based relationship before where she was neglected and ignored, this may seem like a better way to live. She may have never had control, and, seeing the control his mother has over him, she may unknowingly want to have that same level of control over him, which she believes he will give her. If she has played servant to her own dad or mom, she may have liked the accolades she received because of her devotion. This man may feel like her ticket to a life of being respected and admired by others.

3. *The woman may be afraid of an egalitarian relationship.* Playing second fiddle seems safer. She is not a risk taker and does not think the woman should be the one out front in a relationship. Taking a backseat feels very natural to her. This is how she prefers life and is prepared to dedicate hers to it in exchange for safety and sameness.

4. *She may believe that her love is so special that it will win him away from Mom, especially because she can use sex as a tool.* If she could never fix her broken dad or mom, she may feel compelled to fix someone. She may be driven to do for him what she could not do for her own father, which was save him. She believes that she can make everything different for him. She sees the problem and knows that she

is this man's salvation. His strong response to her reinforces that feeling from the beginning of the relationship.

5. *She may think he is noble, kind, and generous in the way he treats Mama; she assumes he will treat her the same way.* If she came from a home where women were treated like doormats, this may seem like a dream come true. This wonderful gentleman makes her feel appreciated and loved and cared for. She is jealous of his mom and the devotion she has endeared from him.

Compared to her past, this all looks so good that she will not look at the motivations behind the relationship or face the reality that this is all bait and switch. Once she has been snared, she will realize that the treatment of Mama is so good that none of the good stuff is left for another woman.

RELATING TO THE MAMA'S BOY

What if you are married to a mama's boy? What if you have been dating one? What should you expect? What should you do? Obviously, if you are dating him, *don't* marry him. No sense putting more time into a relationship that is not going to go anywhere. Your love will not win him over. You must assume you will not be able to defeat Mama. The enmeshment was there before you came along, and it will be there long after you are gone. His need for her is as strong as her need to stay attached to him. You are fighting a losing battle that is rarely won.

If you are married, realize that *you* will not change him. As long as his mom is alive, he will still be married to her. He may say he loves you, but his heart belongs to Mama. Seek the Lord as your true husband and friend. Find an intimacy with Christ Jesus that rivals any you have ever known. Wrestle with God until He blesses you with that closeness. Let Christ remove all bitterness and hurt from you. If you are normal, you have a lot of anger and hurt built up against him and against her. Keep a clear conscience. Do not gossip about her (or him). Ask the Holy Spirit to pour out the Father God's love into your heart (Rom. 5) so that you can be loving and kind rather than spiteful and jealous. Establish a support system outside the family. That way you can have some objective support, not pressure from biased family members.

Learn how you are enabling his behavior. You do not cause his dependence, but you may unknowingly reinforce it. Counseling may help here. When he wants you to solve something for him (as Mom does), say something like: "I have no idea what you should do. But I do have utter confidence in you that you will find the solution." Stick to that stance no matter what.

Try not to make everything a test of whom he loves more, you or her. Accept the fact that he is "addicted" to Mom and that you are the codependent. His problem is his problem, even though it impacts you big time. He is really a scared, unhappy little boy who only wants Mama to love him. He is unconsciously dependent on her for his own sense of self and survival. It really is not about *you*.

You can pray for him and his relationship with the Lord Jesus. He may be placing pleasing Mama over pleasing the Lord, and she has become his god. Pray that the Holy Spirit will separate him from any unhealthy ties to his mom and that God the Father would become his true Father. Pray for healing of any emotional or sexual incest. Bless him in prayer: "Dear Lord, bless this man in his ability to stand and be separate from his mom. Bless him in his ability to be strong in the power of Your strength. Help me accept him as he is so he can become what he is not."

In areas where he hesitates to assert himself with Mom, encourage him to use his "courage muscle." Express confidence in him regularly, especially in areas where he has previously been weak. Encourage him to question old patterns in his relationship with his parents. If he is willing, go to marital counseling. Acceptance of him combined with boundaries for you will encourage his growth.

WHAT COULD THE MAMA'S BOY DO TO CHANGE?

If a mama's boy woke up and realized there was another way to live, and wanted to change, he would need to take certain steps:

1. *Differentiate from other people.* He is too enmeshed with Mama and needs to develop his own identity. He is like a Siamese twin attached at the heart with his mother. He must see that separating from her is not abandoning her. He may not be able to get through, but he can talk with his mother about his becoming his own person and explain that it does not mean he is abandoning her. He needs to allow a woman to set some boundaries with him that will prevent them from becoming Siamese twins as he and his mama are. He must learn that being in a relationship with someone does not mean being fused at the hip or the heart. Connection does not mean consumption.

2. *Get some therapy to settle his masculinity issues.* An older male therapist who is wise can help greatly with this. It is not a quick issue to resolve. First, it requires honesty. If he dreams about men, that is where the process can begin. If he obsesses over them or his own body, he must open up about these feelings so that their origin can be understood. He must also get clinical help for the anger that lies just beneath his gentility. Resolving the anger toward the mother who consumed him and the father who walked away and allowed her to consume him can help stabilize a fragile sense of masculinity.

3. *Strengthen his courage muscle and learn to say no, and then say it to Mama.* This will mean that he will have to get comfortable with her momentary rejection of him. She will not like his new sense of power and will do whatever she can to restore the household to the natural order to which she is accustomed. This is where strong boundaries come in. Again we recommend the book *Boundaries* by Dr. John Townsend and Dr. Henry Cloud, published by Zondervan.

4. *Depend on God and His strength, not on pleasing others, for his self-esteem and confidence.* He does not need to please Mama to be a valuable human being. He was created by God and needs to depend on Him for his sense of worth. This requires working through whatever distrust he has of God because of the lack of trust he has in his dad. He can please God and be confident that He loves him; God's approval is conditional but His love is not. He must allow Jesus to become a model of masculinity for himself by reading and studying

His life and using it as a guide for his own dependency on God. What Jesus did more consistently than any other thing was to seek the wisdom of His heavenly Father. He can depend on his heavenly Father in that same way.

5. *Be accountable to someone else to make and keep commitments to his wife.* He must seek out a male partner in this venture of self-development. A growing friendship is best. A pastor or counselor could help also. This person must be invited to encourage and confront him. They must discuss his need to say no to Mama and say yes to his wife. He must come to understand her needs and meet them. Commitments must be kept, especially when the only conflict is a request from Mama.

CONCLUSION

There is hope for a marriage to a mama's boy. If your mama's boy is also a taker, you have a hard row to hoe. You need to ask yourself why you would want to be with someone who uses others with so little remorse. Do you like being Mom? Does his dependency make you feel powerful? Was your dad a taker, too, and that is what you are used to experiencing? Are you enabling his user behavior? What do you get out of that arrangement? Sometimes, with prayer and divine intervention, a taker can reform. The biblical story of Zacchaeus is a good example. While there are no clues in the account that he was a mama's boy, it would not be hard to imagine the diminutive fellow as one. And for sure, he was a taker. He used anyone and everyone, but when he encountered Jesus, his life turned around dramatically. And not just in his words either. But if you are dating a mama's boy, do not assume he is going to change. He may not be a Zacchaeus.

So pray, take care of yourself, grow in your own character and spiritual life, and perhaps things will change. At some point he needs to make a decision. Is he going to be married to Mama, or is he going to be married to you? You have to be strong enough to handle the truth if Mama's umbilical cord is wrapped tightly around his neck. But if you have some good guidance and God is at work, you may be instrumental in cutting that cord and experiencing a real marriage for the first time.

The good news about mama's boys who are devoted to Mother is that they do want to love. They feel loving inside and do have love and care to give. It is just that the attachment to Mom hinders their ability to give that love to anyone but her. However, if over time a mama's boy senses that it is safe to risk giving love to you; that you are not smothering like his mom; that you love him and yet have a life of your own (unlike Mom); then there may be hope. With work on his part or upon her death, or by chance, should you move away due to job transfer, etc., he may be able to feel safe and comfortable enough to relate more intimately with you. If you can be patient and grow on your own, in time you may find yourself married to a man who will love you deeply.

SNAPSHOT SUMMARY OF THE MAMA'S BOY

CLUES TO HELP YOU SPOT HIM

1. People ask, "When is he gonna get away from his mama?"

2. Either treats his mom too well or terribly.

3. Is unwilling to make a commitment to you.

4. Does more for his mom than you and thinks you are selfish to be jealous.

5. Defends her over you and refuses to accept your emotions while possessing complete understanding of hers.

THE WOMAN TO WHOM HE IS ATTRACTED

1. Is "a girl, just like the girl, that married dear old Dad."

2. Appears willing to take second place to Mom.

3. Is independent enough to handle all inconvenient details of life for him and for her.

4. Has low expectations of him.

5. Will put up with his passive-aggressive behavior.

THE WOMAN WHO FALLS FOR HIM

1. Is used to being used.

2. May enjoy the feelings of power that come with being a mama to a man.

3. May be afraid of an egalitarian relationship.

4. Believes her love will win him over and save him from his mom.

5. Sees him as noble, gentle, and kind in the way he treats his mother and believes she will be treated the same way.

WHAT YOU CAN DO

1. If dating him, don't marry him.

2. Realize he will only change if he decides to or if a crisis, such as her death, moves him toward maturing.

3. If married, attempt to develop relationships with couples in which the man is not playing the role of a boy and the woman is a wife.

4. Accept that you have grown since you married him. But you did marry him, so forgive him and yourself, refusing to allow bitterness to build up.

5. Find a support group that will help you remove all enabling behaviors from your relationship with him.

WHAT HE COULD DO TO CHANGE

1. Learn how it feels to differentiate himself from others without rejecting them.

2. Settle masculinity issues through long-term counseling with an effective, older male counselor.

3. Do a courageous thing and say no to Mama, yes to wife, and increase the frequency with which he takes that risk.

4. Depend on God and His strength and stop depending on pleasing others for a feeling of self-worth.

5. Be accountable to his male counselor and a friend in keeping commitments to his wife.

CHAPTER 7

THE DECEIVER

WHAT IS THE TRUTH, ANYWAY?

Do you find yourself always hoping, always believing, and frequently being deceived by the man you love? Is a good part of your time together spent in his explaining away the obvious or chastising you for not believing him? If so, you are living his lie. Few relationships are more frustrating and few have less hope for success.

Today, more than ever before in history, the truth seems up for grabs. Lying is winked at, overlooked, and enabled. We have seen presidents and pastors, leaders and losers caught in career-ending and career-derailing lies. In every case the truth would have been so much easier and served them so much better, but they did not know how to express the truth. It was not part of their character.

The search for truth amid lies, however, is not new. John's Gospel describes one such query: "Pilate therefore said to Him, 'So You are a king?' Jesus answered, 'You say correctly that I am a king. For this I have been born, and for this I have come into the world, to bear witness to the truth. Everyone who is of the truth hears My voice.' Pilate said to Him, 'What is truth?'" (John 18:37–38 NASB). Pilate wondered what truth was two thousand years ago, and now in this postmodern age, some people think the question is irrelevant. Most Christians would be shocked if they realized the degree to which truth has become irrelevant (or at least relative) in our culture today.

Focused as we are on Scripture and on Jesus Himself as the Truth incarnate, it is difficult for us to conceive of a mind-set that does not believe truth is even possible. The *modern* worldview (from the Enlightenment era to the mid-twentieth century) held that truth is discoverable through reason. By using logic and reason, human beings, it was believed, could discover truth. There may have been debate about what truth *was*, but the assumption remained that it *did exist*, and could be discovered. Hence, the development of the scientific method, and the resulting industrial revolution, which made "modern" life possible.

At the beginning of the twenty-first century, however, we live in a *postmodern* world. Postmodern thought is suspicious of science. It doubts that human beings are getting better. All so-called "truth" is relative. No one view has any claim to be better than another. Truth, per se, does not exist, and those who pursue it are deemed foolish. Truth has become whatever one perceives it to be, and thus, *it may change from day to day, hour to hour!* Therefore, concepts such as loyalty, commitment, and fidelity are defined based on how one *feels* at the time. There are no absolutes against which to judge one's behavior. At least that is the message you will find out there in the world. Don't be confused by it. You have a right to be in a relationship with someone who tells the truth.

Recently, a pastor came for counseling and reported that his board of elders was concerned that some young people at youth camp reported seeing him kissing a female counselor (not his wife). Other accusations were made as well, one being that he had told the youth that it was acceptable to have premarital sex. The problem he presented to the counselor was that he had indeed kissed the female counselor. He reported that he had lied to the board in order to save his reputation and that of the young woman. He was seeking counseling because his marriage was in trouble, and he "felt badly" that he "had to lie." Yet there was no sense of needing to repent of the lie and correct the board members' impression of what had happened. He had broken off the relationship with the counselor (which, he admitted, had been going on for six months) and was willing to work on his marriage; but he did not have any qualms about maintaining what he deemed as a "necessary lie."

Sissela Bok commented about this type of dilemma in her book *Lying: Moral Choice in Public and Private Life:*

> Ordinary decisions can no doubt be made in spite of theoretical beliefs which confuse truth and truth-telling, or which set epistemological certainty ahead of ethical analysis. But the fact remains that moral choice is often harmed thereby; for to the extent that one had radical doubts about the reliability of all knowledge, to that extent the moral aspects of how human beings treat one another, how they act, and what they say to each other, may lose importance. Worst of all, this loss is especially likely to afflict one's own moral choices. For whereas it is only prudent to support morality in others, we are more hospitable to doubts about the possibility of moral choice when it comes to our own decisions.[1]

If we doubt knowledge of truth is possible, as postmodernists do, morality loses its importance. It becomes okay to lie, as long as *I* am the one who is lying. By "lie" we mean intentional deception. Let's be honest. We all will lie in some way under some circumstance. Jeremiah 17:9 states that "the heart is deceitful above all things" (NKJV). We are deceitful in many ways. We may add an embellishment or fail to disclose everything, and both of those are forms of lying. We all do it because we are all human. We all occasionally tell a "white lie." We all fall short of the biblical standard "[Speak] the truth in love" (Eph. 4:15 NKJV). However, there are those individuals (both women and men) who are habitual liars. They cannot tell the difference anymore between their lies and the truth. They may even come to believe the lies themselves. They do not just lie, they live a lie and their whole life is a lie.

WHY DO LIARS LIE?

Why do people tell lies? They lie because they choose to do so. Paul Ekman, in his book *Telling Lies,* commented:

A liar can choose not to lie. Misleading the victim is deliberate, the liar intends to misinform the victim. The lie may or may not be justified, in the opinion of the liar or the community. The liar may be a good or a bad person, liked or disliked. But the person who lies could choose to lie or to be truthful, and knows the difference between the two.[2]

Even though a liar may come to believe his lies, at some level, deep down inside, he knows, or at least once knew, he is lying.

There are two ways to lie: One is to deliberately falsify; the other is to conceal or omit. I may not tell you the whole truth of where I was last night, thus omitting the more damaging information. By doing so, I have concealed the truth from you. In falsifying, I go a step farther and present something as true that is not. Concealing the truth is generally easier than falsifying because nothing has to be invented. To some people, concealment is seen as less reprehensible, since it is more passive than active.[3] It is easier to say about concealment, "I cannot remember" or "I don't recall," as O. J. Simpson did in his murder trial. Falsifying is more difficult because you have to remember what you made up.

Events in the Christian community in the last few years have been illustrative. Any one of us can name prominent Christian preachers, evangelists, and entertainers who have been caught in lies. In the same issue of *Christianity Today* that highlighted the case of the Seattle pastor resigning (July 31, 1998), a dramatic case of affinity fraud was reported. Philip Harmon, a seemingly successful Christian businessman, bilked fellow Christians from his home church of millions of dollars. Harmon entered federal prison in July 1998 to begin serving an eight-year sentence for conspiracy and tax fraud. The $16 million he bilked from an unsuspecting fellow evangelical Quaker community will likely never be recovered.[4] Clearly, even those who profess to be evangelical Christians can have problems with concealment and falsifying.

The deceiver has a lot in common with Mr. Wonderful. There are some big differences though. Mr. Wonderful is more often a narcissist who is so full of himself that he ignores everyone around him. The deceiver is more often a sociopath who is so full of lies he hurts everyone around him. Mr. Wonderful is motivated by looking good while the deceiver is motivated by survival. He lies to hang on to whatever he has. The deceiver lies probably because he lives according to certain assumptions:[5]

1. Dishonesty is necessary between women and men, because women and men are so different. The other person "just would not understand" so he has to lie.

2. Dishonesty protects people from getting hurt. He sees the mate or loved one as so pathetically fragile that he *must* deceive her to protect her.

3. The problem with infidelity (or other dishonest behavior) is in getting caught, not in the act itself. It is too dangerous to be caught, because then someone might be upset or there might be some distasteful consequences.

Compounding the problem, men in general often view dishonesty differently, depending on whom it is against. Male friends, colleagues, and business partners are assumed to be honest with one another because they are on the "same team." Only with competitors or the "other team" is deceit acceptable. Some exclusive clubs used to throw a man out if he cheated at golf, but not if he cheated on his wife.[6] In dealing with women, the assumption is "What she doesn't know won't hurt her." There is an unspoken code that one does not "squeal"—even if one learns a pal is cheating on his wife. Men often see women as fragile and "too easily upset," so they justify concealing the truth from them. Young boys learn to hide the truth if it protects Mom or makes her feel better.

All of this rationalization assumes an inherent inequality or imbalance of power in a relationship. A liar hopes to gain an advantage over the one to whom he lies. By lying, he distracts or disorients her and thereby steps outside the bounds of the relationship. He uses the lie to gain control and maintain it. He sacrifices the joys of intimacy he has never known for control he has never had. By using lying in his efforts to dominate the other person, the liar eliminates all possibility of equal trust or mutuality. Attempting to disorient the partner through misinformation or deceit is a power play that will eventually kill the relationship.

LIARS WITHOUT CONSCIENCE

While all of us have been known to lie at one time or another, most of us who are thirty and over usually feel guilty about it. We have been brought up with values of truth and integrity. And if we were not brought up with those values we have learned them, discovering the emptiness we feel when we have lied. Whether by teaching from parents or personal experience, we know there is some basis for living, some standard to which we are accountable.

People who do not have that conscience have no concept of right or wrong beyond what seems good at the moment: "Whatever works." "If it works for you, go for it." "That's great for you, but it will never work for me. I have to go my way." Sound familiar?

Some people go beyond this seemingly benign approach to a more evil stance. They lie, deceive, and manipulate to achieve their goals, their plans, their aspirations. It does not matter who stands in their way. If they have to lie to maintain their power, so be it. This approach can range from the political machinations of a presidential candidate to the small-town power-grabbing of a pastor more in love with himself than God. The goal is the same: to have power over, to dominate, to control others.

The deceiver has no conscience. That which would produce guilt and shame in most of us produces something far different in him. He feels justification rather than guilt. First, he convinces himself that everyone deceives everyone as he does. That is not too hard for a person to believe, especially if they have a good bit of paranoia going on, which the deceiver usually does. He believes everyone deceives, but because of his status or bad luck or past experiences, people are against him and trying to trip him up and make him fail. So, since everyone does this, and he is the victim of a nasty plot to ruin him, he is justified in lying to protect himself, his career, and his family. In fact, the more formidable the challenge before him, the more deceptive he becomes. The sharper at it he becomes. He is fueled and supercharged by his belief that when he lies he is doing what is right. No one knows what he knows, and if they did, they would encourage him to lie. It is something he just has to do.

As mentioned earlier, this man is a sociopath. That is who the deceiver is. He is a sociopath. Our colleague/friend Paul Meier wrote more about him in his book *Don't Let Jerks Get the Best of You*, published by Thomas Nelson. What we call the deceiver, he calls the "Nth-Degree Jerk." Prisons are full of these guys, but most of them are out here with the rest of us. They are trying to control us and take what we have, even our souls. And all the while feeling justified and right in all they do.

EXAMPLES OF DECEIVERS

While there are many examples we could use, we have chosen two, which, although dramatic, are really not as uncommon as you might think.

ESTHER AND GEORGE

Esther had been married to her first husband for thirty years. They had raised four children, and at the age of fifty-eight, she was looking forward to retirement and grandchildren. One day her husband came home and announced that he wanted a divorce. He had been having an affair with his secretary and had decided to move in with her. Esther was shocked and horrified. *Divorce* was not even in her vocabulary, and she had had no inkling of the affair. She had never worked outside the home and could not imagine being single again at her age. Her kids, though sympathetic, all lived out of state, and so could not give more than moral support. The divorce went through quickly, and before she knew what had happened, her ex-husband moved to Minnesota, and she was living in a new condominium all by herself. Luckily, she had found a good lawyer, and so she was set financially. Her husband had always made good money and invested wisely; there was plenty of money for anything she might need. Despite his callousness otherwise, he had seen to it that she was more than provided for in the settlement. Esther did not know his motive, but at least she did not have to worry about money.

At first, when she was still in shock, Esther just went through the motions of living. She got up every day, got dressed, walked the dog, read the paper, did the dishes, and vacuumed the condo. She saw few friends and became more and more depressed. Then one day an old friend, who was also divorced, sort of kidnapped her and took her to a local church where there was a singles' dance going on. Esther loved it. She laughed for the first time in ages and danced 'til her feet hurt. One gentleman was especially gracious and did not seem to mind that she tripped over herself a few times and couldn't remember all the steps. His name was George, and he said he was sixty-two years old and had just moved to town from the Detroit area. He had family in the South and a couple of kids and grandkids spread around the country. He told her he had been married once but that it had ended six years ago. George had been a salesman all his life and had done well for himself, or so he said. He had decided to retire early, so as to enjoy life, and had chosen Cincinnati because it was in between his northern and southern relatives. George exuded a warmth and sincerity that Esther found compelling. She could not remember the last time she had had so much fun talking with a man. Her ex-husband had always been so busy with work (and his affair) that he had rarely had time to talk to her. It was a nice change of pace to actually be able to relate to someone.

George continued to listen with empathy (or so it seemed) in the next few weeks as Esther poured out her heart about her divorce. He said all the right things and seemed genuinely concerned for her welfare. When the subject of Christ and a personal relationship with Him came up, George's eyes seemed to brighten. He said he had not been to church for years, but that after his move to town, he had wandered into a great little church and decided to give his life to Christ. Esther was thrilled; she loved the Lord with all her heart and wanted only to serve Him in any way she could. George began to attend a couples'

Bible study with Esther, which her pastor and his wife led. They, too, were impressed with George and the seeming genuineness of his faith experience.

Over the next six months, Esther and George continued to see each other. Their friends at church all were delighted at how well they seemed to get along. Some of her women friends were jealous, since George treated her better than their husbands treated them. In the spring, Esther and George decided to get some premarital counseling from their pastor. After eight sessions, they decided to become engaged and were married in the late summer. Everyone who knew them rejoiced. For some reason George's kids couldn't come. Esther's kids came in from out of town and added their approval to the happy day.

Finally, they were alone in their beautiful cabin nestled in the Michigan Lakes District. It was the perfect setting for a honeymoon. It was cool enough to be outdoors without getting heatstroke, and yet warm enough to go swimming. Their cabin opened up to the lakefront, and they could easily slip down for a morning or evening dip in perfect privacy. Esther, like any new bride, eagerly awaited consummating her relationship with George. She had picked out a special negligee and had brought some candles and music tapes from home. She slipped into the bathroom and changed clothes, expecting George to be doing the same thing. When she came out of the bathroom, she was surprised to see him still in his street clothes. He was looking through some papers and seemed totally preoccupied. Using her best feminine wiles, she tried to seduce him away from the papers in his briefcase. He remained unresponsive. Finally, in frustration, she said, "Honey, what is going on? We are on our *honeymoon*. I want to make love to you!" Infuriated, he erupted from his chair, grabbed her by the shoulders, and roughly flung her onto the couch. He shouted, "If you think that is why I married you, you need to think again! I wouldn't make love to you if you were the last woman on earth. I married you for your money and that's *all*. So get used to it!"

Esther thought she had lost her mind. She did not know this monster before her. Where was the kind, loving, attentive man she had married only eight hours before? She tried to protest, to talk to him, but he just slapped her in the face and told her to shut up. Finally, she went to the bedroom, shut the door, and cried herself to sleep. Early the next morning, she awoke with a start. Where was she? Where was George? Then it all came back to her. As she lay in bed, pieces of the puzzle began to fit into place. *So that is why he wanted me to put all my money in joint accounts,* she thought. Fear struck her. What if he had left her there and just went off with the money? Jumping out of bed, she raced to the living room, her heart in her throat. Esther could not believe her eyes. All her luggage was still there where she had left it after unpacking. George and his belongings were nowhere to be found. The rental car was gone. So was all the cash in her wallet. Hysterical, she called her son, who was staying in her condo with his family for a few days after the wedding. He and his wife drove up immediately and brought Esther home. Her family doctor gave her some medication to help her handle the shock. Her friends rotated around the clock keeping her company and never leaving her alone.

In the months that followed, Esther found out that George was really Roger somebody, and that he had not been married once before, but rather four times, and it was not clear if he was legally divorced from the wife before Esther. His kids were aware of his problems but had little contact with him other than some gifts he would send them when he fell into some money. Fortunately, Esther had only put part of her money in joint accounts before the wedding, and so not all of her nest egg was lost. The police have a warrant out for him, but give Esther little hope that the other money will ever be recovered. She has contacted three of his ex-wives, and each told a similar story.

As you can imagine, it has been a devastating experience for Esther, and not one from which she will recover easily. Her kids are supportive, as are her friends. Her pastor feels partly responsible, blaming himself for not being able to see through George/Roger. His guilt is probably irrational, in that George/Roger had conned many people before and probably is doing it again now. Everyone was fooled by this man. He is the consummate liar.

JUDY AND JOSH

Judy and Josh had been married for seventeen years when things really began to unravel. They had married young and had two girls, ages sixteen and twelve. They attended a prominent evangelical church in their area, the one in which Josh had grown up. Her parents were "pillars" of the church and the community. Her dad recently retired, but had been a successful businessman, and her mom still runs a small business of her own. Josh was the kind of man who could sell dog hair and persuade you it was mohair. Judy had dropped out of high school to marry him and always felt a bit intimidated by his intelligence, his gift of gab, and his suave manner. She worked outside the home before her first child was born, but had been a dedicated homemaker and mom since her birth. Josh was in sales—now this product, now that product. He did fairly well, and so Judy did not mind that he went from company to company. She figured that was what salesmen did. Sometimes money was in good supply, sometimes not. She worried at times, but he reassured her that it was just a "cash flow" problem and would be resolved quickly. It usually was.

Then one day, Josh came home especially irritable. When she asked what was wrong, he snapped, "You'll find out soon enough." Startled, she pressed him for an explanation. It all came tumbling out. Josh was about to be indicted for mail fraud. Judy knew that he had started to sell insurance for some company or other and thought things were going well. They had taken a nice vacation, and the money seemed to be consistent. She, of course, was shocked. "What do you mean 'mail fraud'?" she asked. Josh reluctantly explained. He had represented himself as an agent for XYZ Company and sold a large health insurance policy to a local business. He began collecting the $10,000 monthly premiums. The only problem was that he was not yet a representative for the company. So he held on to the money and worked to be appointed. When he was appointed in a short time, he thought his problems were solved. He gave the insurance company the application for the local business and went on to other projects. One day he got a phone call telling him that the local company was not accepted. By this time, three months had gone by and the employees were asking for their medical cards. So Josh went out and fraudulently had some printed up with his own toll-free phone number as the precertification number for the hospitals and doctors to use. He acted as the managed care official and "approved" any requests that were made. He even tried to pay out some of the hospital bills, which he had arranged to be sent to his address, out of the premium money he had collected but not turned in to the insurance company. Of course, he was unable to keep up, and the real XYZ Company began to get phone calls from the employees about their nonexistent policies. Now Josh was about to be indicted.

Judy, trying to be the good Christian wife, stood by her man. They decided to sell their home to pay the legal bills, and she arranged for them to move in with her parents. Josh had the appropriate crying jag in the pastor's office one Sunday morning, and everyone thought things could only get better. The case was settled with suspended jail time, since Josh was able to give the rest of the premium money back to the local business. The court put him on probation for five years.

Judy decided to go back to school to get her GED. They were still living with her folks, which was just as well, because her dad had become sick and needed extra nursing care. Her mom still worked full-time, so it was good that Judy could be there to help out. The girls loved living at Grandma and Grandpa's home because they had a swimming pool, a pool table, and unlimited refrigerator privileges. Remarkably, Josh was able to land a job selling swimming pools. He offered to help out with the in-laws' bookkeeping, since his father-in-law was so ill and Judy's mom had depended on her husband for bookkeeping help in her business. Josh took the bank deposits to the bank for her and investigated some ways that they might invest the lump-sum retirement payment they were about to receive. (Remember, deceivers like Josh are charming, persuasive, and adept at verbal maneuvering. Add to those factors the fact that he was playing the religious experience card like a pro, and we can see how even family were taken in.) He made up some fake investment-annuity forms and had the in-laws sign over the $25,000. To make them think that they were, indeed, receiving their monthly annuities, he would "rearrange" the bank deposits from his mother-in-law's business (she was very disorganized), robbing Peter to pay Paul, as it were. No one ever found out what happened to the $25,000.

During this time, he also helped out by sorting the mail, and whenever his in-laws received an offer for a new credit card with a good limit, he would forge their signatures, get the cards sent, and then forge the checks that were sent with the cards, maxing them out. No one has figured out what he did with that money either. All this time, Judy was nursing her sick dad, Grandma was working her tail off at her job, worried sick about her husband, and the two girls were running wild. The eldest began to get into trouble with drugs, and the youngest was getting into minor discipline problems at school. Neither child was making the grades of which she was capable.

Finally, the credit card companies began to send notices that they were not being paid, but Josh threw them out. So the companies began calling the house, and Judy took the calls. When confronted, Josh claimed to know nothing about it. When the card companies sent copies of the applications, the truth could no longer be denied. Judy's dad, sick as he was, looked into the investment-annuity plan that Josh had set up and found there was no such company. He and his wife filed charges, and Josh was convicted and went to jail for two and one-half years. All the while, he claimed, "It was not really my fault." Judy had *pressured* him to make money, and he was just trying to be a good provider. To top it all off, he professed a renewed faith in Jesus and was leading a Bible study in jail for the other miscreants. He felt *God* had put him there to bless them. He could not understand why Judy decided to divorce him in his hour of need, or why the kids were not crazy about driving up in the mountains to the prison (three hours away) every weekend. His parents, who had mortgaged their home to put up bail for him during the trial, did come to visit every week, but now that he is out of jail, he does not want anything to do with them. At last report, Josh still feels like a victim and tries to justify what he did with comments such as "Well, all those other people scam the system, why should I get punished when they don't?"

While these examples are extreme, there are a lot of women who can relate to these stories. They thought they married one thing but they actually married another. They spent months or years giving the deceiver the benefit of the doubt, but, finally, they had to admit that the whole relationship was built on deceit. Breaking through the denial is not easy. It makes you look foolish. The depression over the reality of who he is can be severe. If you are at that point, do not give up. There are plenty of opportunities for life for you and your children. It just may take a little time and effort to untangle the web the deceiver has woven around you.

CHARACTERISTICS OF THE DECEIVER

1. *Is not able to identify with others as human beings.* He sees himself as superior—more intelligent, more creative, more insightful, more clever than other people. Weakness is the thing he despises most in others and, in reality, in himself. Often any sign of weakness (tears, sighs, illness, pain, sadness) triggers his rage. While he may come on with charm and warmth, beware. It is a false front. The disdain with which he views the rest of the human race is not far beneath the surface.

2. *Is incredibly narcissistic, selfish, and self-oriented.* While, especially in the beginning of a relationship, this type of man comes across as generous, giving, and gracious, in truth his "gifts" all have a purpose. Whether it is to get the woman in bed or to the altar, there is only one purpose: to con her *now* so he can control her later. His motives are always selfish, no matter how much he protests to the contrary. He does not care one whit for others and, indeed, sees them as mere pawns in his grand scheme. When he is done with them, they are tossed aside as if they had no meaning at all (which, of course, to him they did not). He sees himself as the real victim, in that he has to put up with persecution by people who "just don't get it" or who are "too sensitive, too emotional, or too stupid."

3. *Has no shame.* When confronted about some of his cruel or hurtful behavior, he'll most likely respond with a shrug, as if to say, "So what?" Violations of boundaries, broken promises, lies, deception

are all justified or blamed on the victim. He is never wrong (in his view) and so is above shame. There is *always a reason* he did what he did, so that makes it okay. He is above the law and above shame.

4. *Comes across as the consummate leader.* He appears to be able to solve any problem. His affable manner disarms any suspicion of his real motives. He has a boldness and confidence that put others off guard. He seems to know what he is doing, so others abdicate their responsibility to use their brains and get conned. (For example: Two of the victims of Philip Harmon's pyramid scheme mentioned earlier, said the following: "He was a pillar in the church and the community," declared Joy Getty. "He was a success." "I knew him through the church," said Tex Kazda. "He seemed honest and smart and had lots of assets and a happy family." *Christianity Today* reported that Getty and her husband lost $133,000 and that Kazda lost $119,000.[7]

5. *Is cold and emotionless, capable of a heartless hatred of righteousness.* From a biblical perspective, he has a seared conscience. He walks in darkness and does not know it. He is wise in his own eyes and delights to do evil. He takes great pleasure in the cleverness of his schemes. His disconnection from human feeling enables him to do what he does without compunction. He is the kind of man Chuck Colson says he was before his conversion. He'd run over his grandmother if it meant fulfilling his goals.

6. *Is often capable of violence—both physical and psychological.* The Scripture makes it clear that this type of individual *desires* violence. It is like food to him (Prov. 13:2). He uses sarcasm, mockery, shame, and humiliation to control others. He has no problem with tearing someone down in public. He has nothing but contempt for those who oppose him, and he has no qualms about destroying anyone who gets in his way. He systematically destroys joy, hope, and serenity in those around him. This meanness often comes as a surprise to the victim because in the beginning of the relationship, he was as charming as a prince and twice as kind.

What do you look for if you are wondering if your honey is a deceiver? Here are some clues:

1. You suspect that many of the things he says are untrue, at least

partially. Every now and then you find him exaggerating beyond belief. Or he makes a statement that you know is not true. You come to realize that you cannot trust him because his versions, his excuses, do not match with reality.

2. When caught, he is without shame, remorse, or genuine repentance. When something happens that cannot be hidden, he fakes feeling sorry. You have seen him shed tears many times. He is the best at producing tears. But you see no change in him. In fact, the tears are often followed by irritability and then anger. His self-justification sets in, and he is back on his feet and back to his old ways.

3. He has little or no ability to empathize with others. He can actually be cold and heartless. You are often embarrassed by him when with friends; he says things that hurt their feelings. He often uses inappropriate humor. He cannot focus on another person's needs. He wants to be the main attraction, and he will put anyone down who tries to rule in his territory.

4. He is affable, charming, and takes charge easily. Others follow him without a lot of introspection. One of the reasons that you were attracted to him was because he has a way with words and a way with women. He is fun, and he makes you feel good. He seems to have that sixth sense that knows what you like to hear, and he says it, with no regard to whether it is true or not.

5. He has no problem putting you down, even in public, especially if you are questioning the veracity of what he has said. If you question what he says, he feels justified in putting you in your place rather than letting himself look the fool. He will try to make it up to you later, and he will expect you to respond to his apology. He has no connection to how you might have felt when he humiliated you and no understanding of how you could still feel that way after he has apologized.

WHAT KIND OF WOMAN DOES THE DECEIVER WANT?

The deceiver looks for women who are vulnerable. He looks for someone who is naive. Obviously, if his goal is to abscond with her money, he looks for someone well off financially. Usually, these women trust men more than they trust themselves. In their minds, men are smarter, wiser, more savvy than women are. Men just know more. Liars look for women who will accept what they are told with little questioning; women who are overly submissive and subservient. These types of women are good caretakers and nurturers; they get most of their identity from being nice and kind to others. They are usually lonely, widowed, or divorced and have grown kids, who are conveniently out of town or too busy to pay much attention to Mom. If they are religious, all the better. The deceiver knows how to use that to his advantage as well. Robert Duvall's preacher character in the movie *The Apostle* would certainly be an example of how that aspect of the con works.

RELATING TO THE DECEIVER

If you think you are vulnerable, or that you are already hooked up with such a man, GO SLOW. Keep records of discrepancies he cannot explain. Hire a detective to see if he is on the level. Do not give him access to your money. Tell your counselor and your friend that before you can commit to him, both of you have to take a full battery of psychological tests, give a verified, full disclosure of finances, and undergo premarital counseling for as long as it is needed. Talk to his family when he is not around. Press them to be truthful with you. Ask about possible mental illness in the family. Ask him if you can talk to any former wives. If he says no, maybe things are not on the up-and-up.

The deceiver is lacking the basic character traits necessary to build a solid, healthy relationship. He does not have the character to embrace the truth and its consequences. Character can be developed in counseling and through immersing himself in the love of God. Outside help (counseling and God) is his only hope. Get counseling for yourself even if he refuses to go with you. Let him know you are a safe person with whom to share his struggles with the truth. Invite him to be brutally honest with you, and then be prepared to hear it.

One final note: Never believe what a liar says when he is confessing or apologizing. Watch the actions and the behaviors. What he does will tell you whether or not you can trust him, not his words.

WHAT COULD THE DECEIVER DO TO CHANGE?

1. *Turn away from his old ways of doing things and submit to some serious reparenting.* This is best done by a same-sex counselor over an extended period of time. He is a sociopath. The goal is to develop character where none exists. Deceivers are willing to commit to spending the time required to accomplish this difficult work. If he hangs in for the long haul, he will begin to be able to put himself in the place of those he has victimized.

2. *Discover the lies within his own heart that enable and equip him to lie to others.* He has some internal problems and conflicts that he has not resolved. Rather than heal them, he has constructed a web of lies around those painful matters of his heart. A good counselor will help him find these areas and carefully ease the deceiver into exploring them.

3. *Become accountable to someone other than family.* His wife does not need to police him, and he needs other relationships in which he can grow and be honest. He needs a person of integrity who is not afraid to tell him the truth. He also needs someone to pray with him and for him, to help him focus on what God wants rather than what he wants at the moment. This accountability, along with the help of a counselor, can accomplish what seems impossible: the development of an authentic man with character.

4. *Humble himself and ask for the forgiveness of those he has hurt.* If he is sincere he will clear things up with those he has victimized. He will offer to make restitution if he has taken anything from anyone.

5. *Make some new commitments and keep them.* He must commit to a relationship based on truth with his wife. He must commit to God to live in His truth. He must study God's truth in the Bible and saturate

his mind with it through meditation and memorization. He must be accountable to others.

SNAPSHOT SUMMARY OF THE DECEIVER

CLUES TO HELP YOU SPOT HIM

1. You begin to doubt what he says and suspect he lies about most things.

2. He shows no remorse or genuine shame when you catch him in a lie.

3. He is unable to empathize with others and offends often.

4. He can be charming and easy to follow.

5. He often puts you down in public to protect his lie.

THE WOMAN TO WHOM HE IS ATTRACTED

1. Is vulnerable, naive, and very trusting.

2. Appears wealthy or from a family that appears to have wealth.

3. May be someone recovering from the loss of a husband through death or divorce, a child, a parent, or anything that puts her in a desperate situation.

4. Is subservient and comfortable being a caretaker.

5. Has a history of commitment and long-term relationship.

THE WOMAN WHO FALLS FOR HIM

1. Believes his stories and believes life would be very interesting with him.

2. He treats her well, and she responds to his charm when she has doubts about the relationship.

3. Is ruled by her emotions and refuses to think rationally when she feels someone is in love with her.

4. Is drawn to his self-confidence and his smooth way of handling situations that would rattle her.

5. Is comfortable with his style, probably because he is much like her father.

WHAT YOU CAN DO

1. Go slow and do not rush into a relationship with him.

2. Do not let him know about your finances or give him access to any of your accounts.

3. Keep a diary of your relationship, and be sure to document each time a situation comes up where there are discrepancies in his stories.

4. Demand that he get counseling and that you participate in some of the sessions.

5. Do not believe him when he tells you he is going to be different. Watch what he does and not what he says. Do not trust him until he has proved himself over an extended period of time.

WHAT HE COULD DO TO CHANGE

1. Commit to long-term counseling.

2. Resolve the painful conflicts within that have led to the lies.

3. Become accountable to someone who will tell him the truth.

4. Ask for forgiveness and make restitution.

5. Make new commitments to God, spouse, and the truth.

CHAPTER 8

THE ADDICT

Sandy and I (Steve) have a female friend who married the life of the party. As an exciting date, her new love was always looking for a good time. He drank a lot but rarely got drunk. He was in control, and that was all she cared about. If he had stayed in control, life would have just been one party after another. However, with alcoholics and other types of addicts, the party life gives way to hell on earth. When our friend discerned that she had married such a sick person, she tried to please him—she tried hard. She tried everything to get him sober, but her ten-year adventure with him ended with no home, no money, and no marriage. At thirty-four she and her daughters were back home living with her parents. She was so devastated we doubt she will ever marry again. That is what addiction does when it is not treated. It devastates lives and destroys everything around it: homes, jobs, marriages, children, dreams, hopes, aspirations. All are gone when addiction enters the picture. Often the spouse of an addict never quite understands what happened and who this chameleon of a man is that she married.

There is no germ that spreads addiction from one person to another. Yet it is highly infectious, not just to the spouse, but also to the children. Sexually addicted fathers will infect their sons by allowing or even encouraging their involvement with pornography. Their daughters may be infected in numerous ways, including being encouraged to dress seductively and act promiscuously. A man who is hooked on perfectionism, order, and control may drive a daughter to exert control over the one thing she feels she possesses, her body. Her anorexia may flourish in his atmosphere of oppressive demands that can never be met. Nothing destroys a home so completely and thoroughly as addiction, so if you are dating Mr. Addiction he is to be abandoned in the earliest stages of a relationship. You will not fix him, just as you did not fix your dad or brother or whoever led you to be attracted to a man out of control. He may recover, but it will be after he has dragged you through a flesh-ripping thorn patch of torture that you may not be able to endure. Life is too short, too valuable to live in addiction hell.

If you are already married to an addict, I have some good news for you. Of all the men you could have picked, this one has the highest potential for change. This one becomes the most destructive, goes the farthest into despair, drags the most people down with him, and loses more valuable things like jobs, friends, and families. But even with all of that, this man, more often than the others, finds his way back with the help of God and the strength of a spouse who is unwilling to aid and abet his crime of depending on anything other than God and the people who want desperately to have a relationship with him and love him.

UNDERSTANDING ADDICTION

In order to understand the addict, we must know something about addiction in general. When we begin to talk about *addiction*, many Christians voice the concern that we are "letting people off the hook." They are afraid that if we recognize the addictive nature of certain behavior patterns, we are excusing them. While some people may try to use "addiction" as an excuse for their behavior, no one who truly understands addiction of any sort would ever say a person is not responsible for his behavior. Some addictive behavior is thrust upon a person so early in life that they cannot remember a time when it was not a part of their existence. Others chose their addictive behavior out of rebellion or arrogance, thinking they could control it. Once into the vortex, however, they are caught, unable to extricate themselves without God's help. The addiction is a powerful trap that will not let go with sheer force of willpower.

However the addiction develops, whether self-inflicted or induced by an adult, taking responsibility for it is always a part of recovering from it. What is done to us is the fault of others, but what we do with what is done to us becomes our responsibility. Both of us have worked with addicts over the past twenty plus years. We are much less interested in why they started the behavior than why they have chosen to keep it and what they plan to do about it. Responsibility is not admitting "I should have never rolled that first die, or looked at that first pornographic picture, or taken that first drink." Taking responsibility is looking at why I continued to do something that only brought growing levels of pain and destruction to my life and the lives of others. Then, taking responsibility is getting the help that is needed and accepting the direction of others.

Does addiction eliminate the sin factor? Of course not. No addiction can grow out of control without the involvement of many sins. Lying, betrayal, irresponsibility, lust, greed, and idolatry are just a few of the sins that leech off addiction. I have never known anyone who was an addict who was not deeply involved in many sins. By the same token I have never known a sinner who was not addicted to his or her favorite sin. In fact, their identity may center on that addictive sin creating labels for them such as, "gossip, greedy, hypocrite, miser, or cheap." Addiction does not remove the sin factor, and sin produces an addictive process. They are brothers and sisters who grow up in the same family of shameful acts that need to be changed.

COMPONENTS OF ADDICTION

Spiritually, addiction can be seen as a form of idol worship. Whenever someone places a substance, an experience, another person, or a thing first in his life and makes it central to his life, he has turned his substance or behavior of choice into his god. It is his god because it controls him, and he sacrifices his whole life for it. Certainly this is what addicts do. They run their lives not based on God's grace and plan for them, but based on their relationship to a substance, person, experience, or thing. We have all at some time been guilty of placing something or someone ahead of God. As humans we are by nature idolatrous beings. We are all apt to believe the lie that this experience, this possession, this job, this relationship will finally make us happy. It will not. In fact, the more we expect to get from it, over time, the greater our disappointment will be.

Addiction and shame are also linked spiritually. Shame is that sense of lowered self-esteem that I am not all that I could, should, or would like to be. Before the little eating problem of Adam and Eve that got us all into this mess, human pride and glory were totally in God Himself. They had a sense of identity: They were His creatures. Genesis 2 tells the sad story of Satan's deception and their exposure before God, naked and vulnerable. Shame became a universal experience the moment they sinned. They tried to hide behind fig leaves and plants, and we have continued building defense mechanisms ever since. The only solace for Adam and Eve is that if you or I had been in their sandals, we would have done exactly the same thing they did.

Addictive behavior is like Adam's and Eve's fig leaves. It is a defense against the shame we all experience. The addict distracts himself, however temporarily, from feeling the shame by engaging in the addictive behavior. Then the behavior that provided relief ends up causing even more shame than the original feelings that led to it. The strong need to hide the addiction and the shameful acts that grow out of it are stark indications of the strong bond between addiction and shame.

Rebellion is another aspect of the spiritual nature of addiction. Anytime we devote our lives to a substance or a behavior, it is by its very nature rebellion against God. Rebellious individuals want to be in charge, to manage their lives themselves, to be in control. Addicts express their rebellion by putting someone, something, or some experience in the place of God. They contend that they know best and that God doesn't. Just like Cain of old, they think their way is the best way, and they are determined to carry it out.

Psychologically, addiction is multidimensional. Emotional pain and shame seem to be at the root psychologically. Whenever the addict acts out, or even when he acts *in* (i.e., tries to control and limit his behavior), shame and fear of abandonment are at the core of his reality. He is trying with all his might to escape the pain. He is also seeking an identity. Alienated from God, humans no longer experience themselves as created in the image of God. They see themselves as blips in the universe; an accident that just happened. This is further compounded because many do not hold to the traditional Western worldview, which was based on a Judeo-Christian conception of God at the center of the universe. Many do not even see human beings at the center, but rather see humans as an evolutionary mistake, which the planet would be much better off without! Human life in this view is of no more importance than the life of a cricket or a cactus plant. Each has equal value and right to exist, with the earlier species perhaps even having precedence since they were here first. Thus, many young addicts see drugs and alcohol as perfectly reasonable solutions to the meaninglessness of their experience. If we are all protoplasm anyway, what does it matter?

The link between addiction and physiology is becoming stronger every year. New technology is helping us literally see inside the brain, and we are understanding its intricacies more and more. Clearly, while more research needs to be done, certain addictions do have a true physical component.[1]

In their interesting book *Craving for Ecstasy: The Consciousness and Chemistry of Escape,*[2] Milkman and Sunderwirth outline three types of behaviors that human beings use to cope with mental or emotional pain. They are: satiation, arousal, and fantasy. When people feel stress or a sense of shame, they will choose one of these types of experiences as their characteristic way of coping.

Folks whose preferred mode of coping is satiation (relaxation) choose food, depressants such as alcohol or heroin, and television. On a chemical level, the effect of these satiation activities is similar to that of opiates. Other people seek to avoid satiation by seeking arousal. Drugs like cocaine or speed, experiences such as gambling, sexual addiction, or other risk-taking activities are examples of arousal coping strategies. Still others seek to literally escape into a fantasy world. Hence romance novels, video games, soap operas, virtual reality games, preoccupation with daydreaming, mystical experiences, compulsive artistic expression, or drugs like LSD or peyote become attractive.

We would never want to negate the spiritual and emotional components of addiction, but recent research points toward a stronger physical aspect than was once believed. Once addiction sets in, choices become more and more limited, and the outcome often depends more on the family's intervention than on the addict's instant insight into the progression of the condition.

HOW DO YOU KNOW WHEN SOMEONE IS ADDICTED?

Generally, we say a person is addicted when his behavior is out of control and adversely affecting one or more of the following areas of his life: physical, mental, social, emotional, or spiritual. There is a need to escape pain, and the behavior also produces pleasure. Everything else in life becomes subordinate to the behavior in question. The addict refuses to stop the chosen behavior despite many adverse consequences.

An addicted person begins to use denial, manipulation, deceit, and lying to maintain his behavior. He loses touch with God and often is in direct rebellion against Him. He becomes alienated from his support systems, perhaps even losing his job or dropping out of school. Depression, anxiety, panic attacks, paranoia, and psychosis, along with violent outbursts, begin to appear.

TYPES OF ADDICTION

People can be addicted to any number of behaviors and substances, just like the secular world. We have chosen three common examples.

SEXUAL ADDICTION

There are many women, especially those who grew up in church, who have no idea what "sexual addiction" means. Even some clergy, despite their training, have no concept or understanding about sexual addiction. You may think that you will never meet a sex addict because you don't hang around in bars, or frequent dance clubs or other late-night party scenes. You are a *nice* person: someone who goes to church, volunteers for United Way, coaches volleyball at the high school. You look for men at large church social gatherings or at popular singles ministry activities. You ask friends to fix you up with someone. None of *your* friends know any sex addicts. So you are safe.

The problem is that most sex addicts do not fit the stereotype of the guy in a trench coat hanging out at the playground, or of the weird guy who hits on every woman at the office. Yes, there are sex addicts who do those things, but most sex addicts seem like perfectly normal people. Some even seem like ideal Christians. Some are even pastors or elders. They are often gifted, educated, well-liked individuals. Yet they have a secret side; a secret side that causes them to act in seriously hurtful, evil, sinful ways. They are desperate, lonely, and afraid. They try to stop doing these things, but they cannot stop. They are addicts. And there are lots of them out there. Not just in the bars, but in our churches.

We should not be surprised that as people are saved and come into the church, they bring with them the baggage they accumulated along the way. Salvation does not instantly cure a person of all his problems. It is only the beginning. Christians are still vulnerable to sin and temptation. Romans 7, describing Paul's struggle with unwanted behaviors (sin), is certainly illustrative.

I (Steve) was preaching one Sunday at a church in southern California. It was a small Episcopal church. I had never spoken there before and have not spoken there since. While I was preparing before the service, I observed the pastor hugging a woman that I presumed was has wife. When his wife walked in and kissed him on the cheek, I knew something was all wrong. I am not against hugging, but this was not just a friendly hug. Looking at the eyes of this overweight man in a robe, I could see that there were both pain and deception there. When the service started I was on the platform but not seated next to the pastor. As in many old churches, the choir was in the front, but half sat on one side and half on the other side. The ministers and others involved in the service sat on one side or the other. To my amazement I watched this guy mouth the words "I love you" to the woman he had hugged earlier. He did not just do it one time, he did it over and over again. Only a sex addict could be that bold and do something that risky.

On Monday morning I called him and told him I thought there was a problem. He told me he did not think there was. This lady was just someone who had lost her husband and needed someone to help her and encourage her. Well, there must have been a lot of needy women in that church because within a year, due to multiple complaints from multiple victims, Mr. Addict Pastor was removed from the church. I still wonder if he ever got help after losing all for which he had worked and studied so hard. Addiction is alive and well in churches and on church staffs.

This man was like most people in the church when confronted with addictive behaviors; denial is the response of choice. Another example of this was found in the July 13, 1998, issue of *Christianity Today*.[3] The pastor of a large Seattle church resigned amid allegations by at least seventeen men that he had sexually molested them, some as far back as the 1970s. The elders of the church investigated the matter and conceded, according to the article, that the pastor was not "above reproach" and thus needed to resign; but they also found no basis for church discipline against him! *Christianity Today* quoted the response of an area pastor, Jerry Mitchell:

> If the man is not innocent, which they have said, then in my estimation he is guilty. They say, "No, he is not guilty"; therefore, in my estimation he's innocent. Where in the English language and where in the Bible is the in-between stage?[4]

Not only were church leaders responsible to remove this man, they were responsible to help him find his way back through restoration.

Rick Joyner, in his book *The Surpassing Greatness of His Power*,[5] referred to our responsibility to learn where the "gates of hell" are and how to shut them. He defined the "gates of hell" as those places the enemy (Satan) uses to gain access into the world, the church, and our lives. Galatians 6:1 requires us to restore *anyone* caught in *any* trespass (sin), looking to ourselves, lest we, too, fall in the same way. Joyner exhorts us to examine how and why our brothers and sisters have fallen, or we will fall into the same traps. Restoration is the only way to fully understand what has happened to them. This is the area where we have failed as a larger Christian community. Joyner commented:

> Restoring is more than just forgiving. We can apologize to these fallen brothers or sisters to appease our consciences, but this is not enough to pass the test. *They must be restored.* This does not imply in any way that the biblical standards of integrity should be compromised, or that restoration does not involve a process implemented over time. Even so, we must do whatever it takes for the fallen to be restored . . . Until we learn to restore our fallen brethren, even those caught in "any trespass," the gates of hell will remain open against the church in the same areas where the enemy was able to cause these brethren to fall.[6]

One church that has taken the lead in this area of restoring fallen brothers and sisters is the Los Angeles International Church (also known as the Dream Center), founded by Tommy Barnett. They have taken pastors, evangelists, missionaries, and other leaders who have fallen into sin and restored them into ministry in the inner city.

Signs and symptoms of sexual addiction. The signs and symptoms of sexual addiction usually start with the spouse being uncomfortable or uneasy about a secretiveness or distance in the relationship. You want to connect more deeply, but the man who was once so romantic will not allow you to get too close. He says he loves you, and he is often a hard worker, but something about the relationship does not make sense. If sexual addiction is the problem in your relationship it will eventually surface. You will know it when he requests an unusual sexual act that repulses you. Or you will find a video, a magazine, or a receipt he cannot explain. Today, it is common to discover Internet visits to Web sites that are nothing but hard-core pornography. Eventually, behavior will emerge, and you will know that it is not you who has the problem, it is him.

To ensure that you know the difference between sex and sexual addiction I have provided you with some indicators that separate the normal from the abnormal. These come from Steve's book *Addicted to "Love,"* published by Servant Publications.

1. *Addictive sex is done in isolation.* This does not mean that it is always done while physically alone. Rather it means that mentally and emotionally the addict is detached or isolated from human relationship and contact. The most intimately personal behavior becomes utterly impersonal.

2. *Addictive sex is secretive.* In effect, sex addicts develop a double life, practicing masturbation, going to porn shops and massage parlors, all the while hiding what they are doing from others, and, in a sense, even from themselves.

3. *Addictive sex is devoid of intimacy.* Sex addicts are utterly self-focused. They cannot achieve genuine intimacy because their self-obsession leaves no room for giving to others.

4. *Addictive sex is devoid of relationship.* Addictive sex is "mere sex," sex for its own sake, sex divorced from authentic interaction of persons. This is most clear with regard to fantasy, pornography, and masturbation. But even with regard to sex involving a partner, the partner is not really a "person" but a cipher, an interchangeable part in an impersonal—almost mechanical—process.

5. *Addictive sex is victimizing.* The overwhelming obsession with self-gratification blinds sex addicts to the harmful effects their behavior is having on others and even on themselves.

6. *Addictive sex ends in despair.* When married couples make love, they are more fulfilled for having had the experience. Addictive sex leaves the participants feeling guilty, regretting the experience. Rather than fulfilling them, it leaves them more empty.

7. *Addictive sex is used to escape pain and problems.* The escapist nature of addictive sex is often one of the clearest indicators that it is present.

That is what addictive sex is like. Below is a list of observable characteristics of a sex addict:

1. There is a preoccupation with all things sexual. Clues include pornography, incessant desire, constant sexual innuendo, and double entendres and sexual humor.

2. A cycle of withdrawn preoccupation, followed by excitement, acting out, and then despair and shame with the fear of getting caught.

3. Irritable and angry with more frequent episodes of rage.

4. Many acquaintances but no real friends.

5. Inappropriate sexual behaviors in the way they touch others through hugs and greetings.

6. Their eyes will wander and stare at each attractive woman they see.

Of course, I like *Addicted to "Love"* best because it covers sex, romance, and relationship addiction, but there are others who have produced some very keen insights into sex addicts, including Frank Pittman, who has done some interesting work characterizing one type of sexual addict: the philanderer.[7] While other types (the voyeur, the exhibitionist, the rapist, the sadomasochist, etc.) are out there, the philanderer is probably the one most people would recognize as having a problem. Philanderers are noted for their broad sexual range; that is, they need a lot of sexual partners so they can experience *woman* in all her forms (thus validating that they are indeed *men*). They do not believe in monogamy, though they are often married. They just do not expect to be faithful. They could not imagine giving one woman the right to tell them when and with whom they could have sex. Others misuse their religious heritage and believe that since God created *men* in His image, women and their sexuality should be under male control. So they are entitled to have sex with any woman they choose.

Philanderers are also obsessed with their gender. Masculinity is the primary value. They take stereotypes of masculine behavior quite literally and are uncomfortable if not able to prominently display their own (not unlike the male peacock). They believe women have the power to define their masculinity, so they are afraid of women. A woman's response to him is the philanderer's barometer of how masculine he is today. Status and competition with other men (especially over women) are all-important to a philanderer. The greatest loss of status would be to fall under the control of a particular woman. While no one wants to be controlled by someone else, it is the philanderer's perception of what constitutes control that makes him so unusual. A philanderer would be devastated if he "gave" a woman control over who his sexual partners are (e.g., make a commitment to be monogamous). They see their views as natural and normal, and while they may, indeed, marry, they never intend to be faithful.

Pittman makes an interesting observation:

> Men who seek to find themselves as men through chasing women just lose more and more of the masculinity they are seeking. They sacrifice the wife who could know them and love them, and the children through whom they could know themselves . . . But when each woman fails to bestow masculinity, the man feels betrayed and may despair over his failure or lash out in anger. He knows he doesn't have the power to turn himself into a man, and he can't believe women don't have that power either. The man going around in these desperate sexual circles is just chasing his tail.[8]

What kind of women do philanderers go for? They are looking for women who will remain attractive and be "feminine." They want her femininity to contrast with their masculinity, so the more extreme her femininity is the better. They want other men to hit on their wives, but, of course, they do not want her to respond positively. While one would think they would want her to be sexual all the time with them, philanderers do not always want sex with their spouse. They often are asexual with the spouse, acting out with their mistresses or one-night stands. Many times women who are attracted to philanderers are as preoccupied with their femininity as their husbands are. This woman may go to extraordinary lengths not to notice his infidelities and may even defend him if accusations occur. If he is a powerful, wealthy, or influential man, she may be willing to trade his philandering for the perks of being attached to him.

Philandering is an addictive behavior and, like other sex addicts, the philanderer does not like to be confronted. He sees his behavior as normal for him and therefore justified. He resents anything that would imply anything differently. They may stop their activities to get the wife off their back for a while, but they will inevitably pick it up again, unless they receive treatment.

To survive life with a sex addict, you must have your own life. You must not feel responsible for him, but instead take responsibility to create a life that is fulfilling, interesting, and full of people. You must set some firm boundaries for your relationship and not compromise those boundaries. You cannot change him, but you must make some demands on the relationship for your own sanity and safety. These boundaries are things like being accountable to each other with time. Each of you has a right to know where the other is at all times. Each of you has a right to explanations about time and money spent away from each other. Each of you has a responsibility to tell the other if you have been alone with someone of the opposite sex. Each of you has the right to ask the other to leave the home if these expectations cannot be met.

Usually it takes a severe crisis and the potential loss of status for the addict to come to his senses and get help. Trying to change or control him is futile and only brings out the worst in both partners. But agreeing to inform each other is not the same as trying to control him. You have a right to know, otherwise he is unfairly in control of the relationship. If he will not agree that marriage means mutual accountability, then you will be keenly aware of the superficiality of his commitment to you.

While you must not try to control him, you must also refuse to cover up for him. Covering up for him, making excuses for him, bailing him out of jail, or moving with him to another location to escape the shame only enables his addiction. If you are in this position you must be aware that you are at serious risk of exposure to STDs (sexually transmitted diseases) and AIDS. In this day and age, continued sexual contact with an active sex addict can be a death sentence. If you decide to continue to enable his addiction, you must make some serious decisions about your sex life.

CHEMICAL ADDICTION

This addict can be clearly defined if you have all the facts. Many times you have the facts; you just don't know that you do. There is one thing that all addicts have in common. Whether wealthy or poor, heavy or thin, smart or stupid, married or single, Christian or not, they all have one characteristic. They have a high tolerance for the chemical of choice. This is fairly common knowledge when it comes to hard drugs such as heroin. Most people have heard the stories of junkies who could shoot enough heroin into their veins in a day that an elephant given the same dose would surely fly through the air. Crackheads cannot get enough, and they often get so much that the neuroreceptors in the brain begin to function as if cocaine is as vital to their existence as food and water.

With alcoholics we do not often associate tolerance with addiction, but it is always there. Most people get too drunk or too sick to drink at addictive levels. The alcoholic goes beyond normal limits, and that is why he becomes addicted. When I (Steve) meet with a potential alcoholic, I do not want to know why he started drinking or why he drinks now. What I want to know is: How much did he drink when he started drinking? and how much does he drink now? If I am talking to an alcoholic who is telling me the truth, I will hear answers like "a case or more of beer on a Saturday." I will hear about bottles of wine and liquor rather than numbers of drinks. I will hear of consumption levels that are either going up or are already at a level that could not be tolerated by most people.

There are other signs or clues you might look for in someone who may be chemically addicted:

1. *Family history.* It is clear that the use of chemicals, particularly alcohol, runs in families. If you know someone is an adult child of an alcoholic or a grandchild of an alcoholic, you actually have learned a lot about their family without even meeting them. There are many fine books available on alcoholism and its family connection, as well as other chemical addictions. In this day, it is rare to find someone who abuses alcohol who is not also using chemicals of some sort. If Mom was addicted to prescription medications, there is a good chance someone else in the family is an alcoholic. Where there is smoke, there is fire.

2. *Excuses.* The addict uses the excuse that he needs the drug or drink to "chill out" or "relax" or "sleep" or as a "social lubricant." He uses the drug of choice to alleviate emotional pain or fear of abandonment.

3. *Defensiveness.* The addict will defend his usage, and deny it is a problem, even when confronted with evidence to the contrary. Denial is a hallmark of any addiction. He becomes outraged when someone questions him.

4. *Secrecy.* The person hides bottles, prescriptions, paraphernalia, fake ID cards; he starts lying to cover up his behavior.

5. *Escalation.* The person begins not only to increase the amount of chemical taken, he also begins to switch to new and more potent forms of the chemical. For example, first it was wine coolers, then beer, then mixed drinks, then hard liquor, then marijuana, and on and on.

6. *An unexplained lack of funds.* Despite having a good job or a steady income or allowance, the person is always bumming money off friends or even begins stealing. Mom and Dad find money mysteriously gone from their wallets; grandparents find their jar of pennies missing; the secretary cannot find the petty cash box; a friend at the gym cannot find his wallet after coming back from the shower.

7. *Irritability if the supply is interrupted.* When cut off from the source of their supply, addicts get grouchy—real grouchy. Ever see a smoker who is in a smoke-free hospital for a while? Alcoholics and

drug addicts are no different. They do not like it when they are cut off from their source.

8. *Secret or outward resentment if others do not use along with them or stop after one or two drinks or hits.*

9. *Changes in personality.* If someone who was grouchy when they went into the rest room comes out smiling and real mellow, you have to wonder what else they did while in there! Someone who is usually shy and reticent to speak but always becomes the life of the party when they are drinking may have a problem. The nice, quiet gentleman who never has a cross word to say may turn into a monster when he has had a few drinks.

10. *Problems at work, home, or school.* The person begins to have difficulty with finances, physical health, the law. DUI convictions; reprimands at work; failing school; expulsions, suspensions; and relationship troubles all start piling up.

11. *Decreased or increased interest in sex.* Depending on what chemical the person is using, his sexual interest, libido, and performance will be affected.

These are not all the signs of chemical addiction, but are certainly enough to give a person pause. If you notice any of these symptoms in the man you are dating, it would be best that you let him know you won't be dating him anymore. If that causes him to stop drinking and get help, then you might want to patiently wait to see how sincere he is. After a year, if he has stayed sober, been consistent in his recovery, and you have watched his character grow, then you might have a great man with a lot of potential who never had the motivation to step out of the addiction.

If you are engaged to a man with these symptoms, do yourself a favor and break the engagement and request that he get help. If he stops drinking and is consistent in his recovery, and you experience a growth in his character, then you might date again in a year and then get engaged. We realize how few will take this advice because they are so enmeshed and drowning in hopes of changing him. Even so, please call off the engagement and go to work on why you were attracted to a man whose first love is alcohol or a drug.

If you are married to a man with many of the above symptoms, you may feel as if there is no hope. You have threatened and pleaded or tried to be the perfect loving wife and nothing has made a difference. You may be at that point where you have decided that home remedies do not work for something as powerful and deadly as an addiction. There are other options for you. Often an intervention can be done with the help of a trained professional, and your loved one can get help. Rarely do interventions fail when conducted by a trained professional. You can find out about the best ones at 1-800-NEW LIFE.

Your focus though, must be on your survival first of all. You cannot live your life waiting for him to stop drinking and start recovery. You must create a life for yourself, and you cannot do that alone. There are support groups such as Alanon and others like it in churches all over. You must decide that living in secrecy is worse than others knowing you have a problem. Secrecy leads to ongoing sickness; sharing with others and allowing them to help you will lead to healing.

Living with the addict is difficult at best and impossible at worst. No one can go it alone. Interacting with him can be very "crazy-making" as some people call it. The addict will try to convince you that his addiction is your fault; that you made him do it; that his boss or his mother or the dog made him do it. Manipulation is the hallmark of his game. No one can spot all the games without help from someone who has gone through it before. You are not alone, and you need help from those who have been where you are.

It is difficult for many Christians to identify with the possibility that drugs or alcohol could be a problem in their lives. Raised in the church, they may never have had a drink and may be very naive about what is available today. They may think that only uneducated people get addicted to chemicals, or that none of their friends at church drink too much. Their spouse, their child is a good person. He would not use drugs. Or if they are aware of a past history of chemical use, they may believe it has all been taken care of by a religious conversion or the baptism of the Holy Spirit. Or the girlfriend may say, "He only drank because his ex-wife was a witch, and he was under so much pressure living with her. This time, with me, it will be different."

Shame and embarrassment also keep many Christians in denial about the seriousness of their loved one's addiction. You are a good Christian. You teach Sunday school. Your thoughts may go like this: *What would people think if they knew? Surely, no one else in our church has ever been addicted to cocaine! No one will believe me. They will think I am crazy. He's an elder, for heaven's sake.*

Coming out of denial and facing the facts may take time. It is a very painful process. No one who knows the power of God available to us wants to give up hope for the healing and deliverance of someone they love. We want to have tried everything we can think of to offer help and healing. We want to believe his promises. We don't want to find out he is lying again. Yet one day the light dawns. We finally realize we have had enough. One woman reported that the day her crack-addicted husband took the frozen food back to the store to get more money for drugs was the day she knew he was too sick to get well on his own or with only her help. Everyone has their own limit of what they can take. It is important to know your limits and stick to them. Otherwise, you will go down with him.

The next time he promises to quit, tell him you believe he really wants to quit and you will help him. Then do something you may not have done before. Ask him the "What if?" question. "What if it does not work this time?" Again reassure him that you believe he is really going to give it everything, but you would like him to agree right now to get help if for some reason he drinks or drugs again. The goal is to get him to agree to get help at the same time he is about to attempt to prove once again that he does not need it. Then when he drinks again, you pull out a piece of paper that has a date on it showing him where he agreed with you to get help. Often that will lead the addict into treatment. Whether or not he obtains help should not determine whether or not you get help. You need it just as much as he does, so find the help and support that will sustain your strength.

GAMBLING ADDICTION

Christianity Today, in its May 18, 1998, issue, highlighted the issue of gambling in America.[9] Americans legally gambled away more than

$550 billion in 1997 alone. This does not count any under-the-table, illegal gambling. The combo of government, big business, and the media have moved public opinion from the view predominant in the early 1900s that gambling is a tool of the devil and something to be outlawed, to the popular 1990s view that it is fun, relatively harmless, and certainly not immoral. The gambling industry has cleaned itself up, so we are told, and it's practically "family entertainment." Indeed, the big casinos now offer baby-sitting with bright, colorful, child-centered areas all set aside for the little ones. Gambling concerns employ lots of people, donate to local charities, and wave dollar bills under the noses of money-starved politicians. Government gets involved because politicians know they can only ask for so much tax money. At some point, the taxpayer says no. However, if they can dupe the taxpayer into thinking they are having fun and helping "the children," too, why not?

Why are Americans so blind to the social and spiritual ills that accompany gambling? Why do churches feel helpless when a big casino moves into town? *Christianity Today*'s editorial on the subject answers the question thus:

> When it comes to the social cost of gambling, Americans have an acquired blindness. In embracing a philosophy of individualism, we have rightly valued personal achievement, but we too easily view an individual's failure as limited to his or her own life and family. Unfortunately, the cumulative effect of thousands of failed marriages and careers, poisoned by compulsive, addictive gambling brings with it dire symptoms from which all of us suffer.[10]

We like to see the lottery winner as a "hero" who has beaten the system, whereas we see the gambling addict as a stupid fool who could not control himself. Gambling works so well as a mood-altering experience because it gives the person the "high," the spark, the buzz, the arousal for which they will give up almost anything else. People's lives can be ruined by just one short foray into the casino. One casino offered a forty-nine cent "farmer's breakfast." A man wandered in, hungry and, like most of us, wanting something for next to nothing.

He left the casino after losing $18,000, his life's savings. Under normal circumstances, when a casino is *not* in the vicinity, 1.5 to 6.5 percent of the population become addicted to gambling. When a gambling casino is in the area, however, the rate climbs. Estimates of what addicted gambling costs society range from $13,000 to $20,000 per person, depending on who is counting.[11]

Many of the characteristics found in other addictions apply to gambling as well. People deny they have a problem. Money starts disappearing. Time is lost from work. Anger and defensiveness increase whenever the addiction is discussed. Lying and sneaking around begin and later escalate. Denial, deception, and delusion set in. Relationships are disrupted. Jobs are lost. Life's savings are thrown away. Some gamblers end their lives rather than face the shame of what they have done. Others turn to drugs and alcohol to deaden the pain. Marriages break up. Kids go into foster care. People have affairs. Churches become overburdened with requests from members and others who are in financial crisis.

A gambling man is a secretive man when it comes to finances. He would rather talk about anything else, unless he has just had a win. If you look closely into his private affairs, you find all the credit cards maxed out or already revoked. You find unreasonable debts to banks, friends, relatives, and business associates. He is interested in sports and horse racing and is always talking about the odds and making deals with strangers by phone. He is like a manic depressive, up high one day and down low the next. Or on a high for even a month or more and then suicidal for months to come. He tries to explain it away as a bad spell, bad business deals, or just a bad life. The only explanation that makes any sense is that he has gambled what little he has had away. He is likely to have gambled his future away also. Don't allow him to gamble away yours. Find the help you need so he will eventually get the help he needs.

CHARACTERISTICS OF THE ADDICT

Here are some ways to discover that you may be addicted to the addict:

1. *Whatever his addictive substance or experience, you notice that his obsession and compulsions begin to have adverse effects on one or more of the following areas: physical, mental, social, emotional, or spiritual.* The last thing to go wrong is usually the physical. So don't wait for an alcoholic to receive a diagnosis of cirrhosis of the liver before you believe the problem is real. The spiritual portion of his life is what is most likely to disintegrate first. And through it all, he may still be the life of the party and the center of attention. Look carefully and notice that what you see is not normal. At least, it is not normal to most people. You may have become used to it growing up or become used to it since then, but it is not the way most people live and not the way you have to live.

2. *He will deny having a problem despite being preoccupied with it.* He will use many techniques to deny the problem. He will project it onto you, saying your weight or height or attitude or parents or background or anything other than him is the problem. He will rationalize and minimize, and he will become quite good at it. This denial is actually a good sign because it means down deep he still sees some value in himself. He is denying the stereotype that he refuses to believe he is. The key for you is to not accept any form of denial, only the truth.

3. *The addictive behavior escalates from mild to moderate to severe, with greater and greater consequences.* That is the central theme of all addictions. They get worse not better. They progress toward ever-increasing consequences no matter what temporary measures are taken to stop them. The addict can quit anytime and often does, but when he starts back up, he picks up right where he left off. A person's being in control of an addiction at some given point has nothing to do with whether or not he is addicted. Look at the progression, not at momentary control.

4. *The addict acts distant, withdrawn, moody, irritable, and even abusive, especially when deprived of the addictive substance or experience.* Yes, he can quit for periods of time, but his life is miserable when he does. It is really no life at all. Quitting something and starting a process of healing and recovery are two totally separate things.

The recovery process for the addict involves spiritual principles that begin with surrender, then move to accepting the truth about himself and the situation. Openness and confession follow, and they lead to his taking responsibility for his actions and healing. Forgiveness and restitution come next; then there are transformation and protection of the gains he has made. A more thorough examination of these recovery principles can be found in *The Seven Keys to Spiritual Renewal* by Stephen Arterburn and David Stoop, published by Tyndale.

5. *You have a sense that your relationship is full of dishonesty.* You don't feel connected to all parts of him. There is another life you are not privy to. This secret life comes to take more and more of his time, and you don't understand how he spends his time. You catch him in little lies that he explains away, but you know that he is not a truthful man and lacks the integrity you hoped he had.

WHAT TYPE OF WOMAN GETS INVOLVED WITH THE ADDICT?

While anyone can end up with an addict, many times there are family background commonalities when we examine carefully the history of a woman who is married to an addict. These families typically share these characteristics:

1. *Believed in the three Rules: don't feel, don't talk, don't trust.* These rules may never have been spoken out loud, but they were clear to everyone. Certain feelings were okay, and certain feelings were out. Sometimes, all feelings were forbidden, except for the rage spewed out by the parents. Other times anger was the forbidden feeling. Everyone in the family is so nice, so calm, so sweet; at least outside. Many times there is a family history of depression and the caretaking that goes with it. The depression is most likely not acknowledged or even talked over as a family. Children learn it is not safe to talk about certain subjects and if you do, you may be betrayed. So they learn not to trust as well. Insecure, wanting love, wanting to trust, but feeling unable, these kids are ripe to marry an addict, because addicts live by the three Rules all the time. Thus, they get what they have been used to getting.

2. *Had one or more family members "with a problem."* It could be that little sis had leukemia or Mom had multiple sclerosis, or Dad was an alcoholic himself. Whatever the problem, the family functioned in reaction to the problem and the person. Everyone danced around the proverbial elephant in the living room, making accommodations while making sure not to seem too upset. Used to living with some form of stress or chaos, these women grow up thinking the tension of living with a chaotic addict is normal. If things get too calm, it feels scary and even boring.

3. *Had problems with boundaries.* Either the boundaries or limits were nonexistent ("I'm cold. Put on your sweater"), or too rigid ("It's my way or the highway, bud"). Everyone was expected to feel the same, or everyone passed like ships in the night. People were either entangled with each other in a sick way, or they were so detached they barely knew each other. Discipline was somewhere between rare and totalitarian, and often there were double standards for girls vs. boys or parents vs. children.

4. *Had someone who conveyed an exaggerated sense of servant-hood (read: martyrdom).* Being the messiah seemed like an okay occupation when you grew up in this type of home. Your business was to straighten everyone else out—for their own good, of course. You and your ways (the ways learned at your family table) were the *right* ways, and you only wanted to help people. Why should anyone resent it if you offer unsolicited advice? Of course, everyone must acknowledge all you do for them, since you try so hard to please. However, you must always refuse help when someone wants to help you. Can't be a bother you know.

5. *Did not provide an adequate sense of acceptance to each child.* The children in these families often grow up to be compulsive caregivers, eternal people pleasers, and always-ready rescuers. They are searching for approval because, for one reason or another, they never felt their efforts, love, appearance, intelligence, or *something*, was "good enough." Looking for love in all the wrong places is many times a theme they find themselves caught in again and again.

6. *Often presented the children with the idea that "next time it will be different" but were rarely able to fulfill the promise.* These daughters keep looking for the promise to be fulfilled and keep hoping that *this* time it *will* be different. "Maybe I couldn't get Dad to love me, but if I get this alcoholic to love me, then I will have finally done it. I'll make up for the loss of Dad by winning over this guy." Living with unfulfilled dreams and hopes is a way of life in these families, so it does not seem strange to their daughters to keep on doing it by marrying an addict.

Of course, there are situations where a person has no idea that there is the potential for addiction to pop up in their loved one. Addicts are clever at hiding their problem, at first. Some addicts are so in denial that they literally live double lives, and no one in their family finds out until years later. Some women grew up very sheltered and have not a clue about the real world and the temptations and hazards out there. They may have come from a family without a history of addiction and may be totally naive. Some come out of strict church backgrounds and may have never even seen a movie or watched television. Some may have a grasp of what is out there, but never dream it will be a part of their husband's life because he is "a Christian" or "a doctor" or "a good father" or "a dedicated worker."

WHY DOES SHE FALL FOR HIM?

Many times a woman falls for the addict because she is able to see the good in him. She can sense his *potential*. She is sure that her love will make the difference and turn things around. She sees him as a "diamond in the rough." The woman is often used to caretaking and nurturing others and feels comfortable in this role. Loving him seems natural. She is easily duped into believing that "this time it will be different," just as in her childhood. She is an optimist of sorts, always believing, always hoping, always trusting. She feels important and loved because someone needs her, and she may feel equally insecure and frightened on her own. So a relationship with an addict is better than no relationship at all. Or she could fall for him because she is in denial and refuses to see that he has a problem.

RELATING TO THE ADDICT

So what if you are hooked up with the addict? What are the odds you will make it? The odds *you* will make it are good, if you take care of you. The odds of *him* making it, or of *your relationship* making it, are also good, if you will work on you and not on his addiction. You did not cause it. You cannot fix it. But you can get through it. Learn to set boundaries and stick to them. Seek the Lord for yourself and your sanity.

Some people do change. Some people do have miraculous healing experiences. Some people are delivered overnight from their addiction. Sadly, today, most are not. Recovery is difficult, painful, and not always successful. *Can* people recover? Yes. *Do* all people recover? No. What happens to you depends largely on what you decide to do with this information. You can stay in denial, or you can get help. Only you and the Lord know what you need to do to recover yourself. You are probably as addicted to the addict as he is to his substance or experience. You need help for yourself. Only then, when you are clearheaded and in touch with the realities of addiction and recovery, can you make a rational decision. One of the reasons New Life Clinic (1-800-NEW LIFE) was founded was to help people in just this situation. No one can go it alone. We all need help sometimes. Reach out for help. Let others counsel, comfort, and correct you if need be. Help is available if you want it.

WHAT COULD THE ADDICT
DO TO CHANGE?

In order to make lasting change, the addict needs to take several steps:

1. *Come out of denial, face reality, and get help to stop addictive acting out.* If he would use the energy it takes to cover up the addic-

tion to try to uncover what he needs to do to get well, his life would completely change. He is fighting the addiction alone, and he needs to know that you will help him fight for recovery and healing. The payoff for successfully covering up the addiction is more pain. The payoff for accepting the truth and surrendering to the need for help is a new life full of meaning and purpose.

2. *Recognize his powerlessness over the addiction.* If he could have fixed this on his own, he would have done so by now. If he could have kept if from getting worse, he would have done that also. If he could have grown in character rather than watched it disintegrate, he would have. He may own millions, lead thousands, and move mountains, but addiction is the one thing he will never conquer on his own.

3. *Turn his life over to God through Jesus Christ.* Let God renew him, cleanse him, heal him, and deliver him. There really is a God, and the greatest gift that addiction gives many addicts and their spouses is that it forces them to face the reality that there is a powerful God who cares for them deeply and loves them unconditionally. They discover that it is never too late to have a relationship with the God who created them. The addiction path is paved with heartache and leads to destruction. The recovery path is paved with hope and leads to God.

4. *Begin an intensive moral introspection of his strengths and weaknesses, sharing what he learns with a pastor or an elder.* Be accountable to learn new behavior patterns to replace the addictive ones. To learn who he is morally, to discover the defects in his character, he needs to be accountable to someone other than you. He needs to find other men who will mirror the truth to him and help him learn the ways of an authentic man. He needs help in resisting temptation and finding support when discouraged.

5. *Change his circle of friends.* Some call it changing playmates and playgrounds. In the case of the sex addict we are not referring to that kind of playmate. The message here is to turn away from those who have led him down the addiction path. And to stay off the path, he needs to protect himself from people and places that could lead to relapse. If he keeps his old associates, they will be a great threat to his addictive behavior. They will sabotage his recovery. He must say no to

them, even though he may not feel he can ever be happy without his old circle of friends.

SNAPSHOT SUMMARY OF THE ADDICT

CLUES TO HELP YOU SPOT HIM

1. Physical, mental, emotional, or spiritual aspects of life affected by the addiction begin to disintegrate.

2. Denies he has a problem despite increasing preoccupation with it.

3. Addictive behavior escalates and progresses with increasingly destructive consequences.

4. Acts distant, moody, and even abusive, especially when not participating in addiction.

5. You sense increasing dishonesty and that he lives a double life, unable or unwilling to account for his time away from you.

THE WOMAN TO WHOM HE IS ATTRACTED

1. Follows the three Rules of don't talk, don't trust, and don't feel.

2. Is used to living with stress and chaos in a family.

3. Has trouble maintaining boundaries.

4. Is a caretaker or martyr who cares so excessively that she is willing to take on the doormat role in a relationship.

5. Is looking for the acceptance she did not find as a child.

THE WOMAN WHO FALLS FOR HIM

1. Sees his potential and is sure her love will make a difference.

2. Caretaking feels normal and good to her.

3. Thinks this time will be different and she will finally heal someone.

4. Feels incomplete and desperate on her own.

5. Denies his addiction is a problem.

WHAT YOU CAN DO

1. Obtain help for yourself.

2. Seek God's direction for your life and accept His comfort, grace, and love.

3. Admit that you can do some helpful things that will lead him toward treatment but realize that you cannot change him.

4. Stop all enabling behaviors that have allowed his addiction to continue.

5. Set up boundaries and stick to them. Don't just threaten, follow through.

WHAT HE COULD DO TO CHANGE

1. Get out of denial and get professional help.

2. Recognize his powerlessness over addiction.

3. Surrender to God through His Son, Jesus Christ, and allow God to give him the power he does not have.

4. Become accountable to those who can help him grow in character.

5. Change where he goes and whom he goes with to protect himself from relapse.

CHAPTER 9

THE ETERNAL KID

The eternal kid is known by some as "Beetle Bailey," or as "Peter Pan," "Maynard G. Krebs," or the lovable "Gilligan"; others see him as the "Idle Potentate," "the Taker," or "the Bum." He comes in various forms: sometimes the klutz, sometimes the misfit, sometimes the eccentric near-genius. People find it difficult to hate him. He has a charm that beguiles, and his whole persona begs to be mothered. He may infuriate you, but you just cannot hate him. Sometimes he can be *so sweet*. He is the kind of guy that attracts women who like lost puppies. Often he's just there and grows on you, until you finally adopt him.

Raymond was one such man or, more accurately, boy. He was thirty-nine, but most of his family thought of him as a teen. He worked for his dad because he could not stay employed anywhere else. He was not married because he could not figure out how to maintain a long-term relationship with a woman. To Raymond, life was just a place to party, smoke some dope, and drink a great deal of alcohol. His dad, feeling guilty over the divorce with Raymond's mom, kept on rescuing him beyond what other family members thought wise. All in all, circumstances worked out so that Raymond never had to grow up. He eluded manhood and became the eternal kid.

Jack was another eternal kid. He was eccentric—always dressed oddly—uncoordinated, disheveled, rumpled, and baggy. His clothes looked like they came from a cross between the Army/Navy Store and the Goodwill. He was quiet and actually kind of sensitive. He did well in school, especially in science. Jack never dated much, but the girls always thought he was "sweet" and would bake him things and drop by his workshop in his garage after school to talk. (They talked, he just puttered on something or other and at least appeared to be listening.) He would crack the occasional joke and had an endearing wit. You could not help but laugh when you saw him—not unkindly, but rather indulgently, as you would with a small but mischievous child.

Dr. Dan Kiley, in his fascinating work *The Peter Pan Syndrome: Men Who Have Never Grown Up,*[1] outlines what these men were like in adolescence. Understanding what happened at this stage of development is crucial, in that these men *are still in* adolescence. Irresponsibility, anxiety, loneliness, and sex-role conflict are all characteristics that the man who has never grown up begins to manifest during adolescence. Usually, he had laissez-faire parents who did not set limits for him. He came to believe that rules did not apply to him. His parents did not challenge his irresponsible behavior, so he never learned the discipline of self-care habits. Thus, he later developed into an adult who never notices the clothes he dropped all around the bedroom or the pile of wet towels on the bathroom floor. He is not usually dirty, but his clothes never fit correctly and are usually styles and colors most people would find unusual. His grooming is *not* impeccable because he just does not care enough about how he looks to go to the trouble to look good. His beard is scruffy; his fingernails rough and, most likely, chewed; he usually looks as though he slept in his clothes or at least never hangs them up.

As an adolescent, he was very anxious. His home was likely one where tension filled the air because his parents were unhappy. He felt estranged from his dad, who tended to be a macho man who had trouble expressing his concern for his wife or son. Mom felt victimized, though both she and her husband pretended to be happy. They were avoiders: They avoided each other, their feelings, the truth about their lives. They were not critically dysfunctional but often experienced big problems and were miserable. The family looked okay, even well-adjusted, to outsiders. No one outside guessed that the parents were staying together just for the children; but the kids knew and felt haunted by confusion and anxiety.

Isolation is another symptom that sprouts in an eternal kid's adolescence. The affluence of many families doesn't help. These kids are usually handed *things* rather than more *time* with their parents. They take their food, shelter, and clothing for granted. Never having to work hard for anything makes them unable to learn how to feel proud of their own accomplishments. Without the self-confidence that hard, productive work brings, they are more vulnerable to peer pressure. They have too much time on their hands and desperately want to connect, to fit in, to be part of something. Feeling disconnected from Mom and Dad, these boys look to the peer group as the place to find identity. Yet, as Kiley points out, they can take little time to enjoy belonging because they are so obsessed with avoiding rejection. The result is intense, profound isolation.

Another characteristic of these eternal kid men during adolescence is a masculine identity confusion. The boy is told by the masculine culture that sex, sports, and alcohol or drugs are the only acceptable emotional outlets for a male in our society. Any behavior that is perceived as feminine is seen as taboo. The worst put-down you can give to an adolescent boy is to say he is acting "like a girl." So the young boy learns to suppress his human feelings of tenderness, sensitivity, emotionalism, etc., so as to be macho. Sometimes he even begins to question his masculinity, wondering if he is, in fact, gay, since he feels so much and so deeply. This conflict, exaggerated by the severe homophobia many men have, confuses him more.

In his late teens or early twenties, there is often a shift to more severe self-absorption. Narcissism blossoms in a fantasy world designed to revolve around himself. The result is a lack of meaningful relationships and many unique ways to avoid intimate, close connections. Often the young man has a touch of near-genius. He may have been the kid who read at age two or did complicated math at age five. He becomes so enthralled with his mental abilities that he comes to live in his own little universe—the enchanted forest of his mind—blissfully happy, wandering around, oblivious to the real world around him.

Unlike the overt misogynist (woman hater), the eternal kid's chauvinism is more subtle. Bud is an example of this aspect of the eternal kid's personality. Whenever his wife, Ellen, has a problem, he butts in and tries to fix or solve it. Bud has to see her as weaker, more incompetent, less able than he perceives himself, even if Ellen actually is more skilled in the area under consideration. While he does not mind being financially or physically dependent on others, Bud wants his woman to be *emotionally* dependent on him so he can appear to protect her and thus enhance his ego. Another sign of the chauvinism he learned early on is his reactions to Ellen when she gets "upset." His response to her being "upset" will be unpredictable and hard to understand. For example, he will be "perturbed" at her for being "too emotional" or dismiss her concerns as "silly" or "stupid." He tells the woman to "be quiet" (i.e., stop being "upset"). If it were not for these kinds of outbursts no one would know he is actually a very angry man.

The eternal kid learned all this from his dear old dad. He unconsciously figures Dad will eventually praise him for his mistreatment, however subtle, of women. This behavior also allows him to dismiss his mom's complaints about his bungling and irresponsibility as just being "how women are." Thus he is relieved of any guilt he may feel. Attitudes of male supremacy or superiority also allow him to blame any sexual inadequacies or insecurities that he feels on the woman in his life. He sees himself as generous and kind and believes that women take advantage of him (clearly projection on his part). He eventually becomes hardened toward women and wears his callousness like a badge of honor when he is with his male cohorts. He thus believes that his pro-male stance proves he is a real man, and that he is "wise to" women and their ploys in a worldly way.

At age twenty-one, a person is supposed to be an adult, but since the eternal kid has only the body of an adult but the mind-set of a child, this fellow uses his chauvinism to hide his faults and character defects from himself and, hopefully, others. His habit of blaming other people for all his problems only reinforces the attitude, since the *women* in his life become the source of his problems. So, while he is endearing and "sweet" in some ways, underneath is a rather cynical and angry person.

THE BRILLIANT KLUTZ

This is the guy who trips over his own feet and bungles almost every chore, errand, or job he is given. He acts more stupid, clumsy, and ineffective than he really is. He may not be aware of doing so, but he just does not want the responsibility of doing well, at least not at anything about which other people really care. If he does well, someone may ask him to do it again, and then he might even have to be in charge of something, and then he could end up having someone else dependent on *his* decisions. He could never allow that to happen because his whole outlook on life is centered around blaming others and avoiding responsibility. This guy is the consummate buck passer. He just wants to be left alone to tinker in that to which his genius draws him. Living in his own little world, he is blissfully happy, bumbling along unaware of what is going on around him. He commits faux pas regularly but never learns from his mistakes. He just keeps making the same dumb errors over and over. He may actually make money off his spark of genius, but he lets the woman in his life handle it. People like him despite his eccentricities, and he makes sure he gets what he wants—which is to be left alone most of the time. If you are clumsy enough and don't quite get things right, after a while people stop giving you things to do, and you can do what you want to do. The offbeat inventor in the movie *Back to the Future* is a great example of this type of fellow.

This fellow typically marries someone who is strong, independent, and self-sufficient. (She has to be because he spends most of his time alone, doing his own thing.) Even as a parent, he abdicates to his wife, though he may, indeed, adore his kids, albeit from a distance.

THE IDLE POTENTATE, TAKER, OR BUM

This type of eternal kid seems attractive when a woman is young (or thinks she is). He seems like a rogue or a rebel or a gypsy. However, as she matures or wakes up, a woman sees him as a bum. As time moves on, the haze of romanticism lifts, and she perceives him as he really is: totally irresponsible.

The taker believes that the world, and especially women, owes him a living. He is the man who refuses to stick to any one occupation. He is a jack-of-all-trades, master of none. Or he may be the man who never works because he "can't," or he "can't find work," or he had work, but they treated him unfairly—like the people at the job before that and the one before that.

He is the ultimate philosopher-king, who tells the rest of us how the world *ought* to be and blames *others* for his lot in life. He harps continually on the sins of society (especially capitalism) and the defects of all the leaders he has known. He leans on others and commits himself to as little as possible. A great talker on all that is wrong with the world, he can get you off on a tangent before you are able to blink an eye.

He sees hard work as stupid and has a list of reasons why it is foolish to work diligently. He longs for power and glory but will not work for it. He expects it to float down from heaven like a feather from a low-flying bird. The eternal opportunist, he keeps his options open and often is willing to move on a moment's notice. Actually, he's also willing to change wives, homes, jobs, or cars at a moment's notice as well. "Something may come up" is his excuse for why he cannot do whatever needs to be done today.

Rick is a great example of an eternal kid. Rick drives an old, beat-up car that is always needing something done to it. He "forgot" to get insurance for it and doesn't seem to care. He lives at home with his parents and hangs out at the local Burger King after school hours so he can talk to younger girls who might be impressed by an older guy. If he does attach to a young woman, and she is willing, he makes plans to move in with her or with her and her family. He does not do it to rip them off; he does it just to get by. He is self-indulgent and makes sure he does not get the bad end of the stick in anything.

If he cheats he justifies it with statements such as "The government is corrupt" or "Everyone does it." He is into name-dropping to give himself credibility. He shoplifts because "the stores just rip you off." Rick has no qualms about stealing if he can get away with it. He feels entitled to live as well as anyone else, and if it takes shoplifting to do it, so be it. Rebellious or younger women initially find Rick attractive because he offers his woman the chance to "push the envelope" by trying a new sexual thrill, a new drug, a new sensory experience. While coming on to her, he is very lusty and provocative, yet in the long run he gets more than he actually gives. She finds it hard to resist him. He keeps her in a state of utter sexual exhilaration but at the same time does not want a "commitment" (i.e., marriage).

Under all circumstances, he is eager to present himself as the generous one in the relationship. Yet, in reality, he acts incredibly self-absorbed. His actual contribution to the household is minimal, and any money he does manage to bring in somehow mysteriously disappears. The woman becomes *the* financial provider or she learns to live on nothing. Rick is often very critical of how *she* thinks *they* should spend *her* money. When he fantasizes about being a father, he sees himself as generous with his kids and thinks anything they will do for him is his due as their father. Sometimes, men like Rick relate to the kids and their toys as if they are just a big brother. They all go skiing, snowmobiling, stock car racing, rollerblading, or to ball games— because Dad enjoys these activities. Of course, all these fun things are paid for by the wife in one way or another. He rarely acknowledges the woman's contribution to the family and even resents her for what she does do.

CHARACTERISTICS OF THE ETERNAL KID

Are you dating someone who is an eternal kid? Or do you wonder if the guy you are interested in might be one? Here are five clues to look for in someone you suspect may be an eternal kid:

1. *Is basically self-centered.* Whether in a sweet, spaced-out sort of way or an arrogant manner, everything revolves around him. *His* needs are what matter, not yours. He has created a world that allows him to do whatever he wants to do, free of accountability to anyone.

He feels he is owed the ability to live this way. His sense of entitlement is stronger than his sense of self.

2. *Is irresponsible at the core.* Limits and boundaries are unknown concepts to him. He is an avoider: He avoids hard work, intimacy, responsibility, challenges, and blame. He is unable to delay any gratification. His intentions are always good, but his follow-through is always poor. Something within him sabotages his every attempt to do the right thing and turn his life around. Even when he meets someone he thinks he cares about, he is unable to maintain the relationship unless she is willing to take care of everything he is unable to handle. If she is not, he will move on to someone else.

3. *Tends to be chauvinistic.* He sees men as basically more important than women, though he does not always express this crassly or boldly. He dismisses you and your complaints as silly and not worth his precious time. This is an attitude that is often learned from his father. Its main function is to justify his leeching off women and using them to meet his needs. His behavior allows him to be lazy as long as he can find someone desperate enough or empty enough to take him on as a project. Once someone agrees to be his, he literally treats them as his property.

4. *Tends to live in his own little dream world.* He just comes off as a little odd. At first, this is very intriguing to a naive woman. The way he thinks is interesting and often funny. It is hard to resist wanting to get to know more about his unique world. You are so amazed that all the rules you have held so dear mean nothing to him. You find yourself drawn to his free spirit. You are uptight, and he gives you the freedom to let loose and be everything you have wanted to be but were too afraid of rejection by others to try.

5. *Has a growing temper below his easygoing manner.* He resents it if you are too loud or active in trying to get his attention. He wants everyone to be committed to lowering his stress level, and, when they are not, he gets angry. This is why he cannot hold a job. He loses his temper and just walks out. It is why he does not have any long-term relationships. At some point he has run them off with his episodes of anger. When he realizes he has lost control, he explains the outburst

as a result of someone, somewhere, who mistreated him and ruined his day.

WHAT KIND OF WOMAN DOES THE ETERNAL KID WANT?

The eternal kid is on the lookout for a woman whose best skill is taking care of people. If she has a job or family that can support him when he is out of work, that makes her even more attractive. He looks for someone who does not mind being used financially, emotionally, sexually, or mentally. If he eschews self-sufficiency, he looks for a woman who is willing to live in poverty. He just wants a woman who will take all the responsibility and leave him free to do as he pleases. He wants her to be willing to take care of him and then, leave him alone. He does not need her to be wealthy; he just wants her to be responsible enough to handle all his affairs. He feels best when she is both competent to care for him and willing to overlook all his faults and see the good little boy that he really is.

WHY DOES SHE FALL FOR HIM?

There are a number of possible reasons a woman falls for an eternal kid:

1. *She enjoys being in charge, in control, and caretaking.* He seems like the perfect candidate. It does not seem that below his easygoing surface one of his biggest agendas is *not* to be controlled. He looks as though he is begging to be cared for and nurtured. Anyone that has a need feels like a perfect match to her. In the beginning he allows her to do what she wants with him. She loves his response to her care. More than anything she believes that if she cares enough, he will grow up and be a real man.

2. *She may be an oldest child and is used to caring for kids.* This feels very right to her because of her past experiences. She may also be used to caring for her father. Her mother might have died or been sick, or her father might have depended on her to meet his emotional

needs. Once she is grown up and out of the family, she often feels very unneeded. The void is instantly filled when she meets the eternal kid.

3. *She mistakes his irresponsibility for playfulness.* It is fun to be around him. The agenda is always open, and he enjoys relaxing and having a good time. He makes her laugh, and she has not had much laughter in her lifetime. She has had to be responsible, and it feels good to be with someone so young at heart.

4. *She believes "We will grow up together."* She is often very immature and thinks he is someone on her level. Beneath her responsible exterior there is a little girl who was never allowed to grow up. She believes they will have a connection that she could not experience with anyone else. She looks forward to doing what she was never allowed to do because she had to take on an adult role so young. He helps her get in touch with the little girl that never was.

5. *She is a people pleaser and hates conflict.* Initially, he seems to roll with all the punches. He runs instead of confronting a problem. He especially runs when he is confronted. She feels safe with him because his misery and distrust are always pointed toward someone out there, someone out of reach. With her, he jokes away all the issues that would normally be addressed by adults. She likes to please him and is willing to overlook any negatives if it appears to make him happier.

6. *Women who are feeling rebellious themselves are attracted to the eternal kid.* Often she has just revolted against Mom and Dad, freeing herself from their tyranny. Thus, the women he hooks up with are irrational and irresponsible, searching for the unusual and unpredictable. He knows this fact and can smell these women a mile off. He wants a woman who is rebellious, yet willing to take second place to him. He comes across as the ultimate "freethinker" (the type that is so open-minded that his brains fall out). Nonconformity, rebellion, and "originality" ooze from his persona. He may present himself as the libertarian, the maverick, the individualist, the Gandhi of his generation, the lounge lizard, the laggard, the lazy bum, the sloucher, the slacker. Usually, parents are able to smell *him* a mile off.

RELATING TO THE ETERNAL KID

What if you are in a relationship with the eternal kid? Before we present some of the positive things you can do, here are some of the negatives, which at times feel the most tempting.

1. You could say, "Forget this loser!" and just leave.

2. You could leave nicely and hope he changes on his own.

3. You could stay and try to change him through threats and endless hours of nagging.

4. You could punish him for being like he is, treating him worse and worse until he finally understands what a bad boy he is.

5. You could take over every detail of his life and fulfill the role of Mama that he has wanted you to fulfill and allow your sense of injustice and victimization to grow each day along with your pessimism, bitterness, and resentment.

None of these are very good choices, even though, externally, you keep your career, keep your life, and pay all the bills. You raise the kids and do the "right thing." You just feel sorry for yourself, and, indeed, you are in a sorry situation. You may snap under all the pressure and resort to drugs, alcohol, workaholism, or any number of things that will completely destroy you. You may feel justified to do anything you want to do, but there is no justification for ruining your life just because he has ruined his. There are too many other possible positive outcomes to settle for destroying yourself and possibly your children.

A more positive approach with a greater chance for a better outcome for everyone is to stay with him but do some things that have a good chance of leading him into a productive adulthood. Of course, you may not succeed, and one person can never truly change another, but many have taken these steps to help an eternal kid become a real man. Also keep in mind that radical change usually only comes with crisis or divine intervention.

For those who want to help the eternal kid enter adulthood, the following will be helpful:

1. *Communicate instead of manipulate.* With a "kid" in the house you have probably resorted to badgering or at least dropping hints in order to manipulate him into doing what he should be doing. You will do better if you choose to abandon these tactics and become more direct in your communication. Tell him what you want and need. Ask him to do what you need him to do. If he does not respond to a sincere request, stop doing for him what he expects you to do. When he wants to know why dinner is not prepared, explain matter-of-factly that when he decides to help you, you will help him and meet his needs.

2. *Move him to action while taking responsibility for yourself.* It is easy to become parental and condescending with a "Kid." Threats that you would make to a child are not helpful. Talk about what you will do and what you expect him to do. For example, you could say, "I will make us some lunch after you rake the leaves," rather than "If *you* don't rake the leaves, *I* won't fix you lunch." The juxtaposition of request and consequence will make a large difference.

3. *Bring resolution to conflicts and decisions.* Refuse to allow him to procrastinate in settling an issue. Phrases such as "Let's decide . . ." or "Let's get this out of the way" can be door-openers to communication and resolution. If he runs away from conflicts, make sure you bring up the issue when he returns, so he will hopefully understand that running away does not solve the problem. Remember, the eternal kid is more selfish and lazy than passive-aggressive. He just wants to be left alone, unlike the passive man, who wants to display his angry feelings by his nonactions. So when the eternal kid sees that the issue will not go away, he will eventually give in, unlike the passive aggressive, who just ignores you altogether.

4. *Children need their space, and so does the eternal kid.* This can be great for you, especially if you, too, like time to yourself. Be sure that while he is off puttering or playing, you are taking care of yourself. Do some fun things. Connect with groups and get involved in worthwhile projects. As you do these types of activities and stop looking to him for fulfillment, your life will become more satisfying and meaningful. Since

he does not genuinely care about you and your needs, you will need to be responsible for yourself. Reach out to others for support and affirmation. Let family and friends fill in the gaps when you need a hug or a laugh.

5. *When it comes to child rearing, you are going to be the main disciplinarian.* The eternal kid will not want to discipline the children and will want them to have lots of privileges. Sit down with him and develop a list of unacceptable, nonnegotiable behaviors as well as consequences for each child according to their age. That way, even if you are the enforcer, you have him behind you, however silently.

6. *It is crucial when living with someone like the kid that you take the time and effort to look within yourself.* You, like all of us, have some blind spots that need to be revealed. This marriage did not happen by accident. What attracted you to this man? Was it control, power, or some other motivation? When you discover these things, you will be less reactive to him and better able to live in peace, whether or not he matures.

7. *Whatever you choose to do in confronting the eternal kid's behaviors, be sure to stop expressing your fears of abandonment through caretaking behaviors.* Do not appease him with motherly remarks like: "It's okay, honey. You did the best you could. It's not your fault." Do not support any of his rationalizations. Do not feel sorry for him. If he gets mad at you for not feeling sorry for him, say: "I cannot remove or take away your pain." Let him feel his own pain. Ask, "How did you feel when you made that mistake?" Ask open-ended questions such as: "What did you learn for the future?" or "What could you have done differently?"

8. *Do not apologize for him in public or to the kids.* If he does something foolish, just leave the scene or look like a wise old owl, saying nothing or very little. People know what he is like, and your efforts to cover up for him only make you look foolish.

9. *Do not fake your sexual response just to please him.* The chances are he approaches sex in much the same way he approaches everything else in life: He sees it as something good for him rather than for the two of you. Let him know what you prefer and guide him

gently. Do not criticize him or badger him, but focus on what you need and communicate that. Take responsibility for your own role in being sexually satisfied.

10. *Do not expect him to show any concern for you or your problems, and do not whine when he is more concerned about himself than you.* If he does notice your feelings, praise him. Do expect him to *listen:* "I have something important to say. Please listen." Only work on the issues that are high on your "I can't stand it" list of his behaviors. Do not major on the minors.

An eternal kid is nothing but untapped potential. Like all of us, he has skills, talents, and great potential. What he lacks is the character needed to follow through and accomplish the requirements of a normal adult. He is immature, lazy, and wants to be left alone. But he does have flashes of charisma and charm that could one day be part of a wonderful man to have as a husband. The most helpful thing you can do is to help him find a great counselor who understands who he is and what he needs. He also needs a solid church and involvement with mature men. Find that church and become active in it. Then invite him to be part of it with you. God needs to become the center of his life, and Jesus needs to become the model for his manhood. He can make it. It won't be easy and it won't be quick, but he can make it to manhood with your help.

WHAT COULD THE ETERNAL KID DO TO CHANGE?

If the eternal kid should ever desire to change, he would need to make these changes:

1. *Develop a desire to grow up by seeing himself as others see him and as God sees him.* He would take a look at his strengths and assets and determine to develop them and use them. He would practice doing what he needed to do rather than what he wanted to do.

2. *Realize the world does not revolve around him.* The world is not out to get him, nor does it need to make a place for him. He must decide not to be dependent on the world at large for an excuse to fail

or a means to live. While his parents may have either ignored him (making him resentful of everyone), or smothered him (making him expect everyone to cater to him), he must move out of these patterns and develop a new way of reacting to life.

3. *Be proactive, not passive.* He must learn to take the initiative. He can start by reaching out to his wife and children, starting to do for them what he has always expected them to do for him. He must get out of himself and into others. He should practice doing something for someone else just for the pure joy of contributing to someone else's life. This will help him discover that he can set a goal of serving someone and accomplish that goal; he should continue doing this until it becomes second nature.

4. *Let go of his superior attitude toward women.* A lot of this attitude comes from his relationship with his father, but his relationship with his mother may be too closely fused. If so, he needs to break the chains before he can see women in an objective light. Whether his mother was too close or too detached, his reactions to her emotions must be resolved. He probably developed other feelings about women by observing his father's treatment of women. A great counselor can help him identify false beliefs and gain new attitudes about women.

5. *Develop male relationships to break isolation.* Tinkering and television leave little time for developing healthy friendships. Here are some ways for him to make friends: Make a commitment to join activities that involve other men. Attend a men's Bible study. Go to some men's retreats or events. Ask his wife to invite a couple to a movie. Make the effort to get to know the spouses of his wife's friends. An older male counselor can do the most to bridge the gap between isolation and connection.

SNAPSHOT SUMMARY OF THE ETERNAL KID

CLUES TO HELP YOU SPOT HIM

1. Is self-centered, either sweetly or arrogantly.

2. Irresponsible at the core; limits are unknown.

3. Chauvinistic; sees men as more important than women.

4. Lives in a dream world and does not learn from his mistakes.

5. Has a temper and lashes out when confronted and then runs away.

THE WOMAN TO WHOM HE IS ATTRACTED

1. Is best skilled at taking care of people.

2. Doesn't mind being used to make a man comfortable.

3. Can cope with living in poverty during a bad spell when he is likely to be out of work.

4. Will leave him alone to tinker, invent, watch television, or do whatever he wants.

5. Will overlook his faults and see the potential within him.

THE WOMAN WHO FALLS FOR HIM

1. Enjoys being in charge and caretaking.

2. May have been an oldest child who took on adult responsibilities very early.

3. Mistakes his irresponsibility for playfulness.

4. Believes it will be fun to grow up together.

5. Is a people pleaser who hates conflict.

WHAT YOU CAN DO

1. Don't nag or threaten like a mother.

2. Give him a lot of space while you develop your own life.

3. Discover what it is within you that is attracted to him, and resolve that inner need.

4. Don't compromise anything just to keep him from leaving.

5. Expect him to listen but to be unable to understand you or empathize.

WHAT HE COULD DO TO CHANGE

1. Develop a desire to grow up by seeing himself as God sees him.

2. Realize that the world does not revolve around him.

3. Be proactive and reach out to his wife and kids rather than expecting them to meet his needs.

4. Let go of his superior attitude toward women.

5. Develop healthy male relationships through church, accountability groups, men's Bible study, and a prayer partner.

CHAPTER 10

THE UNGODLY MAN

This final type of man could also be one or more of the previous men we have already covered. The problem with this man is that he has no foundation for living, no platform for change. He lives without a knowledge or relationship with God. He has no concept of the spiritual, resulting in a desperate man trying to make up the rules of life as he goes. He is miserable and out of control, and everything he does is an attempt to reassure himself that he is right about life and those who "believe" are not. Here are three very different examples of this wandering man who believes he has it all figured out but has missed the most important fundamental relationship in this life and the life to come.

EXAMPLES OF THE UNGODLY MAN

RALPH

Ralph seems like an ordinary sort of guy—somewhat quiet, but steady, reliable, smart enough, just an average fellow. Ralph is an engineer at a large firm in Denver. He works fifty to sixty hours a week, depending on whether there is a big rush on at work. He comes home, mows the lawn in the summer, rakes the leaves in the fall, shovels the walks and driveway in the winter, and trims the bushes in the spring. He keeps his garage neat, most of the time, and the basement workshop isn't *too* bad. Ralph pays the bills, keeps the cars running, and volunteers at the annual community festival. He heads his son's Cub Scout troop and donates blood to the Red Cross yearly. He does not curse or drink or smoke. He does not beat his wife. He loves his three children, though he does not really know how to relate to them. Ralph looks in on them at night when they are asleep and thinks, *I'm a pretty good dad.* His relationship with his wife is somewhat shallow, but benign. They rarely talk about anything except the kids and even that at no great depth. He leaves the parenting, on the whole, to his wife. Their other conversations entail his work, their house, their finances, and a future retirement: on the fringes of life.

Ralph's one luxury he allows himself is a great car. He loves cars, and every few years he starts pining for a new one. He looks through *Car and Driver* and stops to "window-shop" at the dealerships on Sunday afternoons when they are closed. After a while, he gets excited about a certain model and make and orders one to his exact specifications, never buying one off the showroom floor. The weeks of waiting for it to arrive are filled with anticipation and fantasy about what it will be like to drive this new dream machine. The kids and his wife just nod and smile to themselves, knowing that in a few weeks the joy will be gone, and it won't be long until he will be griping about what a lemon the new car is.

Like his father before him, Ralph places great store in thrift and self-discipline. "Pull yourself up by your own bootstraps" has always been his motto. He figures you'd better get used to doing for yourself because "no one else is going to do it for you." So Ralph diligently saves his money in various plans: His 401K retirement account at work is his greatest source of hope for a secure future, but he also saves money apart from that and invests it in CDs, money market accounts, stocks, and bonds. He watches the stock market with the passion of a gambler with his racing form. He buys a few gold coins so as to hedge against disaster and keeps a locker in the basement full of emergency supplies. Ever since the kids were born, Ralph has had a yearly fire drill with the family. In the middle of the night, he gets everyone up and marches them out of the house as if there were a real fire. He changes the batteries on the smoke detectors every spring and recharges the fire extinguishers regularly. "Can't leave things to chance," he always says. His acts of responsibility are a wonder to those who know him.

Ralph does not think about God much. Well, actually he thinks a lot about God, some god, but not a god that he would be able to accept. Ralph believes that if there were a God, a real God, then that God would have been the one that killed his twin sister in a car crash when they were fourteen. The pain and anger are still not healed, and Ralph wants no part of a god that kills children. His world has been ordered separate and apart from the need for or the reality of God.

To accomplish this feat, he keeps himself very busy and interested in a lot of things. Compared to all that he does and all that he is into, church is very boring. Anytime he has attended for the sake of the kids or his wife, he has left with the feeling that if God is as dead as that church feels, no wonder so many horrible things happen in this world—things that one must be prepared to handle.

Ralph really believes he has more important matters on his mind, and he believes he's got everything under control. He is a good and responsible man who has, thus far, eliminated a need for God. As far as his attitude toward Christians, Ralph believes that they are only fooling themselves, but if somehow it makes them feel better to believe what they believe then that is fine with him. Yet he does shake his head when he reads about those "fundamentalist Christians" in the newspapers. He gets mad that they cannot seem to just let others live and do what they want to do. "It's not my business" is his motto, and it infuriates him that these "holier than thou" people are pushing their religion on others.

Ralph is one of those men who turn away from God because of a loss they think God should have prevented or a hurt God should have healed. They do not go off the deep end; they order their world to prove they don't need God. In a sense, they make their lives so good and solid that they eliminate the need for God. They avoid desperation with planning and responsibility. If everything hangs together as planned, they never come to a point of recognizing the need for God, the joy in a relationship with Him, or the depth of life that comes in living for Him. It is a tragedy that someone so good could miss something so great, but this is a classic example of one type of ungodly man.

FRED

Fred is another type of ungodly man. He is more typical of what most would picture in this undesirable man. Loud, brash, and boorish, Fred would not be on the guest list at the parties given by the university crowd. He loves to put other people down. Comments like "What ya wearing that tie for? Trying to be fancy or something?" or "It's okay, honey. Dave here, he likes his women to have a little meat on them!" are typical, coming out of Fred's mouth. He loves to tell raunchy jokes and lewd stories. It is almost as if he enjoys embarrassing those around him. "Eat, drink, and be merry, for tomorrow we die" certainly fits Fred's mind-set. If it is smooth, fast, and easy to handle, Fred likes it, whether you are talking cars, women, or booze. The thrills may be cheap and the ride short, but Fred thinks, *Who cares? We're all gonna burn in hell anyway. May as well have some fun now.*

Fred lives alone in a duplex. The setup has allowed him to live with almost no overhead. He works long hours on his job at the nuclear plant and goes right to the bar with his friends after work. From there he often goes to a "gentlemen's" club where he watches women strip or dance. He comes home late many nights of the week and gets up the next day and starts the whole routine over. He loves drinking, looking at women, betting on football and horses, and a good hand of poker. On weekends, he rides his motorcycle or works on his truck, which he keeps at a friend's garage. He fills his life with pleasures, running from one fleshly lust to another. He does not acknowledge God because he does not want anyone to get in the way of his "fun."

Fred dates a variety of women, but never for more than five or six months at a time. He always finds them too possessive, too clingy. So he moves on, but not before he has slept with them many times, insulted them over and over, and often abused them emotionally, perhaps physically, and sometimes sexually. This man and all the men like him are repulsive to most people, and only the most broken women would date him more than once. To even want to date him requires coming from an extremely hurtful father/daughter relationship, where father greatly resembles Fred and the cretin he called Dad.

CHRIS

Chris is around the same age as Fred and Ralph. They went to high school together. Chris and Ralph went on to different colleges but ran into each other on vacations and at occasional community functions after graduation. They rarely saw Fred after graduation and did not mind the lack of relationship. Especially Chris. Fred was the antithesis of what Chris wants to be. Chris wants to be described at his funeral as a "pillar of the community." So when he came back to town after graduation, he married his high school sweetheart (making sure they did not have sex before they married); joined the big Baptist church on the corner of Maple and Vine; became a Big Brother to some kid in the ghetto; and began to create himself. Soon he was a deacon and then an elder. He decided that becoming a lay preacher looked good, so he took classes at night at the local Baptist Bible College.

Chris works hard at his job, too. He makes sure everyone there knows he is a *good* Christian. He carries his Bible back and forth to work and makes sure people notice it. He wears a cross pin on his lapel and shows his disapproval if anyone ever happens to swear in front of him. Serving on many church and community committees takes a lot of time, but Chris figures his family understands. They can see, surely, the importance of his calling. He arises early and retires late, all in service to God and the community. Chris requires the same devotion and perfection from his children and his wife. Any deviation from what is expected is met with disapproval and scorn. He gets this hurt "How *could* you?" look on his face whenever someone tries to disagree with him. Everything has to be done just so and to Chris's specifications. "*After all,* we have to do things *excellently* to please the Lord, don't we?" he intones. Everyone dreads his coming home because some petty thing out of place will set him off on an hour's lecture and there will be tension and suppressed rage for dinner. Chris is sure that when all the accounts are examined, God will see how good and righteous he has been and will let him into heaven. After all, he isn't some poor schlepp like Fred.

While Chris does not seem to fit the name ungodly man, Jesus talked about men just like him. Jesus said that there would be people who would claim to know Him and believe in Him. He said that they would even do miraculous things in His name. They would heal people and do a lot of other things that looked good and godly. But in reality, they were not doing these things for God, they were doing them for themselves. Jesus said that no matter what they claim they have done, they have never really known Him. Although they look good, they live a life apart from God.

GODLESS MEN

Godless. Sounds pretty scary; at least to someone who cares about such things. What does it mean to be *godless*? Let's look at Scripture to see what the biblical definition is.

The book of Job has quite a bit of information on the godless. Here are some of the characteristics of the godless person:

- He forgets God (8:13).

- He places his hope in things that perish (8:13).

- He cannot come into God's presence (13:16).

- His relationships are barren (15:34).

- He appalls the innocent and upright (17:8).

- His exaltation or joy is short-lived (20:5).

- He has no hope (27:8).

- When disciplined by God, he stores up anger and does not cry to Him (36:13).

The Proverbs also examine the godless and describe them as

- gnashing their teeth at the righteous (35:16).
- destroying their neighbors with their mouths (11:9).

The prophet Isaiah described the godless man as an evildoer and one who speaks foolishness. As a result, the wrath of God is not abated toward him, and God does not pity him or his family (Isa. 9:17).

The ungodly man or any godless person is someone who does not fear God. Fearing God does not mean being terrified of Him, but rather reverencing, standing in awe, and taking refuge in Him. One of the chief complaints that God had against the Israelites as they wandered in the wilderness was that they "forgot" His wonders, His deeds, His presence with them. In essence, they lived as if He did not exist, despite plenty of miracles to the contrary.

WHAT ABOUT RALPH, FRED, AND CHRIS?

So how do you rate the three fellows described earlier? Would any of them qualify as "godless"? It is probably fairly obvious, but let's look again at some of the criteria. The godless person "forgets God." Because of the loss of his twin, Ralph has almost literally forgotten God or intentionally ignored Him. He is so busy with other things that God and His will do not even occur to him. What about Fred? If Fred thinks about God at all, it is to curse Him for the bum deal Fred thinks God handed him in life. He has no use for God; God is for children and old women. Fred has forgotten who his Creator is. Fred thinks that he himself is at the center of the universe. He is so saturated with temporary pleasures that he has literally forgotten about God. Then there is Chris. Surely, Chris is aware of God. Everything Chris does is for God, isn't it? Or is it? You see, Chris's emphasis is so works-oriented that he fails to see God and His grace. He doesn't think he needs grace from God because he thinks he has been good enough. He has forgotten the holiness and utter perfection of God and arrogantly thinks his pitiful righteousness will add up to be enough to save Him. Chris has forgotten that God is the lover of his soul and that He longs to have a relationship of intimacy and warmth with Chris. Chris thinks God is a savings bank where you deposit your good deeds and someday withdraw the interest you earned. Chris has entirely too high an image of himself, his goodness, and what he can accomplish on his own.

The ungodly man places his hope in things that perish, and his exaltation and joy are short-lived. Where does Ralph place his hope? His hope for fun and enjoyment is placed in his cars. His hope for the predictable future is in his savings and mutual funds. His hope is in himself and his own efforts, all things that are short-lived, perishable, or false. Ralph, in reality, has no hope outside of Christ. How about Fred? Where does Fred place his hope? Fred's hope is in immediate self-gratification. The focus is always on the immediate. The immediate grasp for pleasure is all he has. The past is gone, the future is uncertain, so "grab all the gusto you can" and live for today. Delay nothing, especially gratification. And Chris, what about his hope? Chris's hope lies in the accumulated sum of his own righteousness. He has followed the rules, played the game fairly, and so he expects God to be fair to him in return. His hope is in his ability to do the right thing.

The ungodly man's relationships are barren and even destructive. Ralph knows about barren, though he would not be able to verbalize it very clearly. He rarely talks to his wife except about the children, and when he does, it is superficial at best. His kids are a mystery to him. He cares about them in some vague sort of way, but you would be hard-pressed to call what he has with them a relationship. Fred knows about barren, too. His relationships with women are purely for his pleasure and gratification. And destructive Fred knows well. He is usually the destroyer, but he's taken some hits in his time. He knows about being dumped on. Fred has become pretty cynical through it all: You can't really trust anyone. Better to keep your guard up and the offense ready. The tragedy about Chris is that, for all the barrenness in his relationships, he is clueless. He thinks his family loves him, admires him, adores him. He does not pick up on the tension that fills the house when he walks through the door. He does not notice that the kids stay away as much as possible on weekends, so as not to run into him. He is hardly aware that his wife has moved into the guest bedroom. He figures she just has a cold or something and does not want to disturb him.

The other criterion we looked at for the godless person was that they "gnash their teeth at the righteous." What this conveys is the idea of mocking or being disgusted with or enraged at. When confronted with true holiness or righteousness in a godly person, the unrighteous always are repulsed. Paul said true Christians are either a sweet perfume or a stench to unbelievers, depending on their receptivity to the gospel. Ralph gets mad when he hears about people who take their faith seriously and try to apply godly principles to everyday life. Fred unreservedly mocks and ridicules the Christians with whom he comes in contact. Chris, when confronted with true faith, hope, and love, sees it as sentimentality or mental illness and is deeply offended by it.

Are these men godless? You know they are if you are in a relationship with one. In the beginning it might have been appealing to be in relationship with someone who did not always run to church or discuss religious things all the time. You might have considered it a nice change or something with which you are familiar. But over time you have sensed that this man has many problems, and the biggest is that he claims total control of his life and has no room for anything greater than he.

WHAT ABOUT YOUR MAN?

Perhaps the man in your life is a godless man like Ralph, or Fred, or Chris. Or perhaps he is more blatantly evil like the country preacher who looked holy to the outside world but went home and molested all nine of his children on a regular basis. Or perhaps he is the religious nice guy, who goes to church with you but is not interested in a deep walk with God. He doesn't object to your having one, but he is not interested. He will go to church, sit on the church board, even sing in the choir, but he wants you to keep the talk about Jesus to a minimum.

Maybe he is a Christian who is rebelling right now. He doesn't want to be pushed. He is angry with God or wants his own way. You cannot tell him about your relationship with God because it makes him angry to hear you talk about it. He feels guilty that he is in rebellion and so avoids the subject. If forced to go to church with you for a special occasion, he sits with his arms folded and falls asleep. He won't close his eyes when you all say the blessing at dinner. He stares at the ceiling when people mention God. He refuses to talk to you about it. He just stonewalls.

Living with or being involved with a godless man is a difficult thing for a woman who wants to be a godly person herself. Obviously, if you are a godless person yourself, you are going to be more attracted to a godless man anyway. For a woman who has a dynamic, Spirit-filled walk with God in Jesus, however, it is very painful to have a godless man for a partner. The Scripture is right when it says that we should not be unequally yoked. Being hooked up with an ungodly man is like being in a three-legged race with a two-year-old. It just does not work. Sitting in church on Sundays alone, or with someone who is sulking, is not pleasant. Never having someone to pray with, to share Scripture or spiritual growth with, is very painful. If our partner is antagonistic toward our faith, that is all the worse. Not participating with us is bad enough, but attacking us is something else again.

A tragic example came to light recently in counseling. Years ago, when Sarah was a young child, she went to the local church with her mom. Dad never showed any interest, and she never questioned why he did not attend with them. One day Sarah was all excited because her mom had gone forward to join the church during the service. Sarah was not sure what it all meant, but she knew it must be important because everyone clapped and came up afterward to congratulate her mom. All the way home she hummed happily to herself and enjoyed the glow of the memory. Dinner was at one o'clock as usual on Sundays, and Dad was there, all dressed in his nice shirt and khaki pants. He did not put on a tie on Sundays, but Sarah thought he still looked handsome. All through the meal, Sarah waited and waited for her mom to tell Dad the good news. Finally, she could stand it no longer and she burst out, "Mom, aren't you going to tell Daddy what happened at church today?" Her mother shot her a quick, reproving glance, but it was too late. Dad looked up and said, "Oh, did something happen?" Sarah's mom brushed it off with a negative response, but Sarah interrupted: "*Mom!*" she protested. "*Tell* him. Daddy, Mommy joined the church today! Isn't that great?" Her father's face turned beet red; he stood up, threw his napkin on the table, and stomped off into the living room. Sarah was stunned. Mom was hastily brushing tears away and telling her it would be all right. In a moment, Sarah was sucking on a Popsicle and taking a long walk, as her mom had instructed her to do. When she finally came home, dinner was all cleared up, Dad was asleep in the den, and Mom was sewing in the back bedroom. They never spoke of the incident again, and they never went to church again either.

Over the years, her mom became more and more depressed, more and more withdrawn. Dad handled everything: money matters, grocery shopping, purchasing school clothes. Mom rarely went out and stopped driving altogether. She cooked the meals her husband wanted, cleaned the house the way he told her to do, and was totally submissive and subservient to his every whim and command. Now Sarah is thirty-five, and her mom is clearly mentally ill. She barely speaks anymore, and when she does, it sometimes does not make sense. Her mom gets easily confused and forgetful, and acts more and more childlike every day. Sarah can only wonder what her father did that fateful Sunday to so completely suppress her mother's will and crush her spirit. Her mom let go of her faith, the one thing that could have saved her, and sank down further and further into despair. Sarah's dad was a godless man. Not standing up to him cost her mom everything.

WHAT KIND OF WOMAN DOES THE UNGODLY MAN WANT?

Actually, the type of woman varies depending on the man! Some godless men want truly godly women around. Others want someone on the way to hell with them. Some are like Bonnie and Clyde. They feed off each other. Others are content to have someone who will not rock the boat and will keep her mouth shut. He may or may not want her to share his view of the world. You see, he is so wrapped up in himself that he really doesn't care much what she is like. He just wants to be left alone to do his thing. Whatever that is.

WHY DOES SHE FALL FOR HIM?

As we said earlier, some women are attracted *because* he is god-less. They are rebellious and perhaps evil themselves and want some-one who mirrors their soul. They may be young, naive, idealistic, and think they can change him (the missionary approach to dating). They may feel sorry for him and believe that others have judged him too harshly. They like being champions for the underdog. Or they may be burned out on religion and want someone who is "open-minded" and not hung up on traditional church stuff. Someone who is a "good per-son" is sufficient for them. If he was an Eagle Scout type, and never hurt anyone, why worry about godliness? Others are attracted to his outward religiosity and are unaware of its shallow, insincere, or works-oriented basis. He talks the talk, and she thinks he walks the walk. Outwardly, he looks great. Others vouch for him. He claims to love God, and maybe he does at first. However, other things, other passions, begin to creep in and distort his once-fervent desire to serve God. Maybe he genuinely has faith and has been faithful. She has no idea of the inner turmoil and pain that are beneath the surface, ready to hurl him headlong into rejecting all he once held dear.

RELATING TO THE UNGODLY MAN

What do you do in a situation like the one in Sarah's family, men-tioned earlier? What if your husband opposes your faith? Do you go to church anyway? Do you leave your husband? Did Sarah's mom have another choice? What do you do when your spouse is not actively opposed to your faith, but just won't participate? What if he is a nice guy, good provider, but leaves God completely out of his life?

What if he is a self-righteous son of a gun like Chris? Or a rotten hypocrite? What do you do with a godless man in your life?

This question is not an easy one, nor one that has a single, all-encompassing answer. There are certain principles from Scripture that we can apply, however.

1. *When push comes to shove, we must obey God rather than human beings.* We can love someone, respect them, honor them, and treat them with dignity, but if they ask us to disobey God, then we are to "draw a line in the sand." Picking your battles is the key to this principle. Not everything is a direct request to defy God. For example, asking you to go to the 8:00 A.M. service so you can make the 11:00 A.M. tee time with him would not qualify as asking you to disobey God. Telling you he wants the kids in public school while you want them in a private school associated with a church is not asking you to abandon your faith. Letting your daughter go to the junior prom with her boyfriend is not the same as saying she can sleep with him in your house. Some things are clear violations of God's laws, some are matters of preference, convenience, or choice. Faith or no faith, there will always be disagreements, and it is important that you not turn each one into an argument about faith. You want to be sure to pick some very large hills on which to take your stand, not molehills.

2. *All we do must be done in love.* Even if we have to set boundaries with a person, it must be done with an attitude of love and dignity, not haughty self-righteousness. It is one thing to insist that you will continue to worship God on Sundays, but it is another to do so in a manner that makes him out to be an evil, demonic tyrant. Do not flaunt your faith in front of him. Do not be vindictive with your beliefs. Let him be attracted to you as others were attracted to Jesus.

3. *We should try to keep areas of disagreement from becoming a test of the relationship.* Often couples get into a "If you really loved me . . ." scenario, where one has to prove his or her love by doing what the other wants. Even if the other frames the disagreement in that fashion, we do not have to buy into it. For example: "Well, honey, my going to church has nothing to do with my love for you. I love you

and I always will. I am committed to our relationship. However, I am also committed to our children and to God. My love for them in no way diminishes my love for you. Remember, love is not like pie. With love, the more you give away, the more you have."

4. *We should examine our own motives.* Are you using your walk with God as a contest to prove you are superior to your spouse? Are you trying to shame him into good behavior? Are you more concerned with externals (how things look to others) than with love? Are you patient and kind in your responses to ridicule or indifference? Or do you respond with resentment and bitterness? Do you withhold sex as a way to punish him when he does not live up to your spiritual expectations? Are you judging him without looking at the log in your own eye?

5. *You can pray and pray and pray that God will soften his heart and bring him to repentance and grace in His timing.* Again, this should be a private thing you do, not something you flaunt in front of him.

6. *We have the responsibility to set boundaries and to not allow ungodly behavior in our homes.* For example, we have the right to demand that no pornography come into the home, whether print or electronic or video. We have the right to refuse to participate in immoral behavior with others or with our spouse. We have the right to stop abusive behavior directed at us and/or our children. We must be prepared to follow through with our boundaries, not just threaten, however. If you say it, you must be prepared to follow through completely.

With these principles in mind, we can begin to discern what we need to do in the various situations that come our way when confronted with a godless person.

WHAT COULD THE UNGODLY MAN DO TO CHANGE?

What would constitute change for the godless man? Becoming more religious? Going to church more? Reading the Bible? Singing the songs more enthusiastically? No, you don't want a religious man, you want a man to be more godly. Here are some things he could do and learn to move out of his role of the ungodly man:

1. *Start a search for truth.* It is his ego that allows him to believe that although millions seek a relationship with God and Christ, they are all wrong and he is right. In his unbelief he must somehow come to a point where he at least is looking for truth. The place to start his search for the real God is reading the Bible. The book of John is a good place to begin. Another great book is by Josh McDowell and is titled *More Than a Carpenter*. I (Steve) have just published a book with Waterbrook Press titled *More Jesus, Less Religion*. It and the other resources mentioned will help you understand who Jesus really is, what He expects, and what we can expect from Him.

2. *Have a crisis.* He may never change unless he loses something really big, like his freedom, or his prized possessions, or a job—something that means a lot to him (but hopefully not a loved one). It may take something completely out of control for him to be broken enough to seek God, to finally fix and feed the spiritual dimension of his life.

3. *Realize that godliness is a gift, not a reward we earn.* The Scripture says that no human being is righteous. No, not one. Christ became sin and evil for us, in order that we might become the "righteousness of God" (Rom. 3:5). We put on the Messiah's righteousness, not our own. It is grace, not our efforts, that saves us from our wicked ungodliness.

4. *Fear the Lord, which is the beginning of wisdom and the beginning of seeking to be godly.* Living as if God does not exist is at the heart of godlessness; taking Him always, and in every way, into account is the beginning of godliness. The ungodly man may pride himself in fearing no man, but he can develop a fear and respect for God by starting to look for what He is doing in others' lives.

5. *Place hope in God alone.* Placing hope in things that perish or in one's own efforts is also at the heart of godlessness. So, becoming godly will mean seeking God alone, relying on Messiah's finished work for us, rather than our own efforts. Hope in God means hope in a future. With hope in a future he will no longer need to seek immediate gratification. He can learn to save the best for last.

SNAPSHOT SUMMARY OF
THE UNGODLY MAN

CLUES TO HELP YOU SPOT HIM

1. Has no understanding of God from a personal and intimate perspective.

2. May appear religious in some cases, but it only serves as a cover for his self-reliant actions.

3. Unwilling to delay gratification or think beyond present comfort needs.

4. Often talks of a past event, great loss, or disappointment that is blamed on God.

5. Overly sensitive to and offended by Christians and talk of God.

THE WOMAN TO WHOM HE IS ATTRACTED

1. Will vary greatly among types of ungodly men.

2. A saint—to save him in the end.

3. A person to share his disdain for and disappointment in God.

4. A weak woman who will allow him to play God.

5. A woman who will leave him alone.

THE WOMAN WHO FALLS FOR HIM

1. May enjoy his ungodly ways and is a Bonnie to his Clyde-like personality.

2. May be burned out on religion or church or also blames God for some tragedy.

3. Sees him as a project she can fix for the kingdom.

4. Is attached to his self-assurance if she is haunted by many doubts.

5. May buy into his pseudoreligion if he is active in church, even though he does not allow God to be active in his life.

WHAT YOU CAN DO

1. Lovingly set boundaries that allow you to honor God and bring your children to church.

2. Examine your own motives for becoming involved with him, and resolve the areas that apply to your broken relationship with God.

3. Pray and ask others to pray that God will change his heart.

4. Whatever you do needs to be done in love so it attracts him to you and God.

5. Pick your battles wisely. Refuse to allow every issue to become an issue of faith.

WHAT HE COULD DO TO CHANGE

1. Begin to search for truth by reading the Bible and other materials to find out more about who God actually is.

2. Surrender, realizing that his own efforts have not produced the results in his life he had hoped for.

3. See each new crisis or tragedy as an opportunity to connect with God.

4. Learn to live beyond the immediate need for gratification.

5. Search within himself to discover why God is such a difficult concept for him and why the spiritual side of his life has been neglected and ignored.

CHAPTER 11

AVOIDING MR. WRONG IF YOU'RE STILL SINGLE

Hopefully, the previous material has made you aware that there are certain men whom you may find attractive but who are attractive to you for all the wrong reasons. They are men who look good at a glance but who are not so good once you get to know them—really know them. They are not representative of all men or most men. They are the truly bad apples in the dating supply bucket. Just knowing that the extremely bad guys are out there should make you cautious as you date and look toward the commitment of a lifetime. Just knowing about them is not enough. In fact, in some cases it might just increase your disdain for all men and move you farther away from a deep and lasting relationship.

If you combine your knowledge of men with a new awareness of yourself, you have gone a long way in avoiding Mr. Wrong. It may be painful and it may take a while, but you must look within and rid yourself of those things that lead you to the doorstep and even the bedroom of Mr. Wrong. Let's say you came to my (Steve's) office in Laguna Beach and told me that you wanted some help with something very painful. Let's imagine that I asked you to take a seat but you refused. Upon further inquiry I discovered that the pain you were experiencing was in the very spot I was asking you to sit on. You self-consciously turned around and showed me your backside, and to my amazement I saw about a hundred brass darts with feathered fins sticking out all over your bottom. Even more to my surprise, there was a six-concentric-circle target painted there with a bright red bull's-eye in the middle. When I asked you where you had been, you told me, "Dart World."

It is fairly easy to imagine what my advice would be. Number one, I would tell you to go to a specialist and have those painful darts removed before they become infected. Second, I would tell you not to go back to "Dart World" and find a better place to spend your time. And third, I would tell you to get the target removed from your rear end. Now, that may sound silly, but some of you deeper thinkers already know where this is headed. In order to avoid Mr. Wrong and, further, to avoid going from one Mr. Wrong to another, you need to do pretty much the same thing.

STOP BEING A TARGET

First, you need to see a specialist to deal with any of the current painful realities that exist. Counseling is the place if you are wracked by painful fears, worry, guilt, or anger. Get these conflicts resolved. Do not let your past control your present and lead you to a future you do not want or need. Counseling may seem to be an intimidating and perhaps a frightening experience, but it is a safe place for you to heal your wounds and grow stronger in the process.

Second, you need to find healthy places to meet men. The Dart Worlds of dating are singles bars, couples bars, bars of any kind. These are very unhealthy places to meet someone you would potentially want to spend your life with. People marry who they date, and if all your dates are coming from chance meetings in dark and mood-altering places, you are making it very difficult for yourself to find Mr. Right. Become the most interesting and involved person you can be. Develop numerous hobbies. Take all sorts of classes on writing, painting, dancing, acting, gardening, and anything that interests you. Be involved in civic groups and church organizations. Go and be where people are doing something other than trying to find someone to take to bed for the night. Change where you hang out.

Third, you need to discover if you are a target for the Mr. Wrongs of the world. If you are, you need to change those things that are appealing to the Mr. Wrongs and become attractive to the Mr. Rights. There are exceptions to the types presented below, but these represent the kind of woman most Mr. Wrongs are targeting:

1. *Weak*. She is weak and thinks very lowly of herself. She has a hard time making a decision and is easily carried away by talk and romance. She does not have a mind of her own. The pains of her life have taken away her sense of self, and she plays the role of victim in almost any setting.

2. *Used*. She has a history of being used. All her tales of past relationships are of being caught up in a romance only to be discarded and abandoned. She expects it. It even seems she does not mind it at all. It makes her try really hard to please, but it is never enough. So after the last Mr. Wrong has used her up, he goes on to find a new target.

3. *Has low expectations*. She does not expect much from herself or others. If she is headed for a life of poverty, then that will be okay. If all she has is squalor, then she will find a way to raise her children in squalor. He knows she can handle the bottom of life's barrel and that even when all is dark, she will not abandon him.

4. *Undemanding*. She will leave him alone. He will be free to go out with the boys anytime, and she will not resent it or talk about it. What he gives her will be enough. She will play out her victim role while he plays out his user role, and she will not demand anything other than money for food and some clothes. Anything more will seem like a treat.

5. *Blind*. She will overlook the most blatant problems with his personality. Somehow she will see all the good things about him, even if there are only a couple she can observe. She sees a different person from the one anyone else sees. He just never seems all that bad.

6. *A caretaker*. If he is bad, she is confident she can handle it. She will help him, and the worse he is and the more she has to put up with, the more valuable she will feel. His sickness makes her feel well. His weakness makes her feel strong. She enjoys looking up from hopeless-

ness and finds herself in that position often, taking care of the person who put her there.

Each one of these six descriptions is a big, wide stripe of the target. Look at these characteristics and determine if you are wearing one or all six of the stripes, then do whatever you have to do to stop being such a huge target for the Mr. Wrongs out there who would like to use you for target practice.

WHAT SMART WOMEN DO

When you work on getting rid of the traits that draw the Mr. Wrongs as a dead animal draws buzzards, you will start attracting men who have the potential to become Mr. Right. If you have done the work you need to do, you will develop a healthy relationship and not kill it. If you have not done the work, you won't feel as if you are entitled to be with Mr. Right and you will mess it up. Don't just hope for the best; prepare for the best by ensuring that the worst part of you is out of the way so the best part can flourish in a healthy relationship.

When you start dating some really good guys, there is a good chance you may want to marry one of them. If you are careful, you can not only be assured that the man is a Mr. Right, but you can also lay a foundation for a very powerful and secure relationship. Below are the things that smart women do to make sure they are moving forward with the right man in the right way. They are not easy, but since marriage is meant to be for a lifetime, they are all worth it if you are willing to wait for the right someone.

Here are the ten most valuable things you can do to ensure that you don't end up with Mr. Wrong:

1. *Go slow.* No, really—go even slower than you think you need to go. Did you know that romance and infatuation don't rub off for about two years? If you marry before those two years are up, you won't know if you really love him or he loves you, or if you just love the feelings you create in each other. Go slow. Date at least a year and then be engaged for at least a year. Yes, the clock is ticking, but it is not ticking that fast. You have plenty of time for a great relationship.

What you do not have time for is a bad one that either drags into a lifetime of chronic pain or ends in acute pain and traumatic divorce.

2. *Obtain premarital counseling.* There is nothing better you can do to help discern whether or not you are a good match than to attend a strong premarriage counseling program. One of the best things that could happen, even though it doesn't seem like it at the time, is for a premarital counselor to warn you that some of the things in the relationship do not look so good. Or, on the other hand, you may discover unknown strengths in each other that give you even more confidence in the relationship. Meet with someone who has advised hundreds of couples and knows the best materials for you to study. Go to someone who gives homework assignments and exercises that cause the two of you to talk about the uncomfortable things like money, children, money, sex, money, faith, money, and money. No one has regretted getting too much premarital counseling. Many sure wish they had had more.

3. *Don't have sex before marriage.* Sounds old-fashioned because it is. In fact, it is as old-fashioned as some other guidelines that still work, such as "Don't lie" and "Don't steal." When you have sex with someone, you are proving that you are caught up in romance, infatuation, and the hormones of it all. If you cannot delay gratification now, if he cannot delay gratification now, what makes you think either of you will be able to after you are married? There will be trips and illnesses and times of separation that will require mature delayed gratification on both your parts. Prove it to each other now. Prove it to God now. Make Him and your future more important than your urges. Animals have to act on reflex and urge. You do not. You will not go crazy, and you will not get sick if you delay gratification.

I (Steve) lived a promiscuous single life. I regret that I did not know then what I know now. I regret that I did not know God as I know Him now. When I met Sandy, she dazzled me. I knew there was potential for us, and I respected her from the beginning. We made a commitment to not have sex before we got married. We stuck to it, and it was not easy to do so. But I am so glad we did. Now, this typically jealous and possessive guy never worries about her and her faithfulness to me. It is such a relief to know she can be with men friends at her work or in her hobbies and I can feel confident in her commitment.

When you sexualize your relationship, you are sinking large, sharp hooks into each other. To get away from those hooks will rip your soul and tear your heart. Don't do it. Even if it means not being alone together, do whatever it takes to stay true to yourself so the development of the relationship does not center on sex. Many people on their way to a healthy relationship stopped growing when they entered the world of premarital sex. Everyone is not doing it, and you don't have to either—if you are with a man who really loves you.

4. *Explore your attraction.* Why is he attractive to you? Is it his great body or is it his great faith? Is it his money or his mind? Look at the things that make you feel good about him. Do they remind you of anyone? Is he similar to someone who caused problems for you, like your father, an ex-husband, or an old boyfriend? Search for the real reasons you like this man. Some will be good and positive reasons. Others may not be. If you find that you are attracted to him for some very unbalanced reasons, get the help you need so you can break free of this trap.

5. *Find your motive for marriage.* Are you marrying him because he loves you and you love him, or because you hate something else? Do you hate being lonely so much that you would marry just about anyone who asked? Do you hate living at home so much that you are just looking for a way out? Do you feel so bad about yourself that you need someone else to save you, to make your life complete? Be sure your motives are pure. Be sure you are not trying to trap someone to meet your own needs, which may be less than admirable.

6. *Examine all that you have in common.* Opposites attract; they also tend to attack. Just because opposites attract does not mean that they make good marriage partners. The more you have in common the better. If you are outgoing and love sports and entertainment and being with people, don't rationalize that marrying a quiet man who has no friends and stays at home will be a good balance. Marry someone with whom you can enjoy as many activities as possible. Most

important, if you do not share a common faith, you are asking for trouble. What should be the center of your life will merely remain on the fringe. It may even become one of those areas you do not discuss or an area that produces many arguments. Have a lot in common, and be sure faith is one of those things you share.

While looking at what you have in common, be sure you take special note of what you do not share. What is different about each of you, and are those differences likely to produce huge struggles? Faith is not the only area. If you want children and he does not, how sad that you would move ahead and expect him to come around. He probably won't. If you like to have your own money to spend, but he thinks the man must dole out every cent to his wife, you are headed for huge problems. If you like the city and he likes the country, realize that you may end up living in a place you hate. Differences can make life interesting or they can destroy a marriage, depending on what those differences are.

7. *Agree on full financial disclosure before marriage.* You have a right to know everything about how he has handled his finances. His debts become your debts. If he is up to his ears in credit card debt, that irresponsibility is going to carry over into other areas. If he is reluctant to show you his bills and checkbook, stop. Do not go any farther with this man. Financial secrets are a sign of deeper secrets. Whether he has a lot of money or a little, he should be willing to share the truth with you. Being in debt does not mean you should not marry him. Unwillingness to tell you about his debt and the details of his financial affairs would be a good enough reason to find another man.

8. *Research his life.* You not only need to meet his family, you need to know his family. See him with them in different settings. Look at how he treats his mother. It is a big clue to how he feels about women and how he will treat you. Look at how he treats his father. That will tell you a lot about how he feels about himself.

Spend time with his friends. Find out what he likes about them and what is likable about them. If you do not enjoy them, expect to spend many lonely nights at home. Ask them what they think of him. Ask his friends what they think about his marrying you. Listen carefully and you may discover new information. If they are all telling you it will never work or they reveal an unhealthy pattern, listen to them.

If he was married before, talk to the ex-wife if possible. It will help you judge him and his truthfulness, and it will prepare you for some challenges ahead. If he was not married and you could talk to some ex-girlfriends, it would be very helpful.

9. *Listen to the people who know you.* Those friends who really love you can help you see what you do not see. Ask them to be truthful and then listen to them. Do they think it is a good idea? Or do they see problems that worry them and will lead to trouble for you? Your parents can be very valuable in assessing the potential and pitfalls of the relationship. The more help you get, the more opinions you are willing to listen to, the more likely you will be to make a good decision. Plus, when he sees and hears all that you are doing to make the right decision, it will either run him off or he will feel great about himself and the relationship when you move forward.

10. *Study him.* It is best to keep a diary of your relationship with him. Write down what he says about himself and others. This will reveal patterns and inconsistencies. Most people fudge a bit on the truth, but if he is a liar, your diary will document it. You won't have to wonder. You will be able to go back to what he has told you about his job, family, and other important facts.

In your study of him, you need to know his goals, dreams, and ambitions. When he tells them to you, write them down and be sure they are consistent with the way you want to live your life.

You also want to find out about his fears, insecurities, pains, and hurts. It may be hard for him to just come out and tell you those, but if he can't at all, you have not dated long enough and should extend the engagement. As your study continues, find out how he handles stress. Does it lead to some negative habits? Does he have positive habits? How does he use them to grow and develop?

Remember that in dating, the best foot is always forward. If you don't like some things about him, that is very normal. Everyone has something not to like. Beware that if you hate something now, you will certainly hate them more after you are married. A final piece of research you may want to consider is testing. Many people find it very helpful. There are some insightful tests and surveys such as Meyers-Briggs or the Taylor-Johnson Temperament Analysis Test.

Know who you are marrying. Do not put a blindfold on, move forward, and not expect to eventually walk off a cliff or get hit by a truck. Prayer is good; it is essential. Pray as if God is in complete control, but act as if it is all up to you. Do your homework now, and it will help you create a home that will work for the future you want.

The most profound thing about all of these steps is that you are taking action rather than just praying, hoping, or blindly trusting. You are not allowing yourself to be a victim. You are asserting yourself because you feel important enough to have a lifelong relationship full of love and intimate companionship. You are worth it. God really does want to meet your needs. He wants you to have a great life. Do not rob yourself of a man whom you can love deeply and a man who can love you more than you dreamed possible.

CHAPTER 12

HELPING MR. WRONG
GET RIGHT

HOPE

If you are married, and you know your husband is Mr. Wrong, there is hope. You can do some things that will probably initiate change within him. You cannot change him, but you can do some things to move him toward getting the help he needs. If you have ever tried to give a dog or a cat medicine, you know how hard it is to force the cure on them. You have to wrap the pill in something more agreeable to them. Yes, you have to trick them for their own good to get the pill down the throat.

If you are married to Mr. Wrong, you are going to have to do some things that are a bit tricky, but only after you have been very up front and honest with him about what you want for your relationship. In order for you to have the best chance of saving your marriage, you have to be willing for it to disintegrate. If you have to hold on to your image of a happy couple, then most of this will not help you. If you do not want him to be embarrassed before the people he cares about, then you probably will not be able to help him. But if you are ready to do whatever it takes to help him and your marriage, then there is hope, but this hope does not come without pain.

CAUTION

First, a word of caution. There is a chance that your Mr. Wrong may have already divorced you. You may still be legally married and living in the same house, but he has already broken the ties with you. In reality, he divorced you and began living his own life without you, he just did not complete the paperwork. He has done everything a man does when he divorces his wife, except move out and file the legal documents. You have been living with a man who is not emotionally or mentally living with you. What are ways a person may have broken the marriage bond, yet still be living in the house with you? Some examples of this type of desertion are: the man who uses pornography but would never "commit adultery" physically, the man who is emotionally attached to someone other than you—his drinking pals, his mother, his secretary, his former spouse—the man who is married to his work or his volunteer activities, the man with an addiction or a mistress. If that is the case, you are going to invite him to either be married to you or complete the paperwork that documents the death of your marriage. When that happens, you are not divorcing him, he divorced you. You may have to complete the filing if he is not willing to get help for the condition of separation in which you live. Even in that case, you are not divorcing him, you are just documenting what he did to the marriage years ago.

Divorce is a tragedy. God hates to see people divorce. Divorce hurts everyone who knows the couple. Everything written below is intended to prevent divorce and move a marriage toward healing. It is also intended to help you see the reality of your marriage and do what you have to do to save it, or accept that your husband will not accept help. It is a way to invite him to stop living in his own hell and the one created for both of you. If he does not accept that invitation, it is a way for you to see the reality of your marriage and make decisions accordingly.

A SUGGESTED PLAN

Here are the steps that have the best chance of helping Mr. Wrong move toward becoming your Mr. Right:

1. PROTECT YOURSELF AND YOUR CHILDREN

The first consideration is for your safety. If you or your children are in danger, you need to leave and go to a place where you will be safe. If he has ever threatened you with physical force or death, you should leave. If he has hit you or your children, you should leave. Do not assume that when you start moving toward a healthier you, he is going to move with you. It will probably infuriate him even more in the beginning. So before you take the next steps, make sure you step out of the line of danger.

As I am writing this section, the headlines are reporting a mass killing spree in Atlanta, Georgia. Before he killed himself and people he worked with, this man bludgeoned his wife and two children to death with a hammer. Amazingly, that was how his first wife and her mother were killed. He was never charged in those murders due to lack of evidence. This woman somehow believed the best in him and hoped for change, and now she and her stepchildren are dead. Look at the danger, and don't let anything stand in the way of protecting yourself and your children.

The most common reason women stay in a physically abusive situation is that they do not think they have any alternatives. The batterer tries to eliminate those alternatives. He controls the money and everything else. Do not let this stand in your way. Friends, relatives, and local agencies will all work with you for the sake of your safety and that of your kids. However, do not underestimate the degree of his reaction when you start to initiate change in the marriage. He will not be happy! Be prepared not to cave in to his anger or his tears!

2. OBTAIN COUNSELING HELP FOR YOURSELF AND YOUR CHILDREN

The next step is to find counseling help for you *and* your children. If you have money and insurance, then find the best counselor for you and the best child or adolescent counselor for them. They have feelings and hurts that will either be resolved now or affect them the rest of their lives. A great counselor can help them process their emotions and grow from this experience. The cost of counseling for your kids is some of the best money you will ever spend. Even if you have to sell the TV, VCR, and stereo system to pay for it, counseling is worth it.

You need your own counselor. You are in a battle for your life and your marriage. You won't find that on a call-in talk show or in a book. You need someone in whom to confide. You need someone to help you strategize and adapt to changes as they arise. Find a counselor who also believes in hope for troubled marriages. Ask your pastor or friends for the name of the best they know.

If you do not have money, then ask your church to help. Realize that not all pastors or church elders understand abuse, or even believe that it can happen in Christian marriages. One prominent seminary professor told a recent group of seminarians that they did not need to study abuse in their pastoral counseling class, because it "does *not* happen in Christian homes." One of the biggest problems women have in conservative circles is getting someone to believe them. Meg has received countless letters and phone calls over the last ten years from women who reported abuse to their pastors but were not believed. If this happens to you, *do not give up!* Go somewhere else and find someone who will believe you and help you. If you do not have a church, call your local mental health center. If there is no such thing in your town, go to a town where there is. Ask them to assign a counselor to you who understands marriage problems and your faith. Do not let any obstacle stand in your way of getting the help you need.

3. NAG NO MORE

Nagging has not worked before, it will never work. Give up this ineffective coping mechanism. There are many helpful things you can do, but first you have to decide that you are through with this one. No one has ever been nagged to health. So say good-bye to an old friend that has served you poorly.

4. ASK HIM TO GET HELP

This is the big one. Tell him you are seeing a counselor and you would like him to come with you. If he thinks the whole thing is rigged, then ask him to pick a counselor and you will go with him. You can use many different approaches on why you want him to go to a counselor. You can tell him your counselor would like to help both of you, that she thinks she can help your marriage. You can say the counselor wants to get "his side of the story." Any of these reasons are not only true, but also the least threatening to him.

You may decide it is better to be even more up front. You can tell him that you both know there are problems, and you would like for him to get some help. You can tell him that things are not getting better, and the least he could do is talk to a counselor who could help him. If you have asked before and he was unwilling, tell him you want things to be different and ask him one last time. If for any reason he agrees to go, it is the counselor's job to make the sessions as productive as possible. If you are married to Mr. Wonderful or Mr. Deceiver, however, be sure to alert your therapist to the fact that he will try to charm the socks off him/her. Some counselors are new in the field and are easily swayed by these engaging types. If you think your man has snowed the therapist be sure to speak up and say so clearly.

However, do not be alarmed if the counselor seems to side with him or only cares about his perspective in the beginning. This may be the only way for her to help him feel safe enough to come back. It may take several sessions before the counselor is able to talk about the reality of the relationship and his contribution to the problems. During this process, be willing to look at some of your own problems. His problems may be the main reason you are there, but your problems and your reactions to his problems also need to be discussed.

5. USE AN INTERVENTIONIST

If asking him by yourself does not help, then you need to go to him with someone else. The two of you need to ask him to do what is best for you and him. Whom you choose is very critical to the outcome.

One type of person is called an interventionist. All an interventionist does is work with people like you married to people like him. We work with one man who has done thousands of interventions, and I do not know of any that have been unsuccessful. Many folks who thought there was no hope have found it with his help. Interventionists know what to say and can direct you in what not to say. They train you and the whole family before the intervention is conducted.

If you feel there is no way this man would ever get help, an interventionist might be the only way to go.

Another option is to take a friend. It needs to be someone who is sane and rational and will not escalate a confrontation. Your counselor may be willing to help you also. At least the counselor can give you direction on how best to approach him. You might also ask your pastor to be the one to help you ask your husband to get help.

When you ask him to get help, there is a chance he will tell you he will change. He will try to convince you that all will be better. If he does, tell him okay, then ask him the "What if?" question. "What if you cannot handle this alone and we end up right back where we are now? Will you get help then?" If he will, have him sign a "what if" contract that states that he agrees to get help in the future if his history repeats itself. It could be the final step to his getting the help he needs.

6. WHEN ALL ELSE FAILS, WRITE LETTERS

When you tell him he has some problems and ask him to get help and he does not, then you have someone else go with you to ask him to get help. You are following a very old formula for confrontation that comes right out of the Bible. In fact, you will find it in the eighteenth chapter of Matthew. That chapter lays out the final step of confrontation, and that is to take the problem to those in a leadership position of the church.

There is also another verse that forms the foundation of this last step. It is James 5:16: "Confess your sins to each other and pray for each other so that you may be healed" (NIV). With these two passages in mind, it is time for you to go public with his problem.

You may have protected his image and yours. That may be why he still has the problem. As we said in the beginning, you have to be willing to do some painful things, even humiliating things, if you want the best hope of his getting help. This one can be both humiliating and painful, but it may be exactly what he needs.

A cautionary assumption: if he is violent or abusive, then you will make a phone call for this next step rather than meet with him face-to-face. If you confront him as suggested here, he will do what I suggest you do, he will be furious now, but he will be grateful later once he gets the help he needs. Be sure if you do this face-to-face and he is prone to anger, that you again take someone with you for support and protection.

One way to remember this final step is the ABCs of confrontation:

A. Make a list of all the people who mean something to him, people he has tried to convince that he does not have a problem. Include in that list people who mean something to you. This would include your pastor, the elders, leaders in the church, his parents, his siblings, in-laws, your friends, his friends, and his boss.

B. Write a letter that you may or may not send to these people, depending on his reaction to your final request. In the letter, tell these people that you and your husband are separating and you wanted them to know why. Tell them you love your husband and have asked him to get help for his problems, but he has refused. Tell them you have no choice but to have a time of separation. Outline in the letter why you feel he needs help. Tell them you have your own problems and are getting help for them, but he needs help also. List the problems as objectively as possible (here's an example):

- Randy is full of rage and sometimes hits me and the children.

- Randy spends hours on the Internet, and the sites he visits contain pornography, some of which is too sick to even mention.

- Randy has always had a problem with intimacy and refuses to look at the reasons and get help for it.

- Our children live in fear that he will come home drunk and beat them in a drunken rage.

After you list the detailed reasons why you need to separate, include the fact that you invited him one last time to join you for counseling and he refused, knowing that it meant separation. Tell them you do not want a divorce but that you feel he divorced you years ago but has just never filed the documents. In doing this you are simply asking him to make one of two decisions. Either get help or admit that he is not committed to the marriage.

Don't send the letters, but write them and address and stamp the envelopes, then give them to someone you trust.

C. Make an appointment with a counselor at a time you know your husband could easily attend. This should be a counselor you have been meeting with so the counselor knows your spouse may be with you.

D. Call or confront your husband face-to-face with a support person, depending on whether or not he is physically abusive. Tell him you have made an appointment with a counselor for both of you and you want him to come. Tell him if he does not, if he is not willing to give you even one counseling session, then it is time to separate. Show him or read him the letter, telling him whom you will send it to. Tell him the purpose is to explain why you are separating if that is what *he* chooses for both of you. Let him know that the letters are stamped and sealed and ready to go but you won't have any need to send them if he will join you. Do not listen to his excuses or pleadings. It is either attend counseling, get the help he needs, or there will be a separation and the letters will go out explaining it.

E. If he does not attend the session, do what you said you would do. *Send the letters.* Do not for any reason back down. Send the letters and either move out or move him out and change the locks. If that is an overwhelming prospect, get help from a lawyer to get him out of the house.

F. Continue to go to counseling and invite him to go whenever he makes contact with you. *Do not move back in with him* but always make the counseling an option for him. You will not be aware of what others are saying to him, encouraging him to get help. God is at work on him also. Do not give up, just be firm and stick with your request and your actions.

G. Ask a lot of people to pray for you during this crucial time. You will need that kind of support.

H. We wish we did not even have to include H. But here it is. When he tells you he will go to counseling if he can move back in, *tell him no.* The only way you should ever live together again, even if the separation bankrupts you, is after both of you have received at least six months of counseling and progress is being made. After that, you still should not move in, but you should date, spend time together, and if all goes well for six more months then he could move back in.

These are drastic measures with tough decisions—but that is what is required to know that you have done everything you could to save your marriage. It may not work, but most of the time it does and it probably will. If it does not, better that you are aware of just how hopeless he is now, than to live in denial for another year, decade, or lifetime. You do not deserve to be abused or abandoned. Abuse is not always in the form of hitting, and abandonment is not always when a person changes addresses. It can happen and yet people act for years as though it has not. We are encouraging you to stop acting and start dealing with reality. Facing the truth will either initiate healing or show you how deeply infected the marriage has become.

WHERE IS GOD IN ALL THIS?

This may be your number one question. It may have even become more of an obsession than a question. Because God has not magically or instantly fixed this, you may question if He even cares. He does care. Through all of your pain and trauma, God is right where He has always been. God is there with you and has been there with you through the entire ordeal. You may be angry at God for not preventing all this pain. You may be angry because your Mr. Wrong was not instantly turned into Mr. Right. Most anyone in your situation would have those feelings, but you will heal faster if you move beyond them. They will keep you from a close and intimate connection with God. They will stagnate your relationship with God.

God could have prevented your problem, sure. God could instantly heal it. But God is more interested in something other than your being comfortable and pain-free. God wants you to depend on Him. God wants you to mature. God wants you to grow in character because the only thing you get to take to heaven with you is the character you develop here. And God wants you to receive Jesus as your source of salvation.

God did not cause this problem. It is a result of crummy decisions made in a world where crummy things are allowed to happen. Focusing on the "why" will only keep you living a crummy life longer. Focus on the "what." The "what" is what God can do when this situation is turned over to Him. That does not mean that Mr. Wrong will change, it means that you will change. You will grow, mature, and become a wiser, stronger, more loving person than you ever dreamed you could be. You can look up from your desperation and realize that God really does love you and wants to spend eternity with you.

As you grow through this ordeal, don't simply ask God to change him, ask God to help change you as well.

THE LAST WORD
ON MR. RIGHT

Whom do you think of when you think of Mr. Right? What does he look like? What traits does he possess? You don't want to just avoid Mr. Wrong; you want to end up with a Mr. Right. In this most important search, many women never take the time to determine what and for whom they are looking. They take what comes along. They take what feels good or looks good, and the person they end up with becomes very circumstantial and situational in origin.

You need to develop some principles, some characteristics that you require in a man. You need to think of the things you want and need, and then search for a man who has most of them, not just one or two. Many times in our search for a mate we only think of what that person looks like. Did you know that what appeals to you can change with your menstrual cycle? In the June 24, 1999, edition of the *Orange County Register,* there was an article titled "Mr. Right Image Linked to Cycle." The report was on research that showed women were attracted to more rugged men when they were most likely to conceive and more feminine men when least likely to conceive. While this is not earth-shattering news, it does point out that if you are focused on the superficial, whom you are attracted to will frequently change.

Instead of looking at superficial characteristics, look for substantial and lasting character traits. Look for character. Look for someone who embodies the care and love that you need and deserve. A good example of that someone is a Man who never married: Jesus. Of course, no one is perfect, like Jesus, but let's look at some traits of Jesus that would be good to look for in Mr. Right.

1. *Responsible.* Jesus had a job to do and He did it. He took the responsibility God gave Him and He carried it out, even to the point of death. It is important that your Mr. Right be responsible. If he is, he will want to provide for you and protect you, just as you will want to provide and protect him. If he is irresponsible with his time, money, talent, and work, he will be the same way or even more so in marriage. If he blames others for everything wrong with him, you will be the next in line to be blamed.

A responsible man does not blame. Instead, he admits when he is wrong, accepts responsibility for the wrong, asks for forgiveness, and learns from the mistake. He repents and he changes. The responsible man provides you with consistency and security and predictability.

2. *Delays gratification.* Jesus could have stayed in heaven with all the comforts of Deity, but He chose to come to earth and suffer for us so that He could experience us for eternity. A man who delays gratification will be able to wait for sex. He will be able to save rather than spend all his money. He will be able to walk away from things he cannot afford. He will work hard at a job and not expect to get rich quick. This quality is so important to find in a mate. Encourage him to practice this trait. Help him develop it before you are married. See if he has the strength to delay something that feels good now for something that will feel better later.

3. *Communicates.* Jesus was a great communicator. Whenever He spoke people were attracted to Him and they listened to Him, whether they were doing it all wrong or attempting to live a good life. Whether it was a woman caught in adultery or a large crowd on a hill, Jesus was a great communicator.

You deserve a man who can talk to you. He does not have to draw the masses to a hillside sermon, but he needs to be able to express himself and connect with you personally. Do not think that the communication will get better. If it is not there in the beginning, it will probably not ever be there. Mr. Right needs to know how to talk.

4. *Has supportive friends.* Jesus was connected to other men. He had twelve of them around Him who helped Him accomplish what He wanted to accomplish. He was not a model of the Lone Ranger type of man. Within this twelve, He had three friends with whom He was even more connected. Be sure that your Mr. Right has friends who can help him. And friends that he can help. Meet his friends and do things with them. If you enjoy them, they will be a support to him and you. A red flag for you is either a man who has no friends and no desire to connect with others, or a man whose friends are unsavory.

5. *Has a purpose.* Jesus had a purpose. He wanted to help people, to save them from themselves. Before He left this earth His purpose was fulfilled. Your Mr. Right needs to be a man of purpose. He needs to have a life goal that goes beyond having a lot of money or a fishing boat or making it to retirement. Ask him what his purpose is in life. Ask him why he exists beyond his job. Ask him what he hopes to give back to the world and how he hopes to do it. Ask him why God created him and how his purpose relates to God.

6. *Is kind and comfortable with women.* When you look at the life of Jesus you are astonished at how kind He was to women. Although culturally taboo to do so, He talked to the woman at the well. He refused to heap shame on the woman caught in the act of adultery. He refused to criticize, as others did, a woman who spent her money to anoint His head. He healed women and they were drawn to Him. He appeared comfortable with them and they with Him. There was no talk of women being doormats or slaves. His respect for what He had created was quite obvious.

Mr. Right must be kind to you and respectful of all women. Disdain for his mother or other females will eventually turn into disdain for you. Find a man who appreciates you and all women.

7. *Prays.* Jesus was a Man of prayer. When confronted with a problem or temptation, He prayed to His Father. Your Mr. Right, more than anything else, needs to be a man of prayer. If he prays, it means he is seeking to be better; he is connected to God and wanting

His guidance. If he is not a man of prayer, there is little chance he will grow in his relationship with God. Know that your Mr. Right is a spiritual man and seeks God regularly.

8. *Scriptural.* Jesus knew Scripture and quoted many passages from the Old Testament. He used it to confront temptation and take a stand. Mr. Right needs to be in a Bible study where he is learning more about God's Word. Just five minutes a day spent in reading the New Testament will cover it in one year. Encourage him to read with you. If he is uncomfortable, it might mean that spiritual intimacy will not be part of your marriage. If he is comfortable, it may mean many great hours of coming together and learning more about what God wants for each of you individually and as a couple.

9. *Child-friendly.* Jesus loved children and asked them to be with Him when others tried to move them away. Mr. Right's heart can be measured to some degree by how he responds to children. Talk about kids with him. Know that he is as committed to raising great kids as you are. Determine if he is comfortable around them and enjoys investing some of who he is in children. If children are in your future, be sure your Mr. Right knows how to love them.

10. *Has integrity.* Jesus told the truth. Often He said, "I tell you the truth." And He did. What He said He would do, He did. What He said would happen, happened. Mr. Right must not be a man of white lies and inconsistencies. He needs to be a man of follow-through. Be sure you know that you can trust what he says and can count on what he intends to do. Integrity and character hold hands. You cannot have one without the other. When you have them though, you have a good chance of being with a wonderful Mr. Right.

11. *Loves.* Jesus never met anyone He did not love. He had compassion for them. He was more interested in connecting with them than looking good. In fact, He looked bad to a lot of people because He loved some bad people. Mr. Right needs to love you. It is so simple but so profound: Too many women marry men who do not and cannot love them. In this one area especially, be sure that Mr. Right is like Jesus, that he truly and deeply knows how to love you and meet your needs. That he can put you before himself. That his love leads

him to serve you and lay down his life for you. Now that type of man is Mr. Right.

We hope this has been helpful. Go out there and find Mr. Right and avoid all these Mr. Wrongs. We would love to hear from you; you can contact us by E-mail at Sarterburn@newlife.com, and meg3124@prodigy.net. Finally, if you need help finding a great counselor, call 1-800-NEW LIFE, and they will find someone in your area. God bless you in your search for Mr. Right.

NOTES

INTRODUCTION
1. John Friel, *The Grown-Up Man: Heroes, Healing, Honor, Hurt, Hope* (Deerfield Beach, FL: Health Communications, Inc., 1991), 14.

CHAPTER 2
1. Rick Joyner, *There Were Two Trees in the Garden* (New Kensington, PA: Whitaker House, 1993), 105-6.
2. Les Parrott III, *High Maintenance Relationships: How to Handle Impossible People* (Wheaton, IL: Tyndale House, 1996), 55–60, 83–88.

CHAPTER 5
1. Friel, *The Grown-Up Man*, 18.
2. Ibid., 114–16.
3. Margaret J. Rinck and Jeffrey L. Baker, "Addressing Misogynistic Abuse in the Church: A Strategy for Healing and Helping," paper presented at the Christian Association for Psychological Studies International Conference, St. Louis, Missouri, April 1996.
4. Doris Wild Helmering, *Happily Ever After: A Therapist's Guide to Taking the Fight Out and Putting the Fun Back into Your Marriage* (New York: 1986), 33–35.

CHAPTER 7

1. Sissela Bok, *Lying: Moral Choice in Public and Private Life* (New York: Vintage Books/Random House, 1978), 10.
2. Paul Ekman, *Telling Lies* (New York: Berkley Books, 1986), 26–27.
3. Ibid., 30–31.
4. Chuck Fager, "Unsuspecting Christians Bilked of Millions," *Christianity Today,* 42, no. 8, 24–25.
5. Frank Pittman, *Private Lies: Infidelity and the Betrayal of Intimacy* (New York: W. W. Norton & Company, 1989), 53.
6. Ibid., 52.
7. Fager, "Unsuspecting Christians Bilked of Millions," 24.

CHAPTER 8

1. For more information, see Sidney Cohen, *The Chemical Brain: The Neurochemistry of Addictive Disease* (Minneapolis: Care Institute, 1988); and Katherine Whalen Fitzgerald, *Alcoholism: the Genetic Inheritance* (New York: Doubleday, 1988).
2. Harvey Milkman and Stanley Sunderwirth, *Craving for Ecstasy: The Consciousness and Chemistry of Escape* (Lexington, MA: Lexington Books/D. C. Heath and Company, 1987), 18–19.
3. Art Moore, "Megachurch Pastor Resigns, but Denies Sexual Misdeeds," *Christianity Today,* 42, no. 8, 13 July 1998, 26.
4. Ibid.
5. Rick Joyner, *The Surpassing Greatness of His Power* (New Kensington, PA: Whitaker House, 1996), 60–66.
6. Ibid., 64–66.
7. Frank Pittman, *Man Enough: Fathers, Sons, and the Search for Masculinity* (New York: Perigee Books, 1993), 27–28; and *Private Lies: Infidelity and the Betrayal of Intimacy* (New York: W. W. Norton & Company, 1989), 152–86.
8. Ibid., 48.
9. Tim Stafford, "None Dare Call It Sin: How the Mississippi

Bible Belt Succumbed So Quickly and So Completely to the Gambling Industry," *Christianity Today,* 42, no. 6, 18 May 1998, 34–39; and editorial, 24–25.

10. Ibid., 25.
11. Ibid., 25, 37.

CHAPTER 9

1. Dan Kiley, *The Peter Pan Syndrome: Men Who Have Never Grown Up* (New York: Avon Books, 1983).

	ANGRY MAN	CONTROLLER	WONDERFUL GUY	ADDICT	LIAR LIAR
5 CLUES TO SPOT HIM	1. Is passive or active, subtle or direct w/his rage. 2. You become the target. 3. Sees women as good-bad, madonna-whore, perfect-worthless. 4. Is uptight, obsessive, demanding, perfectionistic. 5. Rages when you have needs. Discounts others & their needs.	1. Doing things "right" more important than relationship. 2. Irritated, angry when you mess up. 3. Critical most of the time. 4. Close-minded; has established ways & will not vary. 5. Uses intimidation to force others to do it his way.	1. He's too good to be true. 2. Goes to extremes. 3. His main goal is to have power over you. 4. Can talk his way out of anything. 5. Self-centered, self-absorbed, grandiose.	1. Physical, mental, social, emotional, or spiritual aspects of life affected by addiction. 2. Denies he has a problem, despite pre-occupation. 3. Addictive behavior escalates w/ greater consequences. 4. Acts distant, moody, even abusive. 5. You sense something is wrong, even if not sure what it is.	1. You're suspicious he's lying to you. 2. When caught, he is w/o genuine shame, remorse. 3. He is unable to empathize w/others. 4. He's affable, charming outside; inside, cold & heartless. Puts you down w/o a chagrin. 5. Takes charge easily. Others follow gladly.
WOMAN TO WHOM HE IS ATTRACTED	1. Caretaker. 2. People pleaser. 3. Someone he thinks will "take it." 4. Someone who lets others dominate her. 5. Someone who is apt to blame herself for any problems.	1. Insecure, unsure of herself (male chauvinist controller wants a confident woman who is willing to meet his every need). 2. Loyal & devoted. 3. Willing to be possessed. 4. Willing to be controlled. 5. Willing to let him make all the decisions.	1. Beautiful. 2. Smart. 3. Willing to give him all the attention. 4. Willing to be used & discarded. 5. Devoted & adoring.	1. Believes in the Rules: Don't fret, don't talk, don't trust. 2. Is used to living in stress and chaos (Usually a family member "had a problem" of some sort.) 3. Has trouble maintaining boundaries. 4. Caretaker-martyr personality. Excessive caring. 5. Did not receive adequate acceptance as a child.	1. Vunerable, naive. 2. Young (if older, gullible). 3. Wealthy if possible. 4. Trusts men more than self; accepts what told w/o question. 5. Overly subservient; caretakers, nurturers. 6. Lonely, widowed, divorced: no kids or kids gone or busy. 7. Honest, to a fault, herself.
WHY SHE FALLS FOR HIM	1. She may mistake anger for strength. 2. Living with an angry person is familiar. 3. She may need an excuse to vent her anger. 4. She may feel special to be the focus. 5. She may think she deserves his rage.	1. Some want to be controlled, so as not to have to grow up, make own mistakes. 2. Others may be used to living with a controlling parent. 3. May mistake perfectionism for efficiency. 4. May believe he will control things, not people. 5. If insecure, want to sap off his confidence.	1. Reasons vary. All are attracted to his seeming power, charisma, wealth, or status. Usually codependent, willing to put up with a lot of junk just to have a man around.	1. Sees his potential. Is sure her love will make the difference. 2. Feels good to be able to caretake. 3. Thinks "This time it will be different." 4. Feels insecure on her own. 5. Denies his addiction is a problem.	1. Is naive, trusting, vulnerable. 2. Is flattered by his charm, attention. 3. Cannot believe anyone would lie. 4. Wants to believe him. 5. Goes on emotion, not logic.
5 THINGS TO DO	1. Realize you can't change him. 2. Learn not to be a victim. 3. Develop your spiritual life. Get support from others. 4. Handle your own anger in mature manner. 5. Get away if he is violent.	1. Acknowledge when he is right. 2. Praise him for who he is, not what he does. 3. Remember, it's about HIM, not YOU, no matter what he says. 4. Stay calm; avoid confrontation if possible. 5. Don't try to fix it if he is upset. Let him stew.	1. Remember you cannot change him. 2. Decide how much you are willing to put up with just to have him in your life. 3. Accept his Jekyll-Hyde cycles, so you don't get your expectations up. 4. Create your own life. Gain control of yourself. 5. Put trust in God, not him.	1. Get help for YOURSELF. 2. Seek the Lord and His security and love. 3. Admit you cannot change the addict. 4. Stop enabling his behavior. 5. Set up boundaries & stick to them.	1. GO SLOW. Do not rush into relationship. 2. Do not give him your money. 3. Keep records of discrepancies. 4. Demand counseling for him and yourself. 5. Never believe him when he confesses or seems to repent. Look for behavior change.
5 THINGS HE COULD DO IF HE WANTS TO CHANGE	1. Quit splitting world into all-nothing, good-bad categories. 2. Accept feelings; handle anger w/o violence/verbal abuse. 3. Deal w/fear of abandonment/dependency by renewing spiritual life. 4. Take responsibility for own actions. 5. Get counseling.	1. Become intimate w/Christ so as to heal insecurity and fears of rejection. 2. Let go of performance orientation so he will be less demanding of self & others. 3. Turn away from the desire to have power over others. 4. Examine own flaws first, look for the good in others. 5. Become humble, not demanding.	1. See the world from others' view. 2. Stop seeing self as master of universe. 3. Become humble enough to profit from criticism. 4. Get security from God's love, not performance. 5. Be guided by love and righteousness, not self-interest.	1. Get out of denial; get professional help. 2. Recognize his powerlessness over addiction. 3. Turn his life over to God in Christ. 4. Begin intense moral introspection. Get a sponsor. 5. Change his circle of friends.	1. Turn from self to God; take others into account. 2. Discover the lies he believes that make him lie. 3. Be accountable to someone outside family. 4. Praise God, soak in Scripture; deepen walk w/Jesus, the Truth. Make amends. 5. Refuse to lie even in small matters.

	ETERNAL KID	MAMA'S BOY	COWARDLY LION	DETACHED MAN	GODLESS MAN
5 CLUES TO SPOT HIM	1. Is self-centered, either sweetly or arrogantly. 2. Irresponsible at the core. Limits are unknown. 3. Chauvinistic. Sees men as more important than women. 4. Is in a dream world; does not learn from mistakes. 5. If a User, he has a temper. Lashes out when he wants to be left alone.	1. People ask: "When is he gonna get away from Mama?" 2. Treats his mom either too well or terribly. 3. Can't make a commitment to you. 4. Does more for mom than you. You are "selfish" to be jealous. 5. Defends her over you. Refuses to see your pain; only sees hers.	1. Remain silent passive when they ought to speak. 2. Think of themselves first; "Take care of Numero 1." 3. Tend to be resentful and passive agressive. 4. Some are chameleons, changeable. 5. His faith in God is very weak.	1. Believes good comes to those who wait, and wait, and wait. 2. Active at work, passive at home. 3. Active with things, passive w/people. 4. Feels trapped, resentful, furious. 5. Often uses work to escape.	1. Doesn't take God into account; acts as if God doesn't exist. 2. Pins hopes on things that perish/are fleeting. 3. Relationships are barren–even destructive. 4. Offended, repulsed by, mocks true holiness. 5. Often verbally abusive, mean spirited.
WOMAN TO WHOM HE IS ATTRACTED	1. Competent; knows what she is doing. 2. Doesn't mind being used financially, emotionally, mentally. 3. Is self-sufficient, or willing to live in poverty. 4. Willing to take all responsibility leaving him free to do as he pleases. 5. Will take care of him but then, leave him alone.	1. "A girl just like the girl" Dad married: a mom. 2. Willingly takes 2nd place to his mom; 3. Is independent, willing to bear all weight of relationship. 4. Has low expectations of him 5. Will put up w/his passive aggression.	1. Complements his weak areas. 2. A risk taker. 3. Solid in convictions, perfectionist. 4. Extroverted; strong. 5. If a bully, a timid woman who will acquiese.	1. The Gal Friday/Ivana Trump type. 2. Successful, eager, independent. 3. Willing to be 2nd place to him despite her career needs, goals. 4. Distracted, busy; leaves him alone. 5. Supports him emotionally, sexually.	1. Varies according to the man. May want a godless person; may want a saint he can mock; may care, just wants to be left alone.
WHY SHE FALLS FOR HIM	1. Enjoys being in charge, caretaking. 2. May be eldest child. 3. Mistakes his irresponsibility for playfulness. 4. Thinks they will "grow up together." 5. Is a people pleaser; hates conflict.	1. Used to being used. 2. May feel powerful being "mom." 3. May be afraid of a egalitarian relationship. 4. Thinks her love will win him away from Mom. 5. Sees him as noble, gentle, kind, in way he treats mom; believes he will treat her the same way.	1. Varies w/woman. 2. Some want to feel strong, superior to her man. 3. Some may confuse his cowardice w/caution. 4. Some see his bluff & bluster, and want to hide behind it. 5. Some are chameleons and just go along like he does	1. For same reasons they fall for the Wonderful Guy: charm, wit, charisma; devotion to work seems admirable at first; flattered he "has time" for her; believes he will make time for her later, too.	1. Varies greatly. 2. May be evil; (Bonnie to his Clyde); 3. May be burned out w/religion, wants indifferent man. 4. May be naïve; thinks she can redeem him. 5. May be godly, unaware of deep turmoil & self-righteousness in him. He may have been godly & rebelled.
5 THINGS TO DO	1. Don't become parental. Don't nag, hint, threaten. 2. Give him lots of space. Develop your own life. 3. Look w/in self: what attracts you to him? Get help. 4. Don't caretake or nurture to keep him from leaving. 5. Expect him to listen, but not empathize. Don't excuse him.	1. If dating, don't marry him. 2. Realize you will not change him. 3. Seek the Lord to be your true husband, if married. 4. Keep a clear conscience; don't let bitterness build. 5. Get some counseling. Learn not to enable. Get a life.	1. If not yet married, reconsider. 2. Focus on God's love for you and His protection. 3. Evaluate your situation: Are you intimidated? Are you or your kids at risk because of his cowardice? 4. Realize you cannot make him into Braveheart, but you can praise his attempts to change. 5. Talk to him; praise him, uplift him.	1. Don't expect much. Aim for realism. 2. Acceptance, not perfection. 3. Cultivate a loving attitude. 4. Guard against bitterness. Get a life. 5. Develop humility and gratitude. Rely on God's ability, not your own.	1. Lovingly set boundaries. Honor God first. 2. Examine own motives. 3. Don't let disagreements be a test of the relationship. 4. Do everything from a loving attitude. 5. Pray God will soften his heart.
5 THINGS HE COULD DO IF HE WANTS TO CHANGE	1. Develop a desire to grow up by seeing self as God does. 2. Realize world doesn't revolve around him. 3. Be proactive, not passive. Initiate. Take responsibility. Reach out to wife, kids. 4. Let go of superior attitude towards women. 5. Develop male relationships to break isolation.	1. Differentiate from others. 2. Settle masculinity issues through therapy. 3. Strengthen courage muscle. Say no to Mom. 4. Depend on God and His strength, not pleasing others. 5. Be accountable to make and keep commitments to wife.	1. Seek the Lord and His strength. 2. Overcome fear thru power of Holy Spirit. Accept Christ's peace. 3. Banish insecurity by experiencing his place in God's family; learning who he really is. 4. Practice taking risks and chances. 5. Read, study, learn, & practice assertiveness.	1. Learn how to connect w/others. 2. Get some therapy to see how his parents influenced his choices. 3. Become proactive, not passive. 4. Be responsible in relationships. 5. Accept God's approval, quit seeking human recognition to boost his ego.	1. Give up self-effort; see godliness as a fight. 2. Seek God diligently. Take God into account. 3. Be ready to suffer rejection, persecution for Jesus' sake. 4. Place hope in God alone; not self or things. 5. Look to things which last, not perish.